Network and System ~~N~~
For Dummies~~®~~

M000159664

NetWare Commands

Command	What It Does
~~Clear~~ NETWare ~~er~~ server	Removes specified NetWare file server from TROY XCD Print server access list
	Sets advertising frequency of print server
~~...~~ware ~~...~~	Enables/Disables NetWare protocol on print server
~~...~~ NETWare ~~...~~name [802.2|802.3| ETH|AL|AU|SNA]	Sets NetWare frame type to 802.2, 802.3, Ethernet II, ALL, AUTO, or SNAP
SET NETWare NEtwork n	Sets NetWare internal network number
SET NETWare NPrinter <pserver> n ON <service>	Sets NPrinter mode on service
SET NETWare PAssword <psw>	Sets print server login password for file server
SET NETWare POlling n	Sets queue polling time in seconds
SET NETWare QServer <fileserver> ON <service>	Sets Queue Server mode on service
SET NETWare REscan	Rescans file servers for new queues
SET NETWare SErver <name> [EN|DIS]	Enables file server
SET SERVIce <servicename> NET [EN|DIS]	Enables or disables NetWare jobs on specified service
SHow NETWare	Shows NetWare parameters
SET SERVIce <servicename> CONtext <string>	Sets NDS Context
SET SERVIce <servicename> TREE <string>	Sets NDS TREE

Windows 2000 Command Shortcuts

Shortcut	What It Does
CTRL while dragging item	Copies selected item
CTRL+SHIFT while dragging item	Creates shortcut to selected item
SHIFT+DELETE	Deletes selected item permanently without placing item in Recycle Bin
F2	Renames selected item
F3	Searches for a file or folder
ALT+F4	Quits the active program
CTRL+F4	Closes the active document in programs that allow you to have multiple documents open simultaneously
ALT+TAB	Switches between open items
ALT+ESC	Cycles through items in the order they were opened
F6	Cycles through screen elements in a window or on the desktop
SHIFT+F10	Displays the shortcut menu for the selected item
RIGHT ARROW	Opens the next menu to the right or opens a submenu
LEFT ARROW	Opens the next menu to the left or closes a submenu
ESC	Cancels the current task

For Dummies®: Bestselling Book Series for Beginners

Network and System Integration For Dummies®

Cheat Sheet

UNIX/Linux Commands and Shortcuts

Command	What It Does
ping	Tests network connection by sending a TCP/IP packet from your computer to another
hostname	Displays the name of the machine on which you are working
last	Shows listing of users last logged in on your system
uptime	Shows amount of time since last reboot
ps -e	Lists all processes
ls	Lists the content of the current directory
cd <directory>	Changes directory. Using cd without the directory name takes you to your home directory
cp <source> <destination>	Copies files
mv <source> <destination>	Moves or renames files
ln -s <source> <destination>	Creates a symbolic link
rm <filename>	Removes files
mkdir <directory>	Makes a new directory
rmdir <directory>	Removes a directory. If you have files in the directory, you'll need to use rm-r
find / -name "filename"	Finds the file on your filesystem starting from the root directory
telnet <machine_name>	Connects to another machine using the Telnet protocol
rlogin <machine_name>	Connects to another machine
ftp <machine_name>	Ftps another machine
netscape	Runs Netscape
halt	Shuts the system down immediately
shutdown -h 60	Shuts down the system, but you can specify the length of time in seconds before shutdown occurs, such as 60 seconds. Must be root to use this command
reboot	Reboots system

For Dummies®: Bestselling Book Series for Beginners

™

BESTSELLING BOOK SERIES

References for the Rest of Us!®

Are you intimidated and confused by computers? Do you find that traditional manuals are overloaded with technical details you'll never use? Do your friends and family always call you to fix simple problems on their PCs? Then the *...For Dummies*® computer book series from IDG Books Worldwide is for you.

...For Dummies books are written for those frustrated computer users who know they aren't really dumb but find that PC hardware, software, and indeed the unique vocabulary of computing make them feel helpless. *...For Dummies* books use a lighthearted approach, a down-to-earth style, and even cartoons and humorous icons to dispel computer novices' fears and build their confidence. Lighthearted but not lightweight, these books are a perfect survival guide for anyone forced to use a computer.

> *"I like my copy so much I told friends; now they bought copies."*
>
> — Irene C., Orwell, Ohio

> *"Quick, concise, nontechnical, and humorous."*
>
> — Jay A., Elburn, Illinois

> *"Thanks, I needed this book. Now I can sleep at night."*
>
> — Robin F., British Columbia, Canada

Already, millions of satisfied readers agree. They have made *...For Dummies* books the #1 introductory level computer book series and have written asking for more. So, if you're looking for the most fun and easy way to learn about computers, look to *...For Dummies* books to give you a helping hand.

IDG
BOOKS
WORLDWIDE

1/99

Network and
System Integration
FOR
DUMMIES®

by Michael Bellomo
and James Marchetti

IDG Books Worldwide, Inc.
An International Data Group Company

Foster City, CA ◆ Chicago, IL ◆ Indianapolis, IN ◆ New York, NY

Network and System Integration For Dummies®

Published by
IDG Books Worldwide, Inc.
An International Data Group Company
919 E. Hillsdale Blvd.
Suite 300
Foster City, CA 94404
www.idgbooks.com (IDG Books Worldwide Web Site)
www.dummies.com (Dummies Press Web Site)

Library of Congress Control Number: 00-107255

ISBN: 0-7645-0774-5

Printed in the United States of America

10 9 8 7 6 5 4 3 2 1

IB/QW/RS/QQ/IN

Distributed in the United States by IDG Books Worldwide, Inc.

Distributed by CDG Books Canada Inc. for Canada; by Transworld Publishers Limited in the United Kingdom; by IDG Norge Books for Norway; by IDG Sweden Books for Sweden; by IDG Books Australia Publishing Corporation Pty. Ltd. for Australia and New Zealand; by TransQuest Publishers Pte Ltd. for Singapore, Malaysia, Thailand, Indonesia, and Hong Kong; by Gotop Information Inc. for Taiwan; by ICG Muse, Inc. for Japan; by Intersoft for South Africa; by Eyrolles for France; by International Thomson Publishing for Germany, Austria and Switzerland; by Distribuidora Cuspide for Argentina; by LR International for Brazil; by Galileo Libros for Chile; by Ediciones ZETA S.C.R. Ltda. for Peru; by WS Computer Publishing Corporation, Inc., for the Philippines; by Contemporanea de Ediciones for Venezuela; by Express Computer Distributors for the Caribbean and West Indies; by Micronesia Media Distributor, Inc. for Micronesia; by Chips Computadoras S.A. de C.V. for Mexico; by Editorial Norma de Panama S.A. for Panama; by American Bookshops for Finland.

For general information on IDG Books Worldwide's books in the U.S., please call our Consumer Customer Service department at 800-762-2974. For reseller information, including discounts and premium sales, please call our Reseller Customer Service department at 800-434-3422.

For information on where to purchase IDG Books Worldwide's books outside the U.S., please contact our International Sales department at 317-572-3993 or fax 317-572-4002.

For consumer information on foreign language translations, please contact our Customer Service department at 1-800-434-3422, fax 317-572-4002, or e-mail rights@idgbooks.com.

For information on licensing foreign or domestic rights, please phone +1-650-653-7098.

For sales inquiries and special prices for bulk quantities, please contact our Order Services department at 800-434-3422 or write to the address above.

For information on using IDG Books Worldwide's books in the classroom or for ordering examination copies, please contact our Educational Sales department at 800-434-2086 or fax 317-572-4005.

For press review copies, author interviews, or other publicity information, please contact our Public Relations department at 650-653-7000 or fax 650-653-7500.

For authorization to photocopy items for corporate, personal, or educational use, please contact Copyright Clearance Center, 222 Rosewood Drive, Danvers, MA 01923, or fax 978-750-4470.

is a registered trademark under exclusive
license to IDG Books Worldwide, Inc.,
from International Data Group, Inc.

About the Authors

Michael Bellomo is certified in UNIX System Administration and has over five years of experience as a UNIX (Solaris and Linux) and Microsoft Windows NT Network Manager serving with software and financial technology companies in the Silicon Valley. He is the author of *Linux Administration For Dummies, MASTER Red Hat Linux Visually, Debian Linux For Dummies, Windows 2000 Administration For Dummies,* and *Unix: Your visual blueprint to the universe of Unix.*

James Marchetti served eight years in the U.S. Navy with advanced electronics and weapons systems. He has over seven years of experience as a Solaris and Windows NT network manager and system engineer with software and financial technology companies in the Silicon Valley and in San Francisco.

ABOUT IDG BOOKS WORLDWIDE

Welcome to the world of IDG Books Worldwide.

IDG Books Worldwide, Inc., is a subsidiary of International Data Group, the world's largest publisher of computer-related information and the leading global provider of information services on information technology. IDG was founded more than 30 years ago by Patrick J. McGovern and now employs more than 9,000 people worldwide. IDG publishes more than 290 computer publications in over 75 countries. More than 90 million people read one or more IDG publications each month.

Launched in 1990, IDG Books Worldwide is today the #1 publisher of best-selling computer books in the United States. We are proud to have received eight awards from the Computer Press Association in recognition of editorial excellence and three from Computer Currents' First Annual Readers' Choice Awards. Our best-selling *...For Dummies®* series has more than 50 million copies in print with translations in 31 languages. IDG Books Worldwide, through a joint venture with IDG's Hi-Tech Beijing, became the first U.S. publisher to publish a computer book in the People's Republic of China. In record time, IDG Books Worldwide has become the first choice for millions of readers around the world who want to learn how to better manage their businesses.

Our mission is simple: Every one of our books is designed to bring extra value and skill-building instructions to the reader. Our books are written by experts who understand and care about our readers. The knowledge base of our editorial staff comes from years of experience in publishing, education, and journalism — experience we use to produce books to carry us into the new millennium. In short, we care about books, so we attract the best people. We devote special attention to details such as audience, interior design, use of icons, and illustrations. And because we use an efficient process of authoring, editing, and desktop publishing our books electronically, we can spend more time ensuring superior content and less time on the technicalities of making books.

You can count on our commitment to deliver high-quality books at competitive prices on topics you want to read about. At IDG Books Worldwide, we continue in the IDG tradition of delivering quality for more than 30 years. You'll find no better book on a subject than one from IDG Books Worldwide.

John Kilcullen
Chairman and CEO
IDG Books Worldwide, Inc.

*Eighth Annual
Computer Press
Awards ≥1992*

*Ninth Annual
Computer Press
Awards ≥1993*

*Tenth Annual
Computer Press
Awards ≥1994*

*Eleventh Annual
Computer Press
Awards ≥1995*

IDG is the world's leading IT media, research and exposition company. Founded in 1964, IDG had 1997 revenues of $2.05 billion and has more than 9,000 employees worldwide. IDG offers the widest range of media options that reach IT buyers in 75 countries representing 95% of worldwide IT spending. IDG's diverse product and services portfolio spans six key areas including print publishing, online publishing, expositions and conferences, market research, education and training, and global marketing services. More than 90 million people read one or more of IDG's 290 magazines and newspapers, including IDG's leading global brands — Computerworld, PC World, Network World, Macworld and the Channel World family of publications. IDG Books Worldwide is one of the fastest-growing computer book publishers in the world, with more than 700 titles in 36 languages. The "...For Dummies®" series alone has more than 50 million copies in print. IDG offers online users the largest network of technology-specific Web sites around the world through IDG.net (http://www.idg.net), which comprises more than 225 targeted Web sites in 55 countries worldwide. International Data Corporation (IDC) is the world's largest provider of information technology data, analysis and consulting, with research centers in over 41 countries and more than 400 research analysts worldwide. IDG World Expo is a leading producer of more than 168 globally branded conferences and expositions in 35 countries including E3 (Electronic Entertainment Expo), Macworld Expo, ComNet, Windows World Expo, ICE (Internet Commerce Expo), Agenda, DEMO, and Spotlight. IDG's training subsidiary, ExecuTrain, is the world's largest computer training company, with more than 230 locations worldwide and 785 training courses. IDG Marketing Services helps industry-leading IT companies build international brand recognition by developing global integrated marketing programs via IDG's print, online and exposition products worldwide. Further information about the company can be found at www.idg.com.   1/26/00

Dedication

I'd like to dedicate this book to Ashley Rothschild, for her joie de vivre, inspirational presence, and incredible wisdom in both perceiving the world and how the world perceives us in turn.

— *Michael Bellomo*

This book is dedicated to my beloved wife, Lisa, and our wonderful children, Crystal, Brandi and James. Their unwavering patience, support, and love contributed to this book as much as my writing, if not more.

— *James Marchetti*

Authors' Acknowledgments

We'd both like to thank Carole McClendon of Waterside Productions for her unflagging devotion to this book in helping to turn this idea into reality.

Publisher's Acknowledgments

We're proud of this book; please send us your comments through our IDG Books Worldwide Online Registration Form located at www.dummies.com.

Some of the people who helped bring this book to market include the following:

Acquisitions, Editorial, and Media Development

Senior Project Editor: Pat O'Brien

Acquisitions Editor: Georgette Blau

Copy Editors: Bill Barton, Nicole A. Laux, Sandy Blackthorn, Rebekah Mancilla

Technical Editor: Michael A. Gibson

Permissions Editor: Carmen Krikorian

Media Development Specialist: Jamie Hastings-Smith

Media Development Coordinator: Marisa E. Pearman

Editorial Manager: Mary C. Corder

Media Development Manager: Laura Carpenter

Media Development Supervisor: Richard Graves

Editorial Assistant: Candace Nicholson

Production

Project Coordinator: Leslie Alvarez

Layout and Graphics: Amy Adrian, Beth Brooks, Joseph Bucki, Brian Torwelle

Proofreaders: Laura Albert, John Bitter, Susan Moritz, Dwight Ramsey, York Production Services, Inc.

Indexer: York Production Services, Inc.

General and Administrative

IDG Books Worldwide, Inc.: John Kilcullen, CEO; Bill Barry, President and COO; John Ball, Executive VP, Operations & Administration; John Harris, CFO

IDG Books Technology Publishing Group: Richard Swadley, Senior Vice President and Publisher; Mary Bednarek, Vice President and Publisher; Walter R. Bruce III, Vice President and Publisher; Joseph Wikert, Vice President and Publisher; Mary C. Corder, Editorial Director; Andy Cummings, Publishing Director, General User Group; Barry Pruett, Publishing Director

IDG Books Manufacturing: Ivor Parker, Vice President, Manufacturing

IDG Books Marketing: John Helmus, Assistant Vice President, Director of Marketing

IDG Books Online Management: Brenda McLaughlin, Executive Vice President, Chief Internet Officer; Gary Millrood, Executive Vice President of Business Development, Sales and Marketing

IDG Books Packaging: Marc J. Mikulich, Vice President, Brand Strategy and Research

IDG Books Production for Branded Press: Debbie Stailey, Production Director

IDG Books Sales: Roland Elgey, Senior Vice President, Sales and Marketing; Michael Violano, Vice President, International Sales and Sub Rights

◆

The publisher would like to give special thanks to Patrick J. McGovern, without whom this book would not have been possible.

◆

Contents at a Glance

Cartoons at a Glance

By Rich Tennant

page 57

page 97

page 295

page 207

page 235

page 151

page 271

page 11

Fax: 978-546-7747
E-mail: richtennant@the5thwave.com
World Wide Web: www.the5thwave.com

Table of Contents

Introduction

●●●

*W*elcome to the third millennium. We're entering a time when clean fusion power, a working space station, and parking meters that take credit cards are either right around the corner or already here. And by picking up this book, you're about to begin working with one of the newest phenomena to beguile, confuse, and generally cause stress in the life of new administrators: the dreaded *mixed network*.

Mixed networks are groups of machines that include more than one operating system. A mixed network of 20 machines, for example, can include 14 computers running Windows 2000, five running Linux, and one running NetWare. Getting each of these machines to communicate, print, and share files can prove a logistical nightmare for a network administrator.

If you get each operating system to talk with the other machines, hand out files, print to your printers, and not kick the other machines in the sandbox, you're performing what's known as *system integration*.

In performing system integration, you get to combine city-planning types of skills to decide how you want to structure your network of different machines, nursery-school teacher types of skills to make sure that all the machines are playing nice, and traffic-cop types of skills to act as the enforcer on the system. How's that for job variety? And to make you feel even better, performing system integration means that you're a part of the wave of the future. Or at least you can take comfort knowing that you're building excellent job security by acquiring these skills.

The bottom line is that, if you're in technical administration of any kind, you can't afford to remain out of the loop about hooking up different machines. Even if your integration needs are minimal, you're likely to see more and more mixing of your network as time goes on. What the excitement and press coverage surrounding the new releases of Windows 2000, Red Hat Linux, and NetWare misses is that each new operating system increases the number of mixed networks out there in the business, academic, and software-development worlds.

Now, most books on system integration assume that you already have your Ph.D. in Obscure Computer Sciences and worked your way into your present job by helping to debug Windows 2000 on your summer break. If that describes you, congratulations — send us a postcard from Seattle the next time that you get a sunny day.

But more commonly, the person responsible for orchestrating an integrated system is someone unfortunate enough to find himself in the wrong place at the wrong time. With little or no warning — *presto* . . . you're the new person in charge of the mixed network. You have users with problems (*lots* of problems), and you need to know what to do — yesterday, if not sooner.

If you fall into this category, you came to the right book. In this book, you get straightforward info on what to do and just how to do it — in plain English. Nothing more; nothing less.

About This Book

We designed *Networking and System Integration For Dummies* to serve as a quick, easy-to-understand reference that helps guide you through the most common commands and challenges that you face in working in a mixed networking environment.

Why quick? Because you need your answers fast if you're in the middle of something important. Why easy? Because if you can't understand why you're doing something with Linux, Windows, Unix, or NetWare, you're just one step above typing commands randomly, which is a dangerous recipe.

The topics you find in this book include the following:

- ✔ The mysterious origins of Windows, NetWare, Unix, and its offshoot known as Linux.
- ✔ Designing and setting up a network.
- ✔ Networking concepts that all machines can handle.
- ✔ Becoming the administrator, wherever you are.
- ✔ Setting up networked devices such as external drives and printers.
- ✔ Getting your machines to communicate.
- ✔ Managing users on a mixed network.
- ✔ Troubleshooting your systems.

If you have a specific question or problem, just turn to the specific chapter that covers it. You don't need to read the entire book if you're out of time before the next manager's meeting or before your next power lunch.

Foolish Assumptions

By no means do you need a complicated technical background to use this book. But you get the most out of this book if you possess one (or more) of the following:

- ✔ A familiarity with the basic components of a computer system — that is, you know your way around a keyboard; you know how to turn the CPU (central processing unit) on and off; and you can figure out whether your screen is off and whether it's running a screen saver.

- ✔ A computer network with at least two different kinds of OSes (operating systems). Obviously, hands-on training helps you practice your commands until you're comfortable with the system.

- ✔ A genuine desire to figure out system integration because you want to see what all the fuss is about or because your job depends on it.

And although not absolute requisites, if you plan to do any work on a network in need of system integration, you can benefit from the following:

- ✔ If you have at least one Unix or Linux machine, you want boot disks, rescue disks, and the installation media for your Unix and/or Linux operating system.

- ✔ Knowing some basic Linux commands, such as commands for changing directories and finding your location, always helps. And you need to know what a *path* is. But if you don't, well, don't panic. We go over some of the basic commands and even talk about a few that you may not know.

- ✔ If you run Windows 2000, you need a copy of the Windows 2000 system on CD-ROM or floppy disks.

- ✔ You need access to a copy of the Windows 2000 Server as well as the Windows 2000 Professional. But if you have Server but not Professional, don't fret. That's all right. If you have only Professional, you can still use this book, but some of the administrative functions that we discuss may not be directly available to you.

Incidentally, if you're still figuring out how to install Linux, check out one of the latest books on the subject from IDG Books Worldwide — *Linux Administration For Dummies,* by Michael Bellomo. If you're still figuring out how to administer Windows 2000 systems, check out *Windows 2000 Administration For Dummies*, also — what a coincidence — by Michael Bellomo (and published by IDG Books Worldwide).

Conventions Used in This Book

What's a technology book without conventions? A *convention* is an established way of handling specific information. We use conventions throughout this book so that you don't need to spend valuable time flipping back and forth through the book or scratching your head while trying to figure out what to type, click, or press.

Commands in the World According to Bill (Gates): Windows 2000 conventions

To administer the latest and greatest of the Windows 2000 world, you use two things: applications designed to simplify your administrative workload and *wizards*, programs that are (to steal a well-known line from a Debian GNU/Linux designer) designed so that a chicken can work them — that is, by hunting and pecking on the keyboard or with the mouse.

We tell you in the text when to click, type, or press anything. And, if you're going to choose a command from a list of several menus, we direct you to do so in the following manner: "Choose Start⇨Programs⇨Accessories⇨Disk Manager."

This example means that, if you click Start and then move your mouse pointer over the Programs selection, your reward is a new submenu that lists options. Move your mouse pointer over Accessories, and you see the next listing of options. From there, you can choose Disk Manager by clicking it or by pressing the appropriate keys.

Typing commands outside the Windows world

If you delve into the other side of the networking world — the Unix/Linux yin to Microsoft's yang — you likely need to step outside of the GUI and use the keyboard exclusively to administer and edit a Unix or Linux system.

GUI (pronounced *gooey*) is an acronym for *Graphical User Interface*. Your Windows desktop and all the menus, windows, and icons are part of your GUI. Although the latest versions of Unix and Linux also come with GUIs today, they didn't always do so. Originally, these two operating systems came without any desktop, icons, or need for a mouse.

Even to this day, you can't complete some functions in Unix or Linux without editing outside the GUI by using the keyboard. Entering commands in this manner is also known as entering commands at the *command line* (or *command prompt*).

In the text, commands, filenames, paths, descriptions of things that you see on-screen, and so on, are shown in a `monofont` type. Here's an example: "The screen displays `/usr/bin`."

In the text, if you need to type something, what you're to type appears in boldface, as in the following example: "Type **echo $PATH** and then press Enter."

If what you're to type appears on a line by itself, you see something like the following example:

```
[root@linuxnet /root]# passwd <name>
```

The following list explains what all those characters mean:

- Text that we don't surround with [ ], { }, or < > you must type exactly as it appears.

  So, in this example, you must type **passwd** exactly as shown.

- Italicized text inside angle brackets < > you need to replace with the appropriate text.

  So, in this example, you need to replace *<name>* with an actual name. Here, you put in your own name that you use to log in to your Linux network. (And, no, you don't need telepathy to figure it out. In the text, we explicitly tell you what you need to type.)

Take a breath and don't worry about this stuff. The vast majority of the time, you can figure out what you type versus what the computer's displaying back at you. And, if you ever forget the conventions, just come back and skim this section.

Keystrokes with less hassle

If you need to press multiple keys together, the keystroke combination is shown with a plus sign (+) between the keys. Ctrl+Alt+Delete, for example, means that you need to press the Ctrl, Alt, and Delete keys all at the same time. And, no, you don't need to use one hand to press this keystroke combination . . . unless you *really* feel ambitious.

Finally, you may see commands with labels as follows:

> ✔ <ESC>
> ✔ <ALT>
> ✔ <DEL>

These commands represent the corresponding keys on the keyboard, which some keyboards also spell out as Escape and Delete. (Hardly ever see Alt spelled out, however.)

How This Book Is Organized

If you expect us to organize this book along the same lines as other *For Dummies* books you've encountered, you expect right.

If you're new to this Brave New World of system integration, you're probably best off reading the first three parts of this book to start off so that you gain the basic system concepts that you need to work with such a system. (Or, at the very least, so that you get an idea of the scope of the task in front of you. Onward, brave soul!)

Of course, maybe you do know some Linux or you've worked with its big brother, Unix. Perhaps you're even certified as a Microsoft Windows 2000 professional (or at least as a seasoned amateur). If you can mouse, `ps`, and `grep` with the best techno-jockeys out there, you don't need to read this book in any order. If you face a problem that you can't solve — for example, adding a user account — simply jump to the appropriate section of the book and tackle it head on.

So don't panic. Figure it out. And if the answer doesn't pop up, remember that you have your handy *Networking and System Integration For Dummies* book to turn to.

Part I: The NOS Isn't Nitrous Oxide!

In Part I, you get a quick once-over about the origins of each of the major operating systems that we cover in this book — including Windows 2000, Unix/Linux, and NetWare. You see what each operating system was designed for and what you can do with it. You also see how you can evaluate your needs for each operating system — if the operating system isn't imposed on you already — and how to adjust your hardware to cope.

You also discover the importance of starting to clear the way for your future network with a plan for how to handle whatever life (or your user community) throws at you.

Part II: Building a Network from the Ground Up

In Part II, you start to see just where you need to begin after you decide to start revamping or laying out your integrated system. Rather than start at the software level, you need to begin with the hardware — specifically, the actual wires and plugs that hook up your system and enable your machines to talk to each other or enable you to surf the Internet.

You also get a quick course on the basic parts that make up your network. Whether you administer a simple network with a modem line and a cord of Ethernet cable or a sophisticated setup with routers and switches, you find the info you need in this part.

Part III: System Administration Basics

In Part III, you see examples of how you can create strong, effective passwords. Passwords are the first step in building good security on your system. You also find out what being the alpha geek on the block is like. In other words, you find out how to stop being a user and start becoming an administrator.

You become the *administrator* (in Windows-speak), or the *root account* (in Unix-speak), a being with the amazing powers to leap tall file systems in a single bound, scan binaries faster than a speeding hard drive . . . well, you get the idea. Avoid Kryptonite if at all possible after reading this part.

Part IV: Administering Networked Communications and Files

In Part IV, you get to know basic protocols. Unfortunately, if you enjoy eating at places such as *Il Fornaio* over *Jack in the Box*, this part's not about how to act at formal dinner parties and on which side of the plate you put your fork and knife. It's about the UDP and the TCP/IP protocol suites, your friends in the networking game.

Also in this part, you see how you can centralize control over your users and the files that they create. (This part is where being a *benevolent dictator* comes in handy. Democracy is fine for the government, but it makes for bad system integration.)

Part V: E-mail and News

In Part V, you figure out how to effectively work with the various e-mail programs that your operating systems can use. You see why e-mail and news are becoming so integral to every organization with computers in it, which is the reason that you need to know how to use and administer the MTAs, or mail transport agents, that run on each operating system.

Part VI: Security and Troubleshooting

In Part VI, you find out about how to lock down special files that you don't want people to tamper with. You also get some simple (and common-sense) techniques to effectively block outside intruders from getting onto your network and causing damage.

And, if you're in the mood to put on your Sherlock Holmes cap and pick up your magnifying glass, you find out how to play detective and track down intruders in your domain. How you decide to punish them is, of course, your choice. Have fun, get creative, and remember that you're the boss.

Part VII: The Part of Tens

Part of the _For Dummies_ tradition is "The Part of Tens," which gives you neat shopping lists of answers to important issues. Here, you find out about ten Web sites that help you cover integration issues, ten tools that increase the usefulness of your integrated system, and ten truths about system integration that span from the urban legends of networking to the tried-and-tested truths — all of which you can use if you're stuck in the middle of a tough networking situation.

Part VIII: Appendixes

In Part VIII, you get a series of lists that you can skim to find useful nuggets of information. Appendix A provides a glossary of network operating system terms that you can turn to if the hard drive between your ears starts to slip (as ours does before that first cup of java in the morning). Appendix B lists the most important contents and freebies that we include on the CD-ROM that accompanies this book. Appendix C recaps and covers more options available to you if you need to refer to system documentation or need outside resources to get help in solving a particular problem. And Appendix D goes over basic instructions on how to make those all-important boot disks that can save your life if your system decides to die on you.

Icons Used in This Book

If you haven't had the opportunity to use a *For Dummies* book before, notice the humorous pictures, known as *icons*, that we sprinkle throughout the text. They're here to give you a heads up about certain types of information, as follows:

Don't forget information highlighted by this icon — it's important. Tie a piece of string around your finger if you need to.

This icon highlights nerd stuff. You probably like this stuff if you know, by heart, every line from either *The Matrix* or *Weird Science*.

This icon showcases shortcuts, time-savers, and generally useful information that we've uncovered from our general experience working with different networked machines.

Watch out! This icon points out a strong warning that you better pay attention to the accompanying information.

Where to Go From Here

Unless you have a burning issue — and we mean *burning*, as in smoke coming out of one of your machines — start with some material on each operating system's background and then move into what you need to become familiar with on your network. Familiarize yourself with what each operating system can do and what it needs to do it, and the rest usually falls into place.

Ready? *Vini, vidi, integrae alla!*

"I came, I saw, I integrated it all!"

Part I
The NOS Isn't Nitrous Oxide!

"I guess you could say this is the hub of our network."

In this part . . .

Y ou may be a network administrator by accident, or
you may have been pressed into service like a sur-
prised draftee. You could be a software enthusiast who
has volunteered to fix, upgrade, and standardize the network. Or you may be a run-of-the-mill administrator
whose system has gradually expanded.

The main assumption is that you've had some operating
system knowledge in the recent past. So we're not going
to spend the section on installation tips. (Besides boring
you to death, to describe the installation of Linux, UNIX,
and Windows 2000 would pretty much be the entire book!)
Instead, we show you exactly what the job of system integration entails — and what you need to know when you're
trying to make two or more operating systems talk to each
other!

We also go over the basic strengths of different network
operating systems, so that you can choose which one to
focus on if you need to decide to standardize the entire
network. We focus on System 5 UNIX, Microsoft Windows,
and Red Hat Linux. (As a bonus, you also see how to pronounce the word Linux so you sound more erudite in your
company meetings.)

Finally, in this first part you find out how to plan out a network from scratch, which will come in handy even if
you're adapting an older system you've inherited. You see
how important it is to talk to your user community and
isolate, prioritize, and budget for your needs. From there,
it's (relatively) simple to roll up your sleeves and begin
hooking machines together.

Chapter 1

Networked Operating Systems: What They Are and What You Need to Run Them

In This Chapter

▶ What system integration and mixed networking are all about

▶ Major operating systems

▶ Hardware requirements

*I*f you've ever spent part of your day trying to get machines with two different NOSes (network operating systems) to talk to each other, you've already performed some type of *system integration*. What's more, you know the challenge that system integration represents. (If not, well, aren't you in for a treat.)

In this chapter, you get a quick dose of various network operating system terminology to make sure that you know what *integration* and *mixed networks* are all about. We also go over the various popular and widely used operating systems that are available. And you find out why knowing more about these operating systems is important and how it enables you to build a diverse but well-rounded set of servers. Finally, we provide you with a handy list of the kinds of hardware that you need to run each operating system on your network.

Understanding System Integration (And Its Pains)

Webster's dictionary describes *integration* as "the act of bringing together parts into a whole." We're certainly not going to argue with Mr. Webster. In fact, that definition is a pretty good description of what you must do if you have a dozen or so machines — some running Linux, others running Windows, and perhaps another with the odd NetWare server thrown in for good measure. As an administrator, you probably must do at least two of the following things:

✔ Make sure that all machines can communicate with each other.

✔ Make files available to all machines.

✔ Make sure that users can print from each machine.

✔ Connect to the Internet from each machine.

✔ Perform administration tasks from each machine.

✔ Do anything else that those higher up in the chain of command at your company request.

Because each operating system has its own way of doing things, integration can prove the highlight (okay, the real pain) in an administrator's day. The reason is that, after you start throwing all sorts of software and hardware together, you end up with what's known as a *mixed network*.

Mixing Up Your Network

So what exactly *is* mixed networking? When we first heard about it, we envisioned some kind of pub for computer professionals, where you could saunter up and place your order for a mixed network. "Network-tender, I need a pair of Ethernet cards on the rocks, a couple of Linux servers, and something running the latest version of NetWare, and I'd like it shaken, not stirred." Ah, if things were only that easy.

Mixing networks isn't like ordering straight up from a menu. Often, you have little choice about what you get off the bat, because you're often inheriting a network (some may call it a *patchwork*) of computers that grew out of your organization's needs. By definition, any group of machines that includes more than one operating system is *mixed*.

A simple mixed network can consist of, say, four computers where three run Windows and one runs Unix. A more complex one can include a couple dozen computers running NetWare and five running Linux, with a bunch of nonstandard printers thrown in for spice. A really complex one may span hundreds of machines and include six versions of Windows, two versions of Linux, and the latest version of NetWare, all running on everything from state-of-the-art computers to an antique TRS-80 to an empty gumball machine.

If you prefer analogies, you can think of a mixed network as similar to what you see on a freeway: You see lots of different cars — some fast, some big, some luxurious, and some limping along smoking out the tail pipe (rather like one of our old jalopies, now that we mention it). A mixed network is similar in that it's a conglomeration of different operating systems with completely different capabilities. What's more, a similar network (the freeway) ties it all together — and today, that network normally consists of Ethernet computer cabling.

Following are a couple general tidbits to keep in mind:

✔ Almost all interactions between computers are really some form of communication. Whether it's just asking "Who's out there?" or sharing files or sending a print job to a printer — or even delivering a piece of electronic mail — the interaction/communication consists of sending information via cable or wire from one machine to another. We grant you that this idea may not seem like a mind-blower today, but back 20 or 30 years ago, it was an *amazing* idea.

✔ Purchasing the right software and hardware to make sure that everything in a mixed network runs together takes time, effort, research, more research, reading, more reading, and a fair amount of shopping around.

The Hands-Down Easiest Solution to System Integration

Although the statement probably sounds like heresy coming from the authors of a book telling you how to hook up different operating systems, you need to know a secret: The hands-down easiest solution to system integration as you're designing a network from scratch is *to avoid the problem entirely*.

Yes, it's true. No matter how many tips and techniques you employ to enable one *OS* (operating system) to talk to another, you simplify matters to no end if you stick with using only one operating system and stay faithful to it.

But here's the reality: 99 percent of the time you don't have that option because you inherit a mixed network from a prior administrator. And besides, if you focus on only one OS, your users may miss out on software that they need to fulfill their tasks in your organization. Many high-end server programs, for example, run only on Unix. On the other hand, good luck finding a copy of your typical shoot-'em-up video game that works on NetWare.

The gratuitous history lesson on network operating systems

Truth be told, *NOS* is an old acronym that Novell coined years ago to define its OS (operating system). The term *NOS* was a marketing ploy to differentiate Novell's operating system from the current competition, which at the time was Unix and DOS (for *D*isk *O*perating *S*ystem, the precursor to Microsoft Windows). But the overall idea was to point out that Novell's operating system enabled groups of computers running NetWare to easily communicate among themselves.

Back then, NetWare was the behemoth of server-oriented operating systems and still commanded a large share of the server operating systems. None of the other operating systems call themselves *network operating systems* anymore, because an operating system that can't interface with other machines by default doesn't sell in today's computing environment. For that matter, Novell's moved away from the phrase itself.

Slogging Through the Different Operating Systems

Choosing an operating system is a lot like choosing a car. But the difference for most people is that you can drive more than one operating system at a time and glean the benefits of each of them to your advantage. As long as you have the right hardware, you can mix up the operating systems you use to get the best features of each and to deliver reasonably fast performance to your end users at a reasonable cost.

One of your first questions may concern which operating systems to use. (We use the term *may* here, because you may be stepping into an administration position where you inherit someone's prior work and network design. Although given the haphazard structure of many networks we've seen, *design* is a pretty loose term to use.) To make your selection, you need to understand a little about the major operating systems on the market today and what each was originally designed for.

Microsoft Windows: The 800-pound gorilla

At the time of this writing, Microsoft is embroiled in enough legal rough and tumble to make an entire legion of attorneys run out and place down payments on that fleet of yachts they've always wanted. The Windows operating system is in for a split from its close family members — Microsoft Office and the many other programs that Microsoft has produced over the years. But make no mistake: The Microsoft world is still a powerful force and is likely to remain so for a long time.

Microsoft first began development of a piece of software known as the *Interface Manager* (subsequently renamed *Microsoft Windows*) in September 1981. Although the first prototypes used menus at the bottom of the screen, Microsoft changed the interface in 1982 to use drop-down menus and dialog boxes, as the Xerox Star computer used. These prototypes were the first in the line of GUI-based operating systems that soon came to dominate the software marketplace.

GUI is an acronym for *graphical user interface*. At one time the Holy Grail of operating systems, providing a user with a virtual desktop made of computer graphics, the graphical user interface became the sure-fire key to selling millions of copies of software. Although the GUI took a little while to catch on, those who bet on this stack of chips (such as one William Gates) hit the jackpot.

At the time, other GUI-based operating systems were in development and in direct competition with Microsoft — for example, the just-released VisiOn and impending TopView. Apple Computer had just released its Lisa model (but not the mind-bending Macintosh). And Digital Research Corporation had announced that it was soon to release GEM, another competing graphical environment.

The original Windows

Against a background of competitors, Microsoft finally announced the release of Windows (on a developer-only basis) in November 1983. Microsoft Windows promised an easy-to-use graphical interface, device-independent graphics, and multitasking support. The first consumer version hit the store shelves (after 55 programmer years of development) in November 1985. The selection of applications was sparse, however, and Windows sales were modest.

Windows 2.0 – 3.1

Windows 2.0 was introduced in the fall of 1987, providing significant usability improvements to Windows. With the addition of icons and overlapping windows (at that time, another revolutionary idea), Windows became a viable environment for the development of major applications. Later versions of Windows began to sell more quickly due to their capability to use applications while running multiple DOS applications simultaneously in the extended memory.

Microsoft Windows 3.0, released in May 1990, was a complete overhaul of the Windows environment. It could address memory beyond 640K, and it had a much more powerful user interface. Independent software vendors started developing Windows applications with vigor. More than ten million copies of Windows were sold, making it the best-selling graphical user interface in the history of computing.

Microsoft Windows 3.1, released in April 1992, provided significant improvements to Windows 3.0. In its first *two months* on the market, it sold more than three million copies. And if you thought — as many people did at the time — that this figure was a sales record that nothing else could break, you hadn't seen anything yet.

Windows 95 and 98

Windows 95 was released in August 1995, with many people waiting at midnight to buy one of the first copies.

Designed to coexist with Windows NT, Windows 95 offers a greater degree of backward compatibility with older drivers and software at the expense of greater stability. If you run Windows 95, ask yourself, "How many times must I reboot my computer in a day?"

Windows 98 was released as an upgrade to Windows 95. It features the same interface and features of Windows 95.

Windows NT

Windows NT is a separate product from Windows 3.*x* and Windows 9*x*. Windows NT is aimed at the enterprise market for use on high-end workstations and servers. The first version, 3.1, and versions 3.5 and 3.51 used the same interface as Windows 3.1. Version 4.0 uses the interface first introduced in Windows 95.

Windows NT runs on Intel and Alpha processors.

Two versions are available: Advanced Server and Workstation. Advanced Server comes with additional software that enables it to perform the role of the enterprise server (that is, a server that runs extremely large and complex network of computers handling complex tasks such as data warehousing). Advanced Server also offers, in addition to the features of Workstation, the following features:

- ✔ Software for controlling and managing domains.
- ✔ Internet Information Server (IIS).
- ✔ Support for Microsoft BackOffice products.
- ✔ DHCP, DNS, and WINS server software.

Windows 2000

Windows 2000 was released as an update to Windows NT 4.0. It isn't an upgrade to Windows 95 or 98. Windows 2000 offers the following improvements:

✔ A full 32-bit operating system.

✔ Support for NTFS or FAT32, with support for hard drives as big as 32GB running FAT32.

✔ Windows File Protection, which prevents installed applications from deleting necessary system files.

✔ The elimination of many reboot scenarios, including program installations that require a reboot to function correctly.

✔ Support for up to 4GB of random-access memory (RAM).

✔ Stronger Internet integration with Internet Explorer 5.0.1.

Three different versions of Windows 2000 are available: Professional, Server, and Advanced Server.

Amateurs not allowed: Windows 2000 Professional

The Windows 2000 Professional version replaces and extends the user base that works with Windows 95 and 98. Microsoft includes the client interface advantages first seen in Windows NT 4.0 Workstation with this version. Microsoft has stated that 2000 Professional is the new desktop standard operating system for the current decade.

To serve and protect: Windows 2000 Server

Windows 2000 Server is the networked version of Windows 2000. This flavor of Windows is slated to replace the Windows NT 4.0 Server. In a nutshell, the Server version of the Windows 2000 suite provides the main administrative core of a Windows network. The product's target market is small to medium-sized application deployments, such as corporate e-mail, shared printers, or World Wide Web development.

Microsoft has two other versions of Windows 2000: the Windows 2000 Advanced Server and Windows 2000 Datacenter Server. Advanced Server is designed to run more powerful servers; it offers support for an additional 4GB of RAM (totaling 8GB). Similarly, the Datacenter Server is designed specifically for production-level server environments and is most likely to challenge installations using high-end Unix environments, including corporate data warehousing and large-scale computing projects in the scientific or financial fields. These products aim at a very high-end corporate and academic market, not the vast majority of Windows 2000 administrators.

The bottom line on Windows 2000

If you're familiar with working in earlier forms of Windows, the most obvious change in the Microsoft world is on the surface. As you open windows and start clicking through the Windows file directories, you see some small but noticeable differences.

Wait a minute! What about Microsoft Windows NT 5.0?

To steal a line from the old Palmolive commercials, you're soaking in it. Windows NT 5.0 *is* Windows 2000. The 5.0 moniker was a casualty of the extremely astute Microsoft marketing department.

Early in 1999, Microsoft simply decided to rename the upcoming release of Windows NT 5.0 as Windows 2000. Windows 5.0 just didn't sound, well, apocalyptic enough for the new millennium.

And before you scoff at the name change, ask yourself whether you think first of a new x586-based chip or a new Pentium.

In what was the most recent incarnation of Windows, Windows 98, the idea of blending the operating system interface with the Internet really began in earnest. You can expect to see a Web-like interface on your windows, which enables you to jump backward and forward between the directories that you visit.

Windows 2000 is also designed as a more stable and user-friendly NOS. The reason is that Microsoft's made a commitment to enter the arena of Web servers, file servers, and data servers with a vengeance. And this strategy is already paying off with its latest products.

On the Internet side of doing business, more than one million Web servers now use some form of Microsoft product. Recently, the *Wall Street Journal* reported that Microsoft's made an official company goal to nearly double the existing installations of its network servers in the e-commerce business world.

Unix/Linux: Less GUI, more filling

Unix, which began life at AT&T Bell Laboratories in the mid-1970s, was barely known to the public 25 years ago. Today, with the Information Age upon us, three-quarters of the technology- or finance-related companies in the Fortune 500 use Unix to help run their businesses. Unix implements trades on stock exchange floors, handles file servers at large banks, and, most notably, runs the network infrastructure for Microsoft Corporation.

From the start, Unix was built around the following three simple criteria:

✔ It's simple and elegant.

✔ It's written in a high-level language rather than in an assembly language.

✔ Programmers can reuse code to write new programs quickly and easily.

Not asking too much, right? Well, in the heyday of the mainframe computer, these ideas were simply crazy and unrealistic. (Much the same way that basing an OS on a GUI was considered insane at the time.) Today, these ideas make sense, but back then, they were truly revolutionary. The byproduct of these bedrock principles was unprecedented stability and scalability more than 20 years ago. In fact, Microsoft's taken those 20-some years to approach these benchmark levels of quality in its products.

The flavors of Unix: Everything but chocolate chips

Baskin Robbins offers 31 flavors, right? Well, over the years, Unix seems to have blossomed into the Baskin Robbins of operating systems. As Unix progressed and developed at different companies (unlike Windows, which was helmed solely by Microsoft), different versions, also known as flavors, began to appear on the scene. In fact, the flavors today include Solaris, HP-UX, SCO, IBM's AIX, and more.

In 1984, the University of California at Berkeley released Version 4.2BSD (Berkeley Software Distribution), which included a complete implementation of the TCP/IP networking protocols. Systems based on this version and on later BSD releases provided a multivendor networking capability based on Ethernet networking. The networking support included the capability to remotely log in, transfer files, send and receive electronic mail, and perform other important tasks.

As Unix was *ported onto,* or written for, more and more different types of computer hardware, the Unix networking enabled many different types of systems to share and mutually use data. After Sun Microsystems added extra software known as *NFS* (*Network File System*) to its version of Unix, Solaris, it significantly enhanced this capability to share and mutually use data.

So what do stability and scalability mean anyway?

We're glad you asked.

Stability refers to the probability of your computer *crashing*, which is when your machine refuses to work anymore. Normally, the only way to continue work on a crashed computer is to reboot it. The more stable a computer is, the less it crashes. Really stable operating systems such as Unix or Linux don't crash even if you're running a gazillion programs on them at once (which is the OS equivalent of juggling and riding a unicycle).

Scalability is a measurement of how well a NOS works in a large network of machines as opposed to a small one. Unix is just as stable and fast on 500 machines as it is on five.

Probably the most notable item about Unix (on the surface, anyway) is that it was designed without a GUI. The reason was partly because GUIs were still a thing of the future. But it was also a design decision that persisted for a long time. After all, why waste valuable computing power on drawing pretty pictures? Unix got a GUI type of look only recently, and even so, you still spend a fair amount of time outside the GUI, where you can truly do administrative work.

The bottom line? Unix is a very mature operating system and integrates well into a small or large network environment. It can *interface*, or connect, to virtually any operating system — large or small, new or old. And because Unix's proven so stable that it rarely crashes, it's become the workhorse of the back-end computing world.

Back-end computing refers to the computing tasks that users rarely, if ever, see. These tasks include handling print queues, sorting files, monitoring data-transmission rates, and so on. *Front-end computing* includes running the user interface and the applications that run on the machine, such as a word-processing program.

Linux: Now the road most taken

Linux is making inroads on Windows and is now a viable option for some administrators and network engineers. People often mention Linux and Unix in the same sentence, if not the same breath. We want to clear up the confusion a little:

Linux is a sort of cousin to the Unix OS. Created by Linus Torvalds and a group of programmers at the University of Helsinki in 1991, Linux began as a response to the high cost and high maintenance of the operating systems available to them. The resulting product took less computer muscle to run.

In fact, people don't usually realize just how little computing power that Linux can operate under comfortably. In this day and age, Pentium Pros are passé, and the next set of personal computers is likely to run on dilithium crystals. But Linux was developed to run on 386 computers. (In case you don't remember those specific machines, they're the ones that used floppy disks that were actually floppy — in other words, pretty ancient history.)

Prior to the recent glut of Linux on the street, Linux was touted as the premier "poor man's Unix" and also served as a direct cross-check to Windows by its dedicated and passionate users. The fact that Linux was, and still is, *open source* (that is, developers outside of a specific corporate body work on it) essentially made it free to those who were willing to dig around for the answers on how it worked.

The typical user of Linux wasn't your usual computer geek. These people were crazy about it — so much so that they met for hours each week to talk about Linux, new features, bug fixes, and so on (and still do). We're not talking chit chat either. These were four- or five-hour meetings with heated discussions about Linux and the plethora of cool things that it can do. These early adopters of Linux were the ones who made Linux an operating system that's much more oriented toward users who may not be so infatuated with their OS.

Today, Linux comes in various flavors, just as Unix does. The major flavors for Linux include Red Hat, Caldera, Debian, TurboLinux, and many more.

 Some people pronounce Linux as *Lynn-necks*, and others say *Line-ucks*. Personally, we like the second variation because it reminds us of one of the characters in the comic strip Peanuts — Linus, the fellow with the unhealthy fixation on his security blanket. But whichever way you decide to pronounce the term is okay, as we haven't spotted any Linux police enforcing one variation over the other.

Linux is very much like Unix. It's easier to install, but after you install it, you can face some different configuration issues. As has Unix, however, Linux is benefiting from adopting a GUI for both the general user's desktop and also by developing LinuxConf, a graphically based application that makes administering any computer running Linux much easier for people who're familiar with Windows.

NetWare: Taking a licking but still ticking

NetWare was a commercial operating system from the beginning. It started out as an operating system that could deliver two somewhat boring but incredibly critical services: file-server and print-server functions. NetWare still delivers these two important services very well and does a lot more now, too, including Web servers, firewalls, and gateways.

In the same manner as Unix and Linux users, NetWare aficionados were — and still are — passionate about their OS. Early on, these people knew that NetWare had a product that delivered. It gave them what they needed — it was fast and reliable. It was hearty and could handle the loads of larger networks while still capable of running on a small network with only a few users.

NetWare today still has a loyal following, but in recent years, it's had difficulty staying ahead and not just keeping up with the other operating systems of recent years. Don't worry, however: NetWare isn't a dinosaur or an obsolete operating system.

Dealing with the Nitty-Gritty Stuff: OS Hardware Requirements

Fortunately, and to Intel's good fortune, most operating systems run on Intel chipsets. These include the 80386, Pentium, Pentium Pro, Pentium II, Celeron (or as James' nephew says, "the Pentium Celery"), Pentium III, and the Pentium III Xeon. Not all the operating systems we discuss run on just any of these platforms, but all run fine on the Pentium II platform. This section covers the minimum hardware requirements of the major operating systems that we cover in this chapter.

NetWare 4 or 5 hardware requirements

The minimum standard hardware requirements for installing NetWare version 4 or 5 are as follows:

- ✔ Personal computer with a Pentium 166 MHz or faster processor.
- ✔ 64MB of memory (RAM); 96MB or more recommended.
- ✔ 500MB free hard-drive space, plus an additional 50 to 100MB per user on the system.

Note: NetWare works with a monochrome monitor just fine. Buying a color monitor isn't necessary.

A *chipset* is a family of microchip designs. Each silicon wafer that does the actual calculating and other functions of a computer can, by design, handle data slightly differently, which is why retailers actually go to the trouble of telling you whether your computer contains a chip from Intel or AMD or another manufacturer, such as Joe's No-Name Chip Center.

Unix (Solaris 8)

Of all the operating systems that we discuss in this book, Unix and Linux have the most fussy hardware requirements. (Although to be fair, the reason stems from the fact that they have so many flavors.) This section lists the most complete guidelines as of mid-2000 that you can use to select hardware to run Unix.

- ✔ The usual CPU alternatives are as follows:
  - Intel or compatible 486DX, 486DX2, 486SL, 486SX, 486DX4.
  - Intel Pentium, Pentium Pro, Pentium with MMX, Pentium II, Pentium II Xeon, Celeron, Pentium III, or Pentium III Xeon.

- AMD 486DX2-66, 486DX2-80, 486DX4-100, 486DX4-100 Enhanced, K5, K6, K6-2, or Athlon K7.

- Cyrix 486DLC-40, 5x86-100GP, 6x86-P120+GP, 6x86-P150+, 6x86-P166+, 6x86MX-PR150, or Cyrix MII.

✔ You can install between 32MB and 32GB memory.

Systems that use the Intel Pentium Pro and subsequently released Intel CPUs can address up to 32GB of physical memory. Individual processes are limited to a maximum of 3.5GB of virtual address space.

 Although individual installation procedures are beyond the scope of this book, if you want to view the Solaris 8 installation guide for Sun Microsystems hardware, go to the following Web site (and, yes, this *is* the Web address — we didn't just fall on the keyboard):

```
http://docs.sun.com/ab2/coll.214.7/SPARCINFOLIB/@Ab2TocView?A
            b2Lang=C&Ab2Enc=iso-8859-1
```

Linux

Because Linux has as many flavors as Unix, each with different requirements for hardware, you're best off referring to the two most popular Web sites that cover the hardware requirements for different brands of Linux, which you find at the following URLs:

```
www.redhat.com/support/hardware/intel/60/rh6.0-hcl-i.ld-
            25.html
```

```
www.linux.com/howto/Hardware-HOWTO.html
```

 The best Web site for you is probably the one run by the maker of your flavor of Linux. If you purchased Caldera's brand of Linux, for example, make sure that you visit the Web site that you find in its user documentation (assuming that the documentation doesn't list the information you need).

Windows 95

Following are the minimum hardware requirements for installing Windows 95:

✔ 486/25 MHz-based system.

✔ 8MB memory recommended.

✔ 40 to 45MB available hard-drive space.

✔ VGA or higher resolution display.

> ✔ MS-DOS upgrade requires Windows 3.*x* or Windows for Workgroups 3.*x*.
>
> ✔ Microsoft Mouse or compatible pointing device.

Windows 98

The minimum standard hardware requirements for installing Windows 98 are as follows:

> ✔ Personal computer with a 486DX 66 MHz or faster processor; Pentium CPU (central processing unit) recommended.
>
> ✔ 16MB memory (RAM); 24MB recommended.
>
> ✔ Installation or upgrade of Windows 98 requires the following varying amounts of hard-drive space:
>
> - Typical upgrade from Windows 95 requires approximately 195MB of free hard drive space but may range between 120 and 295MB, depending on your system configuration and the options you choose to install.
>
> - Full installation of Windows 98 on a FAT16 drive requires 225MB of free hard drive space but may range between 165 – 355MB, depending on the system configuration and options that you select.
>
> - Full installation of Windows 98 on a FAT32 drive requires 175MB of free hard-drive space but may range between 140 and 255MB, depending on the system configuration and options that you select.
>
> ✔ One 3.5-inch high-density floppy-disk drive.
>
> ✔ VGA or higher resolution (16-bit or 24-bit color SVGA recommended).
>
> ✔ Microsoft Mouse or compatible pointing device.

Windows NT

The hardware requirements for a Windows NT Server or Windows NT Workstation depend on the demands that you expect to put on the particular computer. The installation guide for each platform specifies the minimum requirements. This section offers a few recommendations for special cases.

For a production server that's to handle more than 100 users at a time, you probably need at least 32MB physical memory (RAM) plus 1GB disk space to hold the operating system, page files, disk logs, user database, and so on.

Each backup domain controller (BDC) can support up to 2,000 users. A single domain can support up to 40,000 network objects, including user accounts, machine accounts, and group accounts.

The following hardware specifications are the standard recommendations for a computer that you use as a primary domain controller (PDC) or BDC, which can support up to 3,000 users:

- ✔ At least 486/33 CPU.
- ✔ At least 32MB of RAM.

Windows 2000

On the accompanying CD is a tool for evaluating your current hardware for Windows 2000 compatibility. You also find a Windows 2000 Deployment Planning Guide document, which presents a comprehensive and exhaustive look at deploying Windows 2000. *Not* for the faint of heart.

The following Web site gives you an opportunity to tell Microsoft what platform you use and to determine whether it's Windows 2000 compatible:

```
www.microsoft.com/windows2000/upgrade/compat/search/computers
            .asp?HU=1
```

Windows 2000 Professional

Following are the requirements for installing Windows 2000 Professional:

- ✔ 133 MHz or higher Pentium-compatible CPU.
- ✔ 64MB RAM recommended minimum.

  More memory generally improves responsiveness (4GB RAM maximum).
- ✔ 2GB hard drive with a minimum of 650MB free space.

  Additional free hard-drive space is necessary if you're installing over a network.
- ✔ Windows 2000 Professional supports single and dual CPU systems.

Windows 2000 Server

The requirements for installing Windows 2000 server are as follows:

- ✔ 133 MHz or higher Pentium-compatible CPU.

  Windows 2000 Server supports up to four CPUs on one machine.
- ✔ 256MB RAM recommended minimum.

  128MB minimum supported; 4GB maximum.
- ✔ 2GB hard drive with a minimum of 1GB free space.

  Additional free hard-drive space is necessary if you're installing over a network.

Windows 2000 Advanced Server

Yep, more requirements, which are as follows for installing Windows 2000 Advanced Server:

- ✔ 133 MHz or higher Pentium-compatible CPU.

  Windows 2000 Advanced Server supports up to eight CPUs on one machine.

- ✔ 256MB RAM recommended minimum.

  128MB minimum supported; 8GB maximum.

- ✔ 2GB hard drive with a minimum of 1GB free space.

  Additional free hard-drive space is necessary if you're installing over a network.

Chapter 2

Selecting Operating Systems

• •

• •

*P*eople call operating systems many things. In fact, people call them the most amazing things whenever they don't work. Traditionally, people consider the different versions of the Microsoft Windows operating system as *front-end* computing products, meaning that their most common uses are user applications and standalone machines. NetWare enjoys the opposite reputation — as an OS that's a standout running the *back-end* processes that make a network function, which isn't so hot if a user wants to do word processing or spreadsheets.

Unix is traditionally a back-end OS, but like Windows 2000, this operating system's trying hard to make the jump from its current status as a purely one-dimensional operating system to become the one-stop shop for both back- and front-end needs.

Because large companies such as Sun Microsystems and Hewlett Packard have appropriated Unix, most users commonly think of it as a product of the same type of corporate structure as Windows. As for Linux, the closest anyone's come to tacking a label on it is to call it the most *organic* of all the operating systems.

Actually, organic is a really accurate term to use in talking about Linux (and we *don't* mean that you grow it without pesticides and sprinkle it with purified water). Linux is *constantly* growing. As a developer makes changes or additions to Linux, those changes are available via instant access on the World Wide Web.

What a Networked, Multiuser, Multitasking OS Can Do for You

A *networked, multiuser, multitasking operating system* is a real jaw-cracker to say, but it's an accurate description of what you need to run a network of mixed machines. Each part of that OS label tells you that a given operating system can perform tasks that many people consider essential in today's computing environment.

In the following sections, we take each descriptor in turn so that you can see just what treats a networked, multiuser, multitasking operating system holds in store for you.

Networked

Networked systems communicate with each other, passing information back and forth at the speed of light over network cables. A computer that doesn't connect to a network is known as a *standalone* machine. Networked machines enable people to use them even if they're not physically present at the computer's keyboard. A person can log in on a laptop computer in California and access the data on a networked computer in New York City.

Multiuser

A *multiuser* system enables a number of people (hence the *multiple* part of the word) to use the same computer at the same time. Because a multiuser system is by definition networked, a shortage of keyboards at a single terminal is no longer an issue. Users can work from many remote locations simultaneously.

Multitasking

A multitasking system can run many programs, routines, and applications at the same time. This capability enables multiple users to complete their work simultaneously, improving overall productivity.

Operating system

The *operating system* is the software part of the computer that controls 95 percent of everything that you do in making sure that one computer can talk to another. (The other five percent that controls what you do is hardware based, including cables, routers, and so on.) Discussing what an operating system actually is can become a tricky proposition but an essential one. The following section goes into more detail about what an OS is and why you need to become aware of what it does for you.

What an Operating System Is and Why You Need to Care

Okay, here's what an operating system really is:

An interface.

We can see the puzzled expressions everywhere each time that we make this statement. Don't we mean a keyboard or a mouse? Well, you can call these *physical* interfaces, but an operating system is actually more of a *mental* interface between you and your computer.

In essence, it's a collection of all the pieces of software that make a computer run. An operating system manages hardware devices and carries out your wishes by making the hardware do the work that you need it to do. Every application that you use, every click of your mouse, each picture that you draw on-screen or alien invader that you crispy-fry in a shoot-em-up game must go through the operating system.

Choosing a server's operating system isn't simply based on the functionality of a particular version of a product. It's a strategic, long-term decision driven by the organization's demands for a platform on which to build solutions for its business problems. And the demands that organizations place on server operating systems (ranging from larger, more complex print jobs to real-time stock quotes) are quickly expanding.

In addition to basic file and printer sharing, server operating systems must handle the following tasks:

- Communications
- Internet use
- Management
- Large-scale distributed applications

These demands make the server operating system of choice a multipurpose platform capable of providing a comprehensive and integrated set of services while excelling in each individual role.

Whoa! What's all that corporate mumbo jumbo? Those kinds of issues drive an organization toward a certain operating system. Because several good operating systems are available, and different organizations like different features of each system, mixing (that is, *integrating*) operating systems is the new standard.

This realization that you can actually use each system according to its strengths to meet user demands is an epiphany kind of moment, where the cartoon light bulb appears above your head and winks on.

Although you may think (and rightfully so) of system integration as a chore, it's a new world opening up for you. Unlike the generations of network administrators who came before you, you *don't* need to dedicate yourself or your organization to one operating system!

The simplified criteria that you want to use for choosing which operating system to go with can include two main questions.

Is the operating system all of the following?

- Capable of providing the service(s) you need
- Cost-effective
- Well supported

By *well supported*, we don't mean that it comes on a nice stable table. A well-supported operating system is one that a company releases and then backs up with sufficient technical manuals, a toll-free call center, bug fixes, and any other services that give you a warm and fuzzy feeling.

Although operating systems from large software companies tend to offer more of these support services, this general characteristic is no guarantee that your particular product is well supported! Linux, for example, offers only a very primitive support system — nothing more than a large, fanatically dedicated group of users and Linux gurus to answer questions.

On the other hand, Microsoft can supply you with all the perks of a multi-billion-dollar corporation. But ask many a Microsoft administrator, and you find that product support is sometimes difficult to get. And if you're running an older version of a Microsoft product, your chances of support get progressively slimmer as time goes on.

Another criterion to keep in mind is what services you need on your network. Do you need any, or all, of the following?

- Networking services
- Storage services
- Printer services

> ✓ Manageability
>
> ✓ Application services
>
> ✓ Web services

These service questions are very broad in scope, but they do encompass the kinds of things that every administrator considers. (Or at least *needs* to consider in making these decisions.)

The Windows World: Comparing 2000 to NT 4.0 and 98

Windows 2000 was recently released. NT 4.0's been around for a while now, and Windows 98 is pretty mature (in Microsoft years, that is). So how do you choose? In the following sections, we take a look at what you typically use these operating systems for, which can help you in the decision-making process. But in brief, the answer depends on the hardware, applications, and version of Windows that you're using.

Windows 2000

Windows 2000 is newly released and full of new technology. So what does that mean? *Bugs! Quirks!* And to fix them, *service packs* — right? Well, if you guess in the affirmative, you're right! In the past, Microsoft's made a name for itself by releasing "not ready for prime-time" software and operating systems. But everyone can remain ever hopeful that, someday, the folks at Microsoft are going to release something much more refined, right? Nope. Microsoft, unfortunately, is the master of tailoring a product to its real user base. It's philosophy: Release the software so that the users can buy it and try it. Listen to the users scream and make suggestions — or even find a fix themselves. Release a service pack to fix the bugs and problems. Brilliant!

The "cost savings" is to *Microsoft*, not to *you*. Always keep that point clear.

Really, Windows 2000 is certainly a viable option now, even with the possible risk of problems. Fortunately, Microsoft's leveraged its knowledge and experiences with NT and expects 2000 to be full-featured and ready to go. We've been running 2000 for a couple months now, in fact, with few gripes about its capabilities as a desktop system.

Already have NT 4.0? In case you're wondering why you'd want to upgrade, the following sections offer some straightforward reasons for your consideration. (Aside from the fact that Windows 2000 corrects many of the problems that make Windows NT crash and need frequent reboots.)

Shutting down not necessary

Windows 2000 also enables you to change its configuration settings without shutting down and rebooting your server. (To be fair, this capability is something that Unix and Linux have offered for a while.) Table 2-1 lists the settings that you can change without rebooting.

Table 2-1	Items That No Longer Require Rebooting
Item	*Why you don't need to reboot*
Changing IP addresses	The OS now supports a more dynamic IP addressing
Adding and removing network protocols	Improved plug-and-play standards
Changing audio drivers	Improved and expanded plug-and-play standards
Changing video drivers	Expanded DVD and other video plug-and-play standards

Plugging away at plug and play

Windows 2000 offers plug-and-play standards and better power management and security features than does Windows NT. Plus 2000's Advanced Server supports multiple servers in a high-reliability cluster, which is important if you run an NT-based network or Web site. If these features appeal to you, trying Windows 2000 to see whether it works in your situation is definitely worth your time.

Spinning a more Weblike interface

The most obvious change in the Microsoft world is on the surface. As you open windows and start clicking through the Windows file directories, however, you also see some small, but noticeable differences.

In what was the most recent incarnation of Windows (Windows 98), the idea of blending the operating system interface with the Internet really began in earnest.

In opening windows, you quickly noticed that the toolbar at the top began to resemble the earlier forms of Internet Explorer, Microsoft's Web browser. As a rule, this interface was more than just a gimmick — the Back and Forward buttons, for example, greatly simplified movement through multiple directory levels. You can see an example of this interface on the window shown in Figure 2-1.

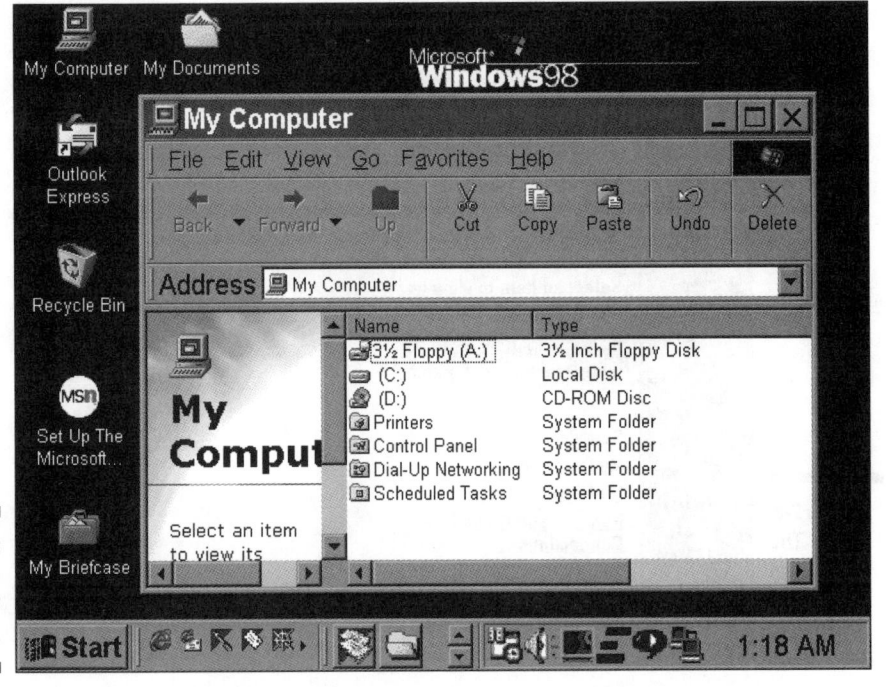

Figure 2-1:
The
Windows 98
environment.

In Windows 2000, you can see the continued growth in this direction. The new icons on the Window toolbar give whole new realms of functionality to the windowing interface. The Folders icon, for example, now enables you to browse file systems with greater ease, much as you can in the Windows Explorer view. You can see this capability in a shot of the Windows 2000 desktop, as shown in Figure 2-2.

Curing your insecurity complex

The Windows 2000 authentication process, which we cover in more detail in Chapter 18, provides extra layers of security for your network. The OS authenticates users before they can gain access to networked system resources or sensitive data.

Windows 2000 also provides network security and system auditing for your Windows resources, including files, folders, and printers.

Multiple processor scalability

The Professional version of Windows 2000 features the capability to support up to two microprocessors (such as on a dual-Pentium II machine). The Server version is the equivalent to the industrial strength version of a product and can handle up to four processors.

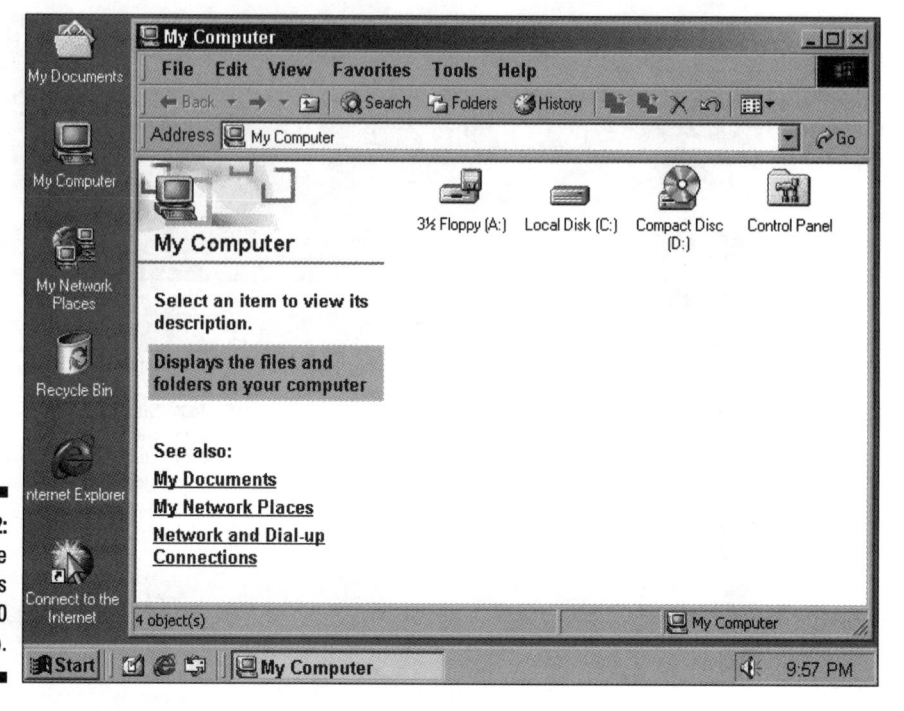

Figure 2-2:
The
Windows
2000
desktop.

Networking and communication

Windows 2000 provides improved connectivity with Novell NetWare, all flavors of Unix (including Linux), and Macintosh AppleTalk. On the scalability side of things, Windows 2000 Server really shines, supporting up to 256 simultaneous inbound dial-up sessions!

Scalability, a fancy name for a simple concept, is how well an operating system works if it's networked to 100, 1,000, or 100,000 machines as opposed to only one. Quite a few OSes in the '70s, '80s, and '90s had a nervous breakdown if you required them to handle multiple network connections, so technology's really come a long way!

Getting on the Universal Bus

Windows 2000 continues the Microsoft tradition of supporting as much plug-and-play hardware as possible, automatically detecting and configuring hardware drivers. More interestingly, Windows 2000 now supports *USB,* (*U*niversal *Serial B*us), which increases the number of computer peripherals on which Windows 2000 works.

Directory services you don't find in your Yellow Pages

Windows 2000 stores information about network resources, such as user accounts, system resources, and security information. The directory service in Windows 2000 resides on the Server version of the software and is known as *Active Directory*.

This directory serves as a kind of database of information on printers, computers, and services that make the system resources available to remote users. One major advantage of the new Active Directory is that it gives administrators more fine-tuned control over how (and to whom) they allocate resources.

2000 Professional versus Server

Microsoft offers several different versions (or, as the truly technical like to call them, *spins*) of Windows 2000 — Professional, Server, Advanced Server, and even a version known as Data Center Server.

Both Advanced Server and Data Center Server are specifically for production-level server environments and are most likely to challenge installations using high-end Unix environments, including corporate data warehousing and large-scale computing projects in the scientific or financial fields. Microsoft is aiming these products at a very high-end corporate and academic market and not at the vast majority of Windows 2000 administrators.

Table 2-2 compares the two versions of Windows 2000 that you're most likely to use, Professional and Server.

Table 2-2	Windows 2000 Versions	
Feature	*Professional*	*Server*
Typical Use	Power users, business desktops, workstations	Small and medium-sized businesses or departments
CPUs supported in one system	2	4
Recommended system requirements	Pentium-133, 64MB RAM, 650MB disk space	Pentium-133, 256MB RAM, 1GB disk space
MSRP	$319 ($219 upgrade from Win 95/98, $149 upgrade from NT Workstation)	$1,199 (includes 10 client access licenses; $599 upgrade from NT Server)

Windows NT 4.0

This OS is a well-established and stable platform that's been around the block. You can find a plethora of information about NT, and Microsoft offers oodles of service packs (which you pronounce *patches and bug fixes*) for free from its Web site, which we list with all the other Web sites in this book in Appendix C.

If you harbor any concerns that NT's going away, don't. Look at the sheer numbers of NT servers installed around the world. For Microsoft to stop production and support of NT for at least another two years would be utter suicide.

Windows 98 or 95

Well, assuming that you're building or adding to a network and you want an operating system that administrators typically use as a server on a network, you're most likely *not* going to use Windows 98 or 95 in such a manner.

Although Microsoft designed Windows 98 or 95 with the capability to connect to a network and make use of many network capabilities — including such tasks as sending e-mail or print jobs to a printer on the network — these operating systems lack the components to actually make files and messages available on a network. This lack of capability isn't a flaw but a conscious design decision that Microsoft made. As merely desktop- or client-operating systems, however, Windows 98 and 95 are reasonable choices. They're just not suitable for the purposes in this book.

NetWare — the Consummate NOS

NetWare *is* the consummate NOS . . . at least as networks were known. Although at times Novell seems ready to drop NetWare completely, this NOS is far from dead. Millions of NetWare servers are running today.

NetWare's always been the superpower of file and print services, and it performs those tasks very well. In addition to those core services, NetWare now includes an Internet/Intranet messaging component known as *GroupWise*, another Novell product worth looking into for complete e-mail and workflow services.

NDS (*NetWare Data Server*) is the backbone of NetWare. Its security model, NetWare SAA, provides gateway services to several types of hosts. NDS provides you with integrated user authentication across all your NetWare servers and you can now use it for authentication into Windows 2000. Additionally, NDS is where you manage file and directory rights. You can even manage Windows NT 4.0 and Windows 2000 accounts from NDS.

The future of NetWare — if it has one

Although NetWare lost a significant share of its market to Windows, Unix, and Linux, don't discount NetWare's talents! True NetWare users believe that the glass is still half full for Novell.

Some of the recent headlines and press releases for Novell products, for example, include the following:

✔ Dot-coms Embrace Novell Caching to Ease Net Congestion, Improve Response Time

✔ Novell Delivers Directory-Based Messaging for the Solaris and Linux Platforms

✔ Novell Internet Technologies Earn Industry Accolades

✔ eDirectory Awarded Product of the Year from Top Industry Publications

✔ eDirectory, NIMS, and NetWare Win Network Computing's Well Connected Awards

Obviously, Novell is still competing and working hard for your business — this statement assuming, of course, that you don't already have NetWare or some other Novell product in-house and running. If you do, you're fully aware of its capabilities and what it offers to your environment. Novell offers the following popular programs, for example, to help you run network operations:

✔ *WebServer* fills the bill for Web-page serving.

✔ *ICS* (*I*nternet *C*aching *S*ervice) caches your most popular pages and graphics for your users.

✔ *BorderManager* gives you the proxy and firewall services that you need these days.

✔ *NIMS* (*N*ovell *I*nternet *M*essaging *S*ystem) provides an Internet mail service that you can manage from a Web browser and that can manage enterprise-wide e-mail flow and control.

Novell even offers a knockout all-in-one product, *Novell Small Business Suite 5*. If you're building from the ground up on your servers, such a package gets you up and running with many of the features that you need for today's small-office environments. This sort of thing is Novell's strength: filling the need of small businesses by not only putting together the components for a network, but also bundling those components together for ease of use and selection.

Unix/Linux

People often mention Unix and Linux in the same sentence, if not the same breath. You also hear people comparing Linux to Solaris, HP-UX, and maybe even SCO. Here's the straight story.

Unix is the basic operating system that's known for its stability, speed, and lack of a *GUI* (*G*raphical *U*ser *I*nterface). Solaris, HP-UX, and Linux are all brands of Unix. In developing its own brand of Unix, Sun Microsystems gave it the name *Solaris* so that you know which company sold you your operating system. Hewlett-Packard's version of Unix is known as *HP-UX*. Linux has a distinctly noncorporate origin — Linus Torvalds developed it off the Unix model by as a cheaper, more configurable form of Unix.

By purchasing one brand over another, you choose a kind of Unix that offers slightly different commands or user interfaces. If you need classes or customer support, you go to Sun Microsystems or Hewlett Packard to get what you need.

The main development rocking the Unix and Linux world is the adoption of a GUI with these operating systems. Until this development, many users were turned off from using Linux and Unix because they saw a GUI's desktop — with its icons, folders, and mouse pointer — as a more user-friendly environment in which to work. And the development of sophisticated, graphics-based word processors such as WordPerfect and Microsoft Word threatened to leave Unix and Linux in the dust among users.

Both Unix and Linux now feature GUIs, although exactly which style of desktop you find in use on your system is an open question. The multiple companies and user groups involved in the development of this operating system make standardization difficult.

The lack of a single standard desktop is one symptom of a phenomenon that's unique to the Unix/Linux world. Because no monolithic corporation such as Novell or Microsoft controls either system, different companies do things their own way.

This lack of standardization is what gave rise to the famous saying about Unix: "The standard in Unix? Sure! We set *lots* of standards!"

The two most common desktop environments are as follows:

- *CDE* (Common *D*esktop *E*nvironment), a Sun product in use on Unix platforms.
- *GNOME,* a Linux desktop that's commonly in use on the popular Red Hat brand of Linux.

You also see Linux graphics desktops such as the following:

- KDE
- Mosaic
- OpenWindows
- X Windows (a basic desktop system that many other graphic environments build on)

And to make further nonsense out of all these different desktop options, a good deal of the time, the GUI doesn't even matter to an administrator. Unix/Linux systems are, of course, getting more and more GUI applications to help you integrate the system into a mixed network environment, but at its base, you go under the desktop GUI to do your real work in a special editor known as vi.

The Advantages of Unix

Because Unix has been around for more than three decades and has a proven record for stability and scalability in handling files or transmitting data, you're likely to inherit a network with at least some Unix machines on it. Don't let the lack of a GUI with most forms of Unix deter you; using Unix also means that you end up with a steady, increasingly employable skill after you master the system. So always remain aware of the reasons for Unix's current ubiquity, which we describe in the following list:

- ✔ Unix can run on outdated machines as ancient as the 386 models.
- ✔ Depending on where you purchase it, Unix can be incredibly cheap.

  Purchasing the Unix flavors of HP-UX or Solaris from HP or Sun Microsystems can prove pricey, but you can perhaps purchase an entire network setup for only a few hundred dollars by using a less popular version, such as SCO.
- ✔ Unix is more reliable than Windows (much as Bill Gates may like to think otherwise).
- ✔ Unix is more flexible than Windows, because the source code is open. If you want to do your own thing, you can — and your creation becomes immortalized in future versions of Unix.

The Organic Operating System of Linux

Linux essentially enjoys all the strengths of Unix but remains far cheaper to purchase — because of a decision made by its creator, Linus Torvalds. After creating Linux, the far-sighted Torvalds made the decision to make all the Linux kernel code freely available. That's why Linux is known as a *freely distributed* operating system.

Because it's free, you can get Linux in a multitude of forms, as the following list describes:

- ✔ As an Internet download.
- ✔ Packaged in various software bundles.
- ✔ On CD-ROMs from software publishers, such as Red Hat and Caldera.

You can either pay a nominal fee for the CD-ROMs and some kind of technical support package or download Linux for free off the Internet.

If you're interested in where to get Linux off the Internet, see Chapter 22.

And in the challenger's corner: Linux!

To say that Linux is on the warpath in the network-operating-system world is an understatement. The growth of Linux has been explosive. To put it into perspective, in 1991, the total number of Linux users could fit on a Greyhound bus, with a few seats to spare.

As of 1999, an estimated 10 million active users were using the Linux operating system. Not bad for an operating system with no parent company, marketing department, or advertising budget!

You often find Linux as part of a file-server system, a desktop workstation, or as a Web server. Cash-strapped institutions (or college students who want to save more money for the deep-dish pizza) can cut their computing budgets to almost zero, because Linux can run on the many outdated machines, such as old XTs.

Because Linux's code is so freely available, people often tag Linux as the most *organic* of all the operating systems. The organic nature refers to the fact that anyone can change the code around and create new features for Linux.

So if you come up with a new, more efficient way to, say, search for files in Linux, you don't need to write to a software company and ask them to add it. You just add it to your own Linux system, distribute it, and if it catches on, your feature becomes part of the permanent Linux landscape.

What exactly is free software?

We suppose that some of the affection that many feel about Linux comes from its revolutionary fervor rubbing off on those who deal with it. Linux is free in more than just the monetary sense — after all, if that was all that was behind the project, you'd have only a few Wall Street types shaking their heads in fascination and wonder. But Linux also is free in the Tinkertoys and Legos sense. You're free to modify and redistribute it.

Free versus Open Source

Software that conforms to this standard of freedom is known (appropriately) as *Free Software* or, more precisely, *Open Source* software. Some semiscrupulous companies however, claim that their software is free even if it's actually only a trial or sample version that entices you to come back and pay for the rest. This kind of stuff doesn't fly with the true Free Software crowd, so the Open Source certification mark was born to distinguish true Free Software from the bait variety.

The Open Source mark means two things, as follows:

- ✔ You *always* can access the source code of an Open Source software product to do what you want with it.

- ✔ The software you're using really *is* free, without any underhanded reservations. Only truly free software can carry the designation Open Source.

You sometimes see the term *Open Source Software* abbreviated as *OSS*.

Your Evaluation Checklists

After you get a rough overview of the relative strengths of the various operating systems from which you can choose, consider which OS to allocate for each task on your network. If you're lucky enough that you're building your network from scratch, you can consider following the second checklist that we offer in this section as a starting point.

Even if you're inheriting an existing network, going through the first of the two checklists that we provide for you in this section is well worth your time. You never know when or how you may need to expand and improve on the existing network that you're administering.

Also, ask yourself and others what features and services you want to provide or add to the network. If, for example, you work for a financial institution where stocks and bonds are traded, stability and speed may prove your main concerns. On the other hand, if you support a network for a publishing house, you may decide on the operating systems featuring the most user-friendly word-processing.

Regardless of which checklist you end up using, don't just mentally jot down your answers to each question. Write them down on a piece of paper so that you can refer to them later. You soon see how you use the facts and figures that you take down to plan out a new network — or to improve on an existing one by removing bottlenecks or phasing in new machines and updated operating systems.

Checklist one: Existing network and servers

Consider the questions on the following list if you're inheriting an existing network and servers:

- ✔ Are the services currently adequate?
- ✔ What are the top five user complaints that I hear on a recurring basis?

- ✔ What products or services do I need to find that can eliminate or reduce these complaints?
- ✔ What's my budget?
- ✔ How much time do I get to build what the users and management are asking for?
- ✔ What's the current reliability of the network and servers?
- ✔ Is physical security something that I need to concern myself with right now?

Checklist two: New network and servers

Consider the following questions if you're building an entirely new network and servers from scratch:

- ✔ What are my objectives?
- ✔ Who are the customers or clients?
- ✔ What do my customers or clients need and/or want?
- ✔ What's my budget?
- ✔ How much time do I get to build what the management and users are asking for?
- ✔ What kind of reliability and backup do I need?
- ✔ How secure must the hardware and software be?

Chapter 3

Ground Zero — Clearing the Way with a Plan

● ●

In This Chapter

▶ Making choices and decisions in planning

▶ Surveying the needs of the users

▶ Selecting and adhering to standards

▶ Laying out and testing a sample plan

● ●

*I*n real estate, the three most important things to consider are *location*, *location*, and *location*. In system integration, the three most important words are *planning*, *planning*, and *planning*. Planning isn't difficult, but the circumstances may dictate that you need to make some tough decisions. You rarely enjoy the luxury of truly building a network from scratch — a luxury that minimizes the integration issues. More likely, you must fix, upgrade, or expand an existing network to bring it in line with what the CIO (Corporate Information Officer) or senior developer for your company wants.

No matter what your situation, however, you need to set priorities and stick to them. If you need to play firefighter and put out burning network, e-mail, or print issues before you can play architect, do so with relish. Remember that no one's going to fault you for your decisions, even if they're incorrect, as long as you can justify them in your plan.

Choices and Decisions — Not Necessarily Easy but Very Important

If you're truly starting from ground zero to plan, design, and install a network, you usually feel as though the world's on your shoulders, and knowing just where to start is frequently difficult. This situation proves especially true if you have no experience in this type of planning. Suddenly, you must make serious decisions that are certain to affect the way that a company, office, or small business operates.

This responsibility results in an incredible amount of pressure, right? No question about it. But as long as you're methodical about your needs and how to meet them, your job gets easier as you progress.

Network design is important enough that, depending on how you set things up, your company's technology becomes (in techie talk) an *enabler* or a *disabler*. In other words, a company can either work efficiently or go down the tubes because of poor technology choices. Mention that as you're in a budget planning session with the higher-ups and you're bound to get a funding increase! (Suuuure you are!)

You may feel more secure if some of this technology is already in place. What if the network you're inheriting is a new branch office, for example, or an expansion of an existing site? Maybe you're adding servers and must move the existing ones to a new data center for the growing office? Perhaps you're replacing network servers and/or cabling.

If someone tells you that you're just going to ramp up an existing network, so the job's not all that difficult, *don't believe it*. If you're working on a running network, you face just as much pressure as in starting one from scratch — if not more. A major constraint on your planning and work time in such a case is that you can't interrupt existing services. And you just can't jeopardize what's already working.

The most critical network functions for a company run 24 hours a day, seven days a week. A networked environment of this sort is also known as a *production environment* or an *enterprise environment*. (All you Trekkies out there, take notice.)

In performing work on a network, understanding just what's part of your production environment — and what isn't — is most important. If you work with servers at a company that develops stock-trading software, for example, the network where employees perform the trades is a critical production environment. A network that your company dedicates to stress-testing beta software or to infrequently demonstrating its products, on the other hand, isn't a production environment, because you can usually schedule some downtime to perform work on it.

Dig out the clipboard and pencil for survey time

With some good planning, lots of research, and some help from qualified co-workers, decision making becomes less difficult. And who can object to simultaneously making a situation bearable and completing a project successfully? Planning is the key; the first step to planning is knowing what you want. You need to realize, however, that what *you* feel that you need to accomplish and what the users you support feel that you need to accomplish are *completely different animals.*

Sure, you may feel that, as the resident network expert, your first priority is to ensure that you make correct backups on the system. But your users (who normally include people who give feedback as to your state of employment and/or the size of your annual bonus) may display more interest in fast, reliable e-mail. Or their top priority isn't waiting in line at the network printer behind the fellow who wants his own print copy of *War and Peace.*

Survey and interview time, folks. Obviously, someone's asking you to get something done or create something new, right? Surely, no one's just saying, "Hey, Jeff, we need more servers. Get some and install them, okay?" or "Hi, Diane, I hear you're a computer whiz. What do you think about helping my company build a new branch office in New Mexico?" Now, you know that these people have expectations, but if you don't probe to find them out, you can never effectively, efficiently, and easily roll out anything for them.

So go on over and ask them! Following are some easy questions to start with during your probe and survey time with them:

✔ What, exactly, are your expectations from this project?

✔ What problems are you trying to resolve with this project?

✔ What priority does the company assign to the project?

✔ Who's the decision-maker? (More important, who can sign the checks?)

✔ What are the criteria for top performance? Speed? Reliability? A cool interface? (Don't laugh. How pretty the user desktop looks can be the primary criteria for choosing an operating system, even at the most technically savvy companies!)

✔ When do you expect me to accomplish this project? ***Note:*** Don't accept vague answers, such as "Sometime in the next year." This kind of vagueness can kill you when your employee review comes up.

✔ Where are you locating the new equipment in the building?

Also ask whether you can secure the environment where the company locates the equipment; see Chapter 18 for information about physical security needs and how to meet them.

✔ Who can explain the business side of this project so that I can use my technical expertise to solve your problems?

✔ Depending on the project, what size, services, features, criteria, and technology do you want to see me use?

✔ Where are the locations of hardware, cabling, circuits, routers, modems, phone lines, and so on for the remote offices (if you have any)?

You get the idea. This data-gathering phase certainly isn't a one-day task. Obtaining the information that you need to even begin a project takes time, energy, and creativity. Even after you think you have enough information, you always find some unplanned changes, additions, removals, budget adjustments, and other problems crossing your path. (Don't you just love our technical terminology?)

Standards? We have plenty of standards!

One way that you can truly tell that you're in the Information Age is that the days of "Wild Wild West" (that is, "anything-goes") technology is coming to a close. Whereas, in the old days, you coded programs by scribbling on the back of a napkin at a greasy spoon, people today build most protocols, software packages, and machines to conform to rigorously applied standards of stability and performance.

Similarly, in today's world of system integration, you need to remain aware of a couple standards that are particularly important to completing your tasks in integration. The biggest hurdles you face are in cabling and power. Those two standards affect your project in ways that you may not expect.

So make sure that you know where to find this information before you need it. The best practice is to gather this information before you're actually purchasing and setting up the network. You want to make such information part of your basic research. To start, take the time out of your busy day and meander down to your local county offices for the scoop on electrical codes for your location. Yes, electrical! You just think that you can slap in all that hardware, daisy-chain a few power bars, shout "*Shazam!*," and watch the network power up? Not if you're working with more than a dozen machines, you don't!

First, each device has its own power rating. You need a ballpark idea of what equipment you're going to need to get this baby chewing on those bytes!

Typically, you measure power ratings in *watts*. Okay, so what is a watt? (Sorry, we couldn't help ourselves; we had to use that joke.) A watt is *voltage* multiplied by *amperage* (or *amps*). You can use 220-volt lighting circuits and bulbs (as in some commercial applications and by folks in some other parts of the world). Normally, a 100-watt bulb uses 110 volts and about .9 amps. In a 220-volt system, however, it draws only .45 amps.

Not that the formula itself is really that important, but it's always good for an occasional trivia question. Really — understanding how much power you're going to use is critical so that you don't overload circuits and cause problems down the road. Understanding your power needs is also something that you need to calculate and understand for purposes of UPS.

UPS stands for *U*ninterrupted *P*ower *S*upply. It's part of what's known as *capacity planning.* (But don't let these scary sounding terms frighten you.) A backup power circuit or even an outside generator can serve as a UPS to keep your systems running in a blackout. And it keeps your system from stopping when the lights flicker.

Capacity planning is understanding how much power you need, assuming that every machine on the network's on at the same time. It also takes into account the size of the generator that you need if you're running one. (A generator does nobody much good if it can't handle the power needs of the company if disaster strikes.)

The need for a backup generator is becoming more frequent in this day and age. Much of California's Silicon Valley, which has a hot, dry climate, suffers from the twin evils of commercial and residential overdevelopment. On hot summer days, the local power grid sometimes can't cope with the electrical needs of millions of air-conditioning units on top of normal power use. Even if you're in the middle of civilization, therefore, a generator may make very good sense!

Okay, after you visit the county offices and get a copy of the local electrical code, you can throw those machines together, right? Not so quick there. Do you have the correct amount of power available in the right place?

You need to look at *space planning* (literally, whether a given machine can fit into a specific room, alcove, or converted broom closet) and tie that in with electrical-capacity planning. Any idea how big an Octellina SuperServer with redundant power supplies and a google-bit hard-drive array is? How much does one (or two!) of those Octellina SuperServers cost anyway? Now you need to know your budget. And how about all that information on what the stuff needs to provide — services, printing, file serving, database storage, and what else?

We think you get the point that we're trying to make. If your task is to carry out some sort of project, you need to move toward it systematically, understanding that one decision you make affects all the others. Sometimes, you can't move forward on one part of the project simply because you don't have the answer or commitment that you need to facilitate that step.

Starting at the crux of the matter, you must identify the issues, problems, and desired solutions for the project. Then you must determine how much money the company's really dedicating to these efforts. After you complete these preliminary steps, you can then assess whether you have enough resources (read: money) to accomplish what the company wants you to do.

After you get this magic figure, you can look at possible solutions. At the same time, however, you still need to straighten out that electrical code, because no matter what, you're surely going to add a load to your current power consumption levels. You still need to estimate the amount of space that you may need and potential locations for it. So while you're dealing with the realities of the project, you can also spend some time estimating (*guessti-mating*, really) these things. Find out the size of that Octellina SuperServer and any other equipment or systems that you think are possible items to add to the list for this solution.

Why do we keep saying *solution*? Well, you don't throw together a huge server room with tape backup and redundant power supplies unless you need something of that order, either now or in the near future. People and companies, large and small, don't spend their hard-earned dollars unnecessarily. (Okay, so maybe some do, but most don't.) Anyway, the concept here is looking at a current or expected problem and trying to find the "right" solution or answer for it. Hard indeed!

Laying Out and Testing a Sample Plan

Although the constraints of a project vary greatly depending on the factors that we describe throughout this chapter, the basic principles of planning and organization remain the same. An example can help to illustrate how to use the information that you acquire in the preceding sections of this chapter.

Suppose, for example, that you're working for a company that resides in a small- to mid-sized office in a single building. The company is growing quite fast and needs a few things in the near future. Right now, it has a simple, peer-to-peer network with no centralized file server or authentication method for the network.

Say, too, that you're the *de facto* technical wizard at the company (lucky you!) and have come to master what you can best describe as a loosely put-together network with the following characteristics:

- ✔ No operating-system standards.
- ✔ Cables taped to the carpet between offices.
- ✔ Printers that were old when New Kids on the Block was hot.

You have about 15 PCs to support, and soon the company expects to add an additional 25 employees, which means more PCs down the road. To make this example more difficult, assume that you can't find any prior information from the former network administrator, who had a photographic memory (and took no notes) and who disappeared into the Amazon rain forest last year without leaving a forwarding address.

Your two most pressing issues are the mind-numbingly slow speed of printing and the lack of disk space for storing files and data. And, of course, machines go offline frequently and sometimes corrupt files as a result — mainly because you're saving files wherever you can fit them, including on another user's machine!

To run this network correctly, you need to put out a few fires first. Unless you get a directive from a higher-up on the corporate ladder, the most critical problems are as follows:

- ✔ A severe lack of disk space.
- ✔ Frequent machine outages.
- ✔ Lack of desktop standards.
- ✔ A substandard cabling scheme.

That's a common scenario. The following sections describe how to address it.

Solving the disk-space issue

Although the disk-space issue may lie at the bottom of other problems, such as that of the machine outages, it's one that you must solve for both the short and long term.

Start by getting an estimated time of when these new 25 employees are coming on board. What about office space? Twenty-five people are going to more than double the current office space, right? Where's the company going to put them? Expand into additional space on the same floor? Add new offices elsewhere in the same building? Find a new place altogether? For the example's sake, say that the company's going to expand to a new floor in the same building.

If you're in charge of the network, don't consider "floor planning" as the realm of the HR department alone. You're the one most likely, for example, to receive the assignment of laying out the cable to each office that the new employees inhabit!

In solving the problem of the lack of storage space, you need to determine how much each user is currently using and figure out what amount the average user is consuming. Then you want to increase that figure by 40 percent each year. The reason for this increase is that, as people continue to use an account, they tend to store more and more material, such as old reports, diagrams, and schematics — even e-mails from friends.

This calculation gives you a baseline to use for predicting the disk space that the new employees are going to need. For this example, say that the necessary space is 250MB per user now (including your initial 40 percent addition). That total comes out to 3.75GB of disk space that you need right now.

Add those 25 employees, however, and that figure grows to 10GB. Begin to add 40 percent for each year, and you see that, in one year, you're going to need 14GB; the next year, you need 19.6GB; the year after that, it's 27.44GB! To use the technical term for people who take up excessive amounts of disk space, what a bunch of Disk Hogs! We have some good news to share on this topic, however: Judging from the price of hard drives these days, this solution is a cheap one to achieve.

The following table gives you a breakdown of how much disk space you need for from one to 40 users at current use levels and in the next three years.

Users	This Year	Next Year	Second Year	Third Year
1	250MB	350MB	490MB	686MB
15	3.8GB	5.3GB	7.4GB	10.3GB
40	10GB	14GB	19.6GB	27.5GB

You still have one more issue to keep in mind, however. In a loosely config-ured network where you store files on many disk drives, you may not even have a central server for file storage! Having files spread across 15 different PCs is both difficult to manage and risky. Besides, the entire situation begs the question of how organized the company *really* is if its data is spread all over the place?

If you have a file server, you need to purchase and install a new hard drive to handle the increased space needs. If you need to purchase a server to store these files in an organized manner, however, allocate this cost in your budget. Determine which operating system you want to run on the file server by asking the questions that we outline for you in Chapters 1 and 2. Purchase a server with the capacity to handle the 27GB that you expect to need for the current and new employees.

Downtime is a technical term for the time that you spend fixing or upgrading a system whenever it's *down* (that is, inaccessible to the user community). In a production environment, you may need to schedule downtime on a weekend, holiday, or at least during a lull in the business period — after work hours.

You're best off scheduling downtime after hours instead of allocating yourself a block of two or three hours in the middle of the day. This scheduling takes some of the pressure off you, reducing the chance that you may make a mis-take in your rush to get the system back up for your users. It also gives you time to test out the new installation before everyone's back at the office!

Although this statement may seem a tad cynical, boasting about how much faster the system's going to become or how much more space everyone's going to have available after you upgrade usually isn't a good idea. People normally don't notice a speed increase unless it's by more than 20 percent. Furthermore, files often tend to expand to fill the space available. After you tell people that they have 50MB more to play with, we can guarantee you that, within six months, it's sure to become jam-packed with reports, e-mails, and pictures of employees' favorite movie stars.

To make things a little more difficult, say that you happen to have a machine that can handle the job for now while you order the server of your dreams. (Someone in the company, for example, always seems to have the newest PC at his desk. And as a corollary, this person normally has the least to run on it!) If you can pull it into service as a temporary file server, not only does the presence of this machine save money up front, but it also makes you look like a miracle worker if the space shortage is truly as acute as it seems. In this example, too, most of your users run Windows 95 on their PCs — but this one came with Windows NT 4.0 on it.

So go ahead and use this PC as your temporary file server. Even better, if the frequent outages are corrupting files with no way to retrieve them, you can use an additional stopgap measure to alleviate the problem. This same machine probably also has a tape backup and thus can perform your back-ups each afternoon.

Remember that the future capacity you need in this example is in excess of 27GB, so ensure that your choice for a tape backup system can handle that amount of storage — on one tape, if possible. One tape is best for small offices because you don't need to change the tape while you're midway through the backup process.

Stopping the outages

What about those frequent outages? Do you any idea why they happen? If the outages happen on single machines on a regular weekly cycle, for example, they may indicate that the disk-space shortage is causing the outages. If a hard drive fills up, the computer normally crashes.

In this case, however, after a lot of questions and observation, you find that user machines running Windows 95 frequently lock up the entire PC and the users must reboot in the middle of the day. Oddly enough, the only pattern that you can discern is that the outages are happening to only a small group of users in one corner of the building. While looking around, you find out that an entire set of four cubicles draw their electrical power via a triple daisy-chained set of power strips!

Not only is this setup against nearly every fire code in the United States, it's simply against the rule of common sense! Essentially, power strips are the equivalent of having an open wire in a high traffic area. You find out that the people in those cubicles must take care not to kick one of the strips, but they forget from time to time and *whack!* — there goes a machine or two as they twirl around in their chairs while taking a stretch break.

Now that you know what's causing the outages, you can fix it. First, get rid of those strips; then get an electrician into the office and ask him for an estimate of what you need — and how much it's going to cost — for sufficient power to all the current cubicles. You probably have others in similar conditions. Fix them now and save yourself a lot of grief later.

Standardizing the standards

If you haven't yet read Chapters 1 and 2, now may be a good time for you to go back and do so. Whenever you decide to standardize the office environment, you want as your end goal to have as many machines running the same operating system as possible. Although individual users may complain that they prefer one word-processing program to another, nothing's better in reducing your administration time than reducing your integration time!

Say, for example, that out of all the machines on the floor, only the last two machines in the office came with Windows NT. You may, therefore, need to budget for 13 Windows NT upgrades. You're also ordering new machines for the 25 new hires. All those need something more stable than Windows 95, which adds to your costs because Windows NT is more expensive. You need to budget accordingly.

Windows 2000 is now out, so you may want to look at that as a possible desktop and server standard and just bite the bullet now. Whatever you decide or that someone else decides for you, make sure that you *agree on a standard operating system*.

Laying the cabling

Contributing to the outage problem that we outline in this example is the cabling. As you look at the cables for the PCs, you find that they're all using Ethernet as their network *topology*, or architecture. All are running at 10 Mbit (Megabit) and you have four hubs in the office, each with four machines connecting to them (except for one with only three machines). So far, this setup doesn't look out of the ordinary.

The hubs all have eight ports and interconnect through crossover cables that someone else built prior to your arrival. Most of the cables were hand-built and crimped with an old crimper. Each cable is a different length. They represent yet another "patch job" that you must re-do from scratch if you want things to run smoothly!

A *hand-built cable* is one that you strip the end off of, exposing the tips of the wires, so that you can use the cable as a connector. You can identify most hand-built cables by looking at the cable tip, where someone's removed the cable cover; if the cut is anything less than machine straight and perfect, what you're looking at is likely a hand-built cable.

A *crimper* is a special tool that (unsurprisingly) crimps the cable end so that it fits snugly into a telephone-style jack that you can insert into a machine or a wall socket. Hand-built cables aren't themselves inherently bad — but don't use them as the basis of your network, because they're less durable than new cabling.

Purchase prefabricated cables for all machines — and that includes prefabricated crossover cables for the hubs. Unless you have very little network traffic (a rarity in this days and age), increase the bandwidth for each machine to 100-Mbit cabling. Because all the new PCs come with this standard, not taking advantage of the speed increase for so very little extra cash is foolish.

A few tips can save hours of frustration, as the following list describes:

✔ Make sure that you don't create new network bottlenecks; install new 100-Mbit hubs.

✔ Pick a single color of cable and stick with it for workstations. Use a different color for servers and a third color for crossover cables. You probably want any mission-critical cables in *red*.

✔ Buy some new crimpers so that you can create new cabling if you're in a jam.

You can purchase entire Ethernet wiring kits that come with strippers, crimpers, cutters, and other network niceties.

Part II
Building a Network from the Ground Up

The 5th Wave   By Rich Tennant

©RICHTENNANT

"No, the solution to our system being down is NOT for us to work on our knees."

In this part . . .

*N*ow you're ready to handle what can be the most ticklish part — getting every one of these rambunctious machines to sit down, talk to each other, and play nice. You'll be starting from the ground up (under the desk, underneath the carpet, and so on).

As important as the wiring under the carpet is the network service and hardware that you have in your wiring closet. And you see several different ways you can get your users' computers to communicate with the server that stores and hands out the information needed to keep your user community happy.

Chapter 4

Wiring — Like Spaghetti but with Fewer Calories

. . . .

In This Chapter

▶ Guide to network cables

▶ Ethernet concepts

▶ Types of Ethernet cabling

▶ Networking hardware

▶ Sample network shopping lists

▶ Cabling standards guide

. . . .

*I*n any network, your cabling is as strong only as its weakest point. Your cabling setup can prove a weak point in any network integration, even in the simplest of networks. Ever try to deal with a string of Christmas lights that doesn't work because one bulb's burned out? You may very well run into a similar problem on a network.

If you have one cable that someone's routed wrong or that has a slightly loose connector, it may jeopardize your entire network. Cabling is what the bits and bytes flow down from computer to computer, and if these things aren't in good condition, you lose data, corrupt files, and endure other inexplicable disappearances of data. This chapter shows you how to arrange your network cabling. You also see exactly what materials you need to correctly outfit a small, medium, or large network.

And, of course, in this chapter, we expose you to the various kinds of cables that you may want to use on your network. Not only is this knowledge helpful as you're setting up your network, but it also enables you to hold your own if you end up at a cocktail party and you hear various technical types tossing about certain technical terms. At the very least, you can nod your head sagely and say, "Why, yes, I'm quite familiar with that setup; I worked with it yesterday."

The Down 'n' Dusty Guide to Your Network Cables

Locating the first part of the Ethernet network is easy; just reach around the back of a computer and find the cable sprouting off the back that doesn't plug into a power socket. (This method is known as the *Down 'n' Dusty* way of figuring out what's on your network because of all the dust that collects behind computer cases.) In case you find multiple cables that fit this category, the cable that plugs into what looks like a phone jack on the back of your computer is the one that you want.

Every time that you turn around today, you seem to see a new kind of cable in the network universe. You're likely to find only three main kinds of cable in your system, however, if you inherit it from someone else. If so, you need to make yourself aware of the following items, especially if you're inheriting a system that looks as if it was in use while Eisenhower was President:

- **Thicknet:** A thick, black or brown cable that looks like the kind of cable engineers use to lay transoceanic phone lines. No longer in use, this variety is an old type of 15-pin connector cable that you want to replace if it's in your system. About the only thing good about Thicknet cable is that it's very easy to spot — it's the only computer cable that you can't cut through with anything smaller than a chainsaw.

- **Thinnet:** Also known as *co-axial cable*, or *co-ax* for short, Thinnet works on a *series-circuit* model. On a co-ax network, the cable is basically one long wire that attaches all the machines and that branches into each computer's Ethernet connection by adding *taps* or *T connectors* along the entire length of a wire. You see this setup very rarely these days, but you can spot it by looking for the T-shaped connectors coming from the network cable.

  If you have Thinnet, we recommend that you get rid of it. Although it's very cheap, it has the potential to cause major headaches, because any break, anywhere along the line can cause the breakdown of an entire section of the network. This situation is similar to that of a series circuit that you use with Christmas tree lights, as we mention in this chapter's introduction. If one light goes out, all lights on that entire segment go out — because they're all part of the same circuit. If you've ever spent hours with a string of these flickering bulbs on your garage floor trying to figure out which one is causing the problem, you know the torture that you can face by using Thinnet.

- **10-Base-T:** This cable, also known as *RJ-45* in the elite circles of cable experts, is the current standard of the Linux world. Your basic 10-Base-T cable looks like a standard phone cable, and it's only moderately more expensive. It also doesn't work on a series-circuit model, so if one machine suffers a broken wire, the rest of the network stays afloat.

Best of all, 10-Base-T offers the capability to run at either 10 Mbps (Megabits per second) or 100 Mbps. The faster rate is more expensive, but it gives you the option of basing your choice of a cable system on price versus performance needs. We provide more in-depth information on this cabling in the following section, because it ties so closely to your understanding of what Ethernet does for you.

Getting Caught in the Ethernet: Basic Ethernet Concepts

As an administrator, you need to know what *Ethernet technology* is and with what parts of it you need to familiarize yourself on a physical and an application level. Ethernet connectivity, on the physical level, consists of two parts — the *cabling* and the *Ethernet card* inside each of your computers. The application part is easier (unless you consider typing strenuous work), because it involves testing out the connection by using utilities such as `ping` and `spray`.

Several *LAN* (*Local Area Network*) technologies are in use today, but Ethernet is by far the most popular. Industry estimates in late 1997 indicate that more than 100 million Ethernet nodes were installed worldwide by that year. The widespread popularity of Ethernet ensures a large market for Ethernet equipment, which also helps keep the technology competitively priced. (In other words, it's cheap!)

Ethernet emerged from the last two decades of chaotic system-network design as the standard way to connect large numbers of networked computers. Developed in the early '70s as one of the first networks based on the *broadcast model*, it had the advantage of being incredibly cheap compared to the other method available at the time.

Ethernet originally suffered from the following two main problems:

 ✔ **Signal strength:** Signal strength was an issue in hooking up computers that lay more than 50 meters apart from one another physically, because signal strength dissipates quickly over long wires. This problem was solved with the introduction of signal amplification devices known as *repeaters* and, eventually, by the introduction of *bridges* and *routers,* which have amplification built into them.

✔ **Packet loss resulting from collisions:** Collisions occur if two or more computers send information out on the network simultaneously and their information packets crash into each other. Packet loss remains a problem on Ethernet but is no longer an issue with the common use of the TCP/IP protocol. We cover the uses of this protocol — another cocktail party buzzword favorite — in Chapter 11. With these two issues out of the way, Ethernet quickly became the dominant force in the networking world.

From the time of the first Ethernet standard, the specifications and the rights to build Ethernet technology have been easily available to anyone. This openness, combining with the ease of use and relatively low cost of the Ethernet system, resulted in a large Ethernet market and is another reason that the computer industry uses Ethernet so widely.

The low cost-to-performance ratio is something that really comes into play if you're building a network with hundreds or even thousands of connections. Ethernet is especially popular, therefore, if you're working with *WAN* (*W*ide *A*rea *N*etwork) links and multibuilding campus networks.

Tens, hundreds, and gigas — your Ethernet cable choices

During the next couple years, network decision-makers (which probably means you!) need to carefully balance their investments in cable-plant installations to avoid unnecessarily investing in obsolete components. An example is the current choice you face between the standard Ethernet cable, known as *10-Base-T*, and the extra-fast version, *100-Base-T*.

According to the Ethernet industry, 100-Base-T offers ten times the performance for twice the price of 10-Base-T. Advances in integrated-circuit chip technology make this improvement possible. As chips get smaller, they run faster, use less energy, and become cheaper to produce. Early Ethernet controllers used 1.2-micron chips. State-of-the-art technology uses 0.45-micron chips. This latter figure represents an almost eight-fold reduction in chip size.

Your 10-Base-T cables and 100-Base-T cables look exactly the same on the outside, so how can you tell them apart? Sometimes, some kind soul or manufacturer labels the cables; at other times, fate is fickle and no labels are in evidence. Looking at the *NIC* (*N*etwork *I*nterface *C*ard) in a PC usually tells you whether it's 100-Mbit compatible.

The war of the ring (the token ring, that is — not the Tolkien ring)

The *broadcast* model that Ethernet uses replaces the older, *token-ring* format that was the mainstay of computing in the '80s. On a token-ring network, an electronic packet, known as a *token*, passed around a network of machines like a discount subway pass.

Only the machine that actually had the token at the exact time it transmitted a message could talk on the net. After it finished, it passed the token on. This system got to be too cumbersome and prone to failure, so people began switching to the broadcast model.

On a broadcast model, every machine gets to talk — that is, send out message packets — all the time. If two machines send out a packet at the same time, a *collision* results and both machines go into reset mode and send the packet again after a random reset time. The buzzword *network bandwidth* comes from this setup. If you have too much network traffic — from a hypertalkative machine, for example — your collision rate becomes too high and people start noticing the slowdown.

Notice that all these transactions we're talking about take place at the speed of light, so many, many computers can talk on a network without colliding.

Most 100-Mbit NICs provide two labeled LEDs to indicate the following characteristics:

- ✔ A good link
- ✔ 100-Mbit operation

Say that you inherit a system with 10-Base-T cabling; do you want to upgrade or can you stick with the older cables if you (and your budget) must attend to other needs first? Luckily, 10-Base-T is still plentiful and available as of this writing (mid-2000), but 100 Mbits is the going standard these days. So if you have 10 Mbit, you can still work with it for now, as plenty of hardware's still compatible with it. We strongly recommend, however, that you think ahead: Any new hubs that you purchase need dual-speed ports and autosensing to handle both 10-Mbit and 100-Mbit speed for future growth and ease of upgrades.

Adding to your choices is the latest cabling breakthrough: *Gigabit Ethernet*. This type of cable offers another tenfold increase in performance. Although the initial price of gigabit Ethernet technology is more expensive, the cost-performance difference is worth looking at if your environment warrants this type of speed.

Pick a card, any card

The second part of the Ethernet is the *Ethernet card*, or *NIC* (Network *I*nterface Card). You need to install an Ethernet card inside your computer so that your 10-Base-T (or 100-Base-T) line can plug into the phone-jacklike plug. If you don't know how to install the card, don't worry. Most vendors of Ethernet cards, such as 3Com, provide support and instructions for how to do so.

After you install the card on a computer, reboot the system so that it can recognize the card. The vast majority of the time, operating systems use a program or script (such as the `/sbin/ifconfig` program in Linux) to register your card with your system files automatically.

If you can't get a computer to recognize the card or experience problems setting the network address, you have one more drastic but effective solution. Save all your important files to floppy disk or tape. Then reboot the machine by using the installation CD-ROM or boot disk and reinstall the entire operating system. Keep in mind that, whatever you don't save off the system on floppy disk or tape, you erase in a reinstallation.

Because the operating system detects the new card during the installation process, it's ready for you to make your changes after installation is complete. On completion, all you need to do is put your files back into place. This procedure is pretty drastic, however. You don't want to use it on a major server that's been in use for some time (unless you have a backup server waiting in the wings).

Bits and Pieces: Other Networking Hardware You Need to Know

In Chapter 1, we liken Ethernet to a highway that data travels on between various machines. Even the best highways, however, can't take you to every single destination in one hop. If you're integrating different networks, you need to become aware of a few more bits of hardware.

These pieces of hardware include *patch panels*, *hubs*, *bridges*, and *routers*. To continue with our highway analogy, these pieces are much like the exits, entrances, and interchanges on your personal information superhighway. And just as you can see a substantive difference between a merge lane and a cloverleaf interchange on the freeway, so these pieces each serve a slightly different purpose. Even if you're semi-familiar with some of these pieces, taking a quick overview of each one is worth the effort, especially if you're building or expanding a network, so that you're sure that you're buying the right hardware for the job.

Two pieces of hardware that we don't examine in detail here are *taps* (or *T connectors*) and *repeaters*. Both these pieces of hardware are old, and you rarely see them nowadays. If you do find these units on your system, consider replacing them or gathering the information that you need about them from the manuals that came with the hardware.

Patch panel — plugging the gaps

A *patch panel* is a device that enables you to easily connect network cables from location to location inside a building and even between floors. You usually describe them by the amount of ports they have — somewhere from 8 ports up to 24 (or even more!). The back of the panel reveals an open structure with a bunch of network cables inside. These cables connect to the smaller patch panels in another area of the same room. Sometimes you find this device in a data closet or server room, making things easier and neater for your cabling needs.

If your office is small enough, using a patch panel to fan out the cabling to the machines is a good idea. A patch panel's also a good idea if you have multiple servers in a server room or closet. Patch panels run the gamut from little 8-port panels to full-blown 120-port units. You use patch panels mainly for efficiency and neatness. They help organize and group your wiring as you begin to add more and more cables to your setup.

Hubs, switches, and repeaters — the long haul

A *hub* is a piece of hardware that handles data arriving from one or more directions and then forwards it out in one or more additional directions. A hub usually includes a switch of some kind.

To make matters a little confusing, people sometimes use the terms *switch* and *hub* interchangeably. As you get down to splitting the finer hairs of network definitions, however, they're actually different from one another. A *hub* is a place where data comes together. A *switch*, on the other hand, is the device that determines how and where the system forwards data from the hub!

Long ago, *repeaters* were in-line devices that you could plug your Ethernet cable into and then plug another cable into the other end of the device and thus extend the overall reach of your Ethernet cable. (You need to use such an extension because Ethernet signals can travel only 328 feet, or 100 meters.)

Why the limit to signal strength down a wire? To get a really detailed answer, you need to dig up an electrical engineer. In a nutshell, however, sending a *signal*, which is an electrical impulse, down a wire encounters what's known as *resistance*. Across an estimated distance of 328 feet, the resistance dampens down the signal strength so that a computer can no longer detect it. Thus the early need for repeaters.

The length of a twisted-pair segment (from computer to wiring closet) may run up to 100 meters (328 feet). This distance is identical to the distance that 10-Base-T links use. Early on, before fiber-optic technology, offices in multiple buildings needed to use the repeaters to link all the buildings together and keep the data flowing throughout the company.

The way of the repeater is to the bone yard now, however, for two main reasons: First, hubs nowadays are self-contained repeaters. And second, if you need to run connections between buildings, fiber optic is now the way to go. Why? Because the 328-foot range of a signal for copper Ethernet pales in comparison next to the 500-*meter* range for Gigabit Ethernet traveling through fiber. That's a major difference in length, which translates to substantial savings (and less of a headache) for you or any network administrator worth his weight in silicon wafers.

Bridges? No, they don't fall down

Bridges are pieces of hardware that connect a Local Area Network (LAN) to another Local Area Network that uses the same protocol, such as TCP/IP. Any bridge hooking into your network examines each message on a LAN, automatically forwarding the messages to addresses known to lie within the same LAN and forwarding those known to lie on the other interconnected LANs.

Bridged networks tend to be interconnecting Local Area Networks, because broadcasting every message to all possible destinations sends too many network messages over the entire network, resulting in unnecessary traffic. (Such a situation is also known as *flooding* the network, for obvious reasons.) To avoid flooding, routing networks, such as the Internet, use a scheme that assigns addresses to nodes so that a message or packet can travel forward in only one general direction rather than in all directions.

Flooding is one of the main reasons why a directionless communications protocol such as UDP gave way to the current standard, TCP/IP. We discuss this subject in more detail in Chapter 11.

If you're inheriting an old network and you discover that a bridge connects two or more networks, don't make the mistake of assuming that computer or node addresses have a specific relationship to location on the network. Although, logically, the idea that all machines in network A are, say, on floor 1 and all machines in network B on floor 2 makes sense, a system that's grown without planning can branch al! over the place.

For this reason, messages go out to every address on the network, but only the intended destination node accepts them. Bridges "learn" which addresses are on which network and develop a learning table so that they can forward subsequent messages to the right network.

Route to the router

A *router* is a device (or, in some cases, a software product that acts as a router) that determines the next network point to which the system forwards a packet toward its destination. The router connects to at least two networks and decides which way to send each information packet, basing its decision on its current understanding of the state of the networks it connects to. A router is often part of a network switch.

A router creates or maintains a table of the available routes and their conditions and uses this information, along with distance and cost algorithms, to determine the best route for a given packet. Rather than acting as a set item, routers are intelligent enough to constantly monitor available routes and conditions and to vary the path of a packet depending on the current conditions.

If a router can send a packet along either route X or route Y to get to the same destination, for example, it can — and often does — make the call as to which route to use. (And no, the router doesn't consult anything written by Robert Frost about "two paths in a wood.") If route X is congested, flooded with network packets, or out of commission, the router sends the packet down route Y.

Now How Much Would You Pay? (But Don't Answer Yet!)

The preceding section gives you a quick run-through of the parts that can potentially make up your network. Exactly what components, however, do you want to pick at your local Radio Shack, Fry's Electronics, or Miracle Network Components (motto: "If it works, it's a Miracle!")? We include some suggestions in the following sections for a shopping list of components, following these possibilities with some guidelines on physically setting up the cabling in your office.

Because your needs are unique — and, we hope specific, if you follow the suggestions that we offer in Chapters 1 and 2 — the only final bit of advice that we can offer is that you don't skimp on network components. The five dollars you save buying a no-name brand of hub, made in Upper Nerdistan or West Dakota, is going to repay you in hours of frustration if it breaks on the evening before you're due for your vacation to Tahiti. Trust me — it never fails. So do yourself a favor and splurge a little.

The following sections provide a selection of shopping lists and ballpark costs associated with building a few different network configurations. Of course, yours is probably different than ours, and the next person's is most likely different, too.

Home network of 2–3 computers

Following is what you may find in a small home office where someone works at home, possibly with one or two other employees or co-workers:

- ✔ (3) Cables, 14 feet each, Cat5 (Category 5 rating), prefabricated
- ✔ (1) Hub, 10/100 Mbps, eight autosensing ports
- ✔ (0–3) 10/100 Mbps NIC (Network Interface Cards), if not already built in

Small office of 16–24 computers

The following setup is what you may find in a small office where several people work together in one building, usually on the same floor:

- ✔ Cables, 10 feet each, Cat5, prefabricated
- ✔ Single-outlet surface block
- ✔ Minihub, 10/100 Mbps, five autosensing ports
- ✔ (1) Main hub (stackable), 10/100 Mbps, 16 autosensing ports
- ✔ 10/100 Mbps NIC (Network Interface Cards), if not already built in

Medium or large office of 24–60 computers

The following setup is what you may find in a small company where several people work together in one or two buildings:

✔ (8) Cables, 25 feet each, Cat5, prefabricated

✔ (24–60) Cables, 10 feet each, Cat5, prefabricated

✔ (1–3) Main hub (stackable), 10/100 Mbps, 16 autosensing ports (= $330 each)

✔ (6–15) Minihub, 10/100 Mbps, five autosensing ports

✔ 10/100 Mbps NIC (Network Interface Cards), if not already built in

This size office is where you may consider a "structured" wiring scheme, where looking intro contracting some of the work out becomes a wise course — unless, of course, you have a lot of experience in this type of wiring system. (A *structured wiring system*, by the way, is one where you have several individual cables on a *trunk*, or group, of wires, and you bundle them together to a certain region of the building and then fan them out to the individual workstations or cubicles.

Each location is physically different in its layout and in what *barriers* may prevent you from connecting the computers that you need to talk with one another. A barrier can consist of walls, cubicles, hallways, fire barriers, false ceilings, power conduit, water pipes, concrete floors through which you may need to drill a *core* (a big hole through the concrete floor) and so on.

Surveying the place is key to making sure that you put in a good, solid cabling plant, or system, and that it lasts for a long time. Surveying is simply looking around, drawing diagrams of the floor space and furniture placement, and taking notice of any possible problem areas or things that may make your installation more or less difficult. While surveying, you may find a nice little hole in which to route some cabling. You may also find that certain walls are fire-code barrier walls and that you can't penetrate them without prior approval of the county fire department or city inspector.

Dos and Don'ts of Running Cable

Cabling is an area where you can't afford any mistakes. One kinked or pinched cable, if it's running to a critical server, can make your life a living heck. This area is one where erring on the side of caution pays off exponentially in saved time, cost, and maybe even your job! If you have no clue about wiring, study this section and ensure that you have someone to watch over your shoulder to guide you along this part of building your network infrastructure. Cabling is a slippery slope for the inexperienced. Level the slope by seeking guidance when you can.

Electrical sources

Running your cables near or across any power sources, wires, or connectors is sure to cause unreliable data transmissions and errors. Electrical sources radiate energy, and this energy can penetrate typical cabling and cause fluctuations in the voltages on the network cabling, thereby corrupting or even erasing the data.

Fluorescent lights

Fluorescent lights run at a high frequency and cause very erratic behavior in network cabling. Running your cables closer than 18 inches to one can cause such problems and give you no end of trouble on that segment of your network.

Water (the wet stuff)

Sources of water, such as in restrooms, steam rooms, pipes, and other places where water may come into contact with your cables, are obvious areas to avoid. Water in its gaseous state can corrode cables; and it can condense to its liquid state and conduct power and signals away from where you want them and into something — or someone! — else.

High-traffic areas

You don't want to run cables across walkways or hallways, through doorways, or in any other area where people or objects (such as doors) move around a lot. Cables in such areas are an obvious safety hazard for people who travel the area, and the cables themselves suffer damage from constant trampling, kinking, yanking, rolling, stretching, and similar mistreatment. Cables are sensitive. You need to treat them with the respect that they deserve. Are you aware of the requirements for becoming a cable? We didn't think so! Enduring the melting of the copper, the pulling into a wire form, the heat of the plastic shielding, and finally, being cut into pieces! Not an easy life.

If you need to cross over one of these areas, such as a passageway, you need to get creative and start looking above and below the area for solutions. Looking above tells you whether you can find ways to route the cables in a false ceiling or to install some sort of hanger system that's not too unattractive. In a data center or computer closet, the looks aren't as important as remaining organized and neat. Looking below for ideas is not as easy because many office buildings are concrete and have no "below" to speak of. Some offices do have raised floors that you can possibly route some wiring through.

Best Practice: No matter where you're laying your cabling, act as if it's a place where the CEO or owner walks by several times each day. If you keep this attitude while planning and, later, installing the cabling, you install a neat and clean set of cables. And people can see how much care you're showing over their work environment and that the work you're doing is good, quality work — and neat, too.

Cabling Industry Standards

Because you're transmitting data over what amounts to glorified telephone wire, your network is subject to several standards set down by the government and the telecommunications industry. Among the first of the standard types that you need to know about are *Category5* (or *Cat5*) and *Category3* (or *Cat3*). Although these terms sound as if they're describing animals that someone made in a secret facility in the Nevada desert, don't pick up the phone to call Scully and Mulder just yet.

If you're running a small- or home-office environment, you can safely bypass this section. You run afoul of these standards (rather like removing the *Do Not Remove* tag off your mattress) only if you run a network for a company in a commercial building.

Cat5 is a Commercial Building Telecommunication Cabling standard that specifies a generic telecommunications cabling system. Cat5 supports multiproduct, multisupplier environments. It's the fastest-growing application for networking today!

The Cat5 standard establishes minimum requirements for telecommunications cabling within a commercial building, up to and including the telecommunications outlet/connector and between buildings in a campus environment.

Cat5 refers to performance levels and cable characteristics that transmit voice and data at up to 100 Mbps (Megabits per second) or more.

Cat5 cabling systems can accommodate virtually all applications, including voice, modems, RS-232, ISDN, four- and 16-Mbps token ring, 10-Base-T, 100-Base-T, and ATM (Asynchronous Transfer Mode).

Cat3 cabling is the performance level for voice and data transmission at up to 16 MHz and 10 Mbps, such as 4-Mbps UTP and 10-Base-T.

Of course, the government had their hand in cabling way back in the days of ARPANET. ARPANET was the governmental organization that, along with universities, created the original version of the Internet. A nongovernment body, *EIA/TIA*, governs cabling standards today. (This wonderful acronym stands for the *E*lectronics *I*ndustry *A*ssociation and the *T*elecommunications *I*ndustry *A*ssociation.)

These people discuss this stuff until they're blue in the face and, with the input from hundreds and thousands of experts and regular people, make decisions and recommendations on where the standards are going.

The Specific Cable Standards

As you install your cabling you need to make sure that you use the recommended standards for outlets at the cubicles, in the walls, and in the area where you locate your servers. Following these standards in a small office environment may seem a little ridiculous, but you're best off using them. (That's not the best reason, however. Using a standard helps *you*. Using a standard enables you to easily know later on exactly how you built the cables.)

A variety of standards-setting bodies throughout the world govern the integrity of the cabling itself and of its associated components. Among these organizations are the International Standards Organization (ISO) and the Telecommunications Industry Association (TIA). From a practical standpoint, the cabling industry also acknowledges that even the best cabling and components can't provide the necessary performance levels if you install them incorrectly. To refer to these standards verbatim, see the information at www.eia.org on the Web.

Full compliance to the current cabling standards requires the following setup:

✔ Two modular jacks minimum/outlet (drop). These are the jacks to which you eventually connect your servers and client PCs to your network wiring.

✔ You must wire jacks according to T568A or T568B pinout.

T568A or *T568B pinout* means the way that you build the jacks, or in other words, what wires go to what pin numbers in the connectors. Wiring is cool and all, but trust us, *hire someone* who's an expert in network wiring. T568A and T568B differ only in which color-coded pairs connect — pairs two and three reverse. Either work, however, as long as you don't mix them! If you always use only one version, you're okay, but if you mix T568A and T568B in a cable, you get crossed pairs! The result? Your cabling doesn't work. Table 4-1 shows the standards for wiring.

✔ Residential building permits six-pin modular (RJ11 type).

✔ Commercial buildings require eight-pin modular (RJ45 type).

Table 4-1		T568 Wiring Standards	
Pair number	*Pin numbers*	*T568A colors (telco)*	*T568B colors (Ethernet)*
1	5,4	blue/blue-striped	blue/blue-striped
2	6,3	orange/orange-striped	green/green-striped
3	2,1	green/green-striped	orange/orange-striped
4	8,7	brown/brown-striped	brown/brown-striped

Chapter 5

Clients: Like People, They're All a Little Different

In This Chapter

▶ Getting the scoop on *client* and *server*

▶ Connecting through `telnet`, `ftp`, or Samba

▶ Choosing gateway services

*O*ne of the challenges of system administration is making different operating systems communicate with each other and pass information. These interactions take place between the computers supplying the bulk of the information (the *servers*) and those that your users access to demand the information (the *clients*).

Utilities connect the dots on your cables, transforming your computers from unconnected machines to a living, breathing network. Which utility you choose depends on the operating systems in your system and the demands of your user community. This chapter gets you up to speed on what clients and servers are all about and helps you sort out the utility choices.

The last thing you want on your network is the cybernetic equivalent of the TV show *Survivor,* where, one by one, your machines are kicked off the network.

Do I Wine and Dine My Clients?

The clients you're dealing with aren't ones to whom you must make presentations or take to three-martini lunches. Instead, your clients are the information hounds that you operate on a networked set of computers. And, actually, *client* is a loose term that can have several shades of meaning to different people.

Any computer that isn't a server for example, you can consider a client. And to some people, a client is any machine that runs only front-end processes; servers, on the other hand, are machines that run mainly back-end processes. (Take a gander at the sidebar if you have any interest in what front-end and back-end processes are.)

Front end, back end . . . what's the difference?

"Jeez, isn't it simple? The front end of a computer depends on which way the monitor is facing."

Uh, not quite. As a matter of fact, these bits of terminology have nothing to do with your hardware and everything to do with your software.

A *front-end* application, or process, is one that's primarily designed for the end user. This admittedly broad definition includes the programs Microsoft Word, Excel, Netscape Communicator, and other applications that users normally access to do office or financial work.

A *back-end* application, or process, is one that mostly runs on the server machines of your network. An even broader definition of a back-end process is any application or utility that only an administrator can use, such as a process that checks file-system integrity or monitors the security of the network.

As a general guide, any machine that does more requesting of information than storing of information is one that you can consider a *client*. The reverse is true of a *server*.

What about Tipping the Server?

You need to tip the server only if it's messing up big time. Tip it right over. Then kick it a few times for good measure.

Not, of course.

Server machines have one purpose in life: to hand out data or information. They act as the central point of contact between the clients that use the data and the data itself, which you normally store on or administer from the server.

The importance of the server machine varies from operating system to operating system, depending on the design of its software (see Chapters 1 and 2 for details), as the following list describes:

- ✔ On a Windows-oriented network, for example, the clients tend toward more independence.

- ✔ On a network-oriented Unix system, the vast majority of the storage and the work on the system takes place on the server machine.

Connecting Clients and Servers

The entire purpose of client-server functionality is to connect your desktop computer (a PC running Windows or a PC running Linux or even a Sun Microsystems Ultra 1) to some sort of server computer. The usual list of suspects for these servers includes the following:

- ✔ Windows NT Server
- ✔ NetWare
- ✔ Solaris (Sun Microsystems's flavor of Unix)
- ✔ Red Hat Linux
- ✔ Windows 2000 Server

You want as much connectivity as possible to as many of your servers at the same time so that your users can access all — or most of — the data that they need to perform their jobs. To make a long story short, if users can't get their data, they can't do their jobs. It's that simple. Now, part of the whole idea here is that we're hoping you don't operate in a crazy, mixed-bag environment, but even if you do, we're going to help you make the connections as painlessly as possible.

Choosing clients

Exactly which clients you connect to the servers is a varied topic and site-specific. Making specific recommendations is difficult considering the vast number of methods and machines on the market, but you can get to know the basics about connecting to these servers. Usually, you run into only a few client-side operating systems — primarily those in the following list:

- ✔ Windows 95
- ✔ Windows 98
- ✔ Windows NT
- ✔ Windows 2000

You may occasionally see the following systems in that category as well:

- ✔ Solaris workstations
- ✔ Linux systems

Seven out of eight times on a site, some form of Windows is the client OS of choice — for the following two reasons:

✔ **Windows has a really nifty desktop.** As much as it makes the fans of OS/2 and Macintosh grind their teeth, Windows is as comfortable and familiar to most people as a slice of home-baked bread.

✔ **The Microsoft juggernaut dominates office applications.** For office managers to buy a word-processor application that the people who *made* the OS designed to work *with* the OS simply makes sense. (Of course, Unix, Linux, and NetWare fans also claim that Windows is ideal for clients because it isn't stable enough to run such an important machine as a server.)

In connecting from Unix to Linux or vice versa, you don't really have a client the same as you do if you connect from Windows 95 to NetWare. The client is really a Unix/Linux native utility — `telnet`, `ftp`, or whatever type of connection or service that you need at the time. Additionally, you have clients for special services, such as the following:

✔ Mapping a drive from a Windows machine to Unix.

✔ Connecting a Linux drive to a Windows PC.

Choosing connection methods for clients and servers

The best way to get a handle on anything is to look at it in an organized manner. So apply the following process to planning your connection:

1. **Choose a client.**

2. **Choose a server.**

3. **Figure out how best to connect them.**

Connecting to Unix from Windows 95/98 doesn't go the way that you may expect. Because Unix isn't anything like Windows, you have limited ways to log in to Unix or to connect to Unix from Windows 95/98.

telnet: Marketing-hoopla name, hard-core technology tool

The `telnet` utility provides a method of connectivity to Unix that enables you to log in to the Unix system and then, in a *CHUI* (*character user interface*) manner, navigate around the Unix file-system structure. While using `telnet`, you can kick off programs, scripts, and other processes on the Unix system that you're logged in to. In executing the `telnet` command, you start up a daemon (known, sensibly enough, as `telnetd`) that handles the specific byte-to-byte operations of setting up a `telnet` session with the remote host of your choice.

Because the name is a little too cute for a software engineer to think of, an old joke has the marketing department naming `telnet`, not the IT department. Actually, `telnet` is a combination of the terms *telephone* and *network*, which sort of shows its age; those engineers originally designed it to work solely across telephone lines.

The `telnet` utility is very popular on all platforms. Computers running Linux use `telnet` to communicate. Computers running Unix also use `telnet`. Macintoshes use `telnet`. Windows 95, 98, and NT computer users can use `telnet` by looking in the Accessories directory.

TCP/IP-based `telnet` sessions are the most widely accepted method of opening communication between different computers because `telnet` is simple, reliable, and easy to use. To start a `telnet` session with any machine, perform the following steps:

1. **At the command prompt (or in the telnet window on a PC), type** `telnet` *<name of machine you want to connect to>* **and press Enter.**

   The system asks you for your user account name.

   If you don't know a machine's name, you can also `telnet` into an IP address. Instead of typing **telnet** *myserver*, for example, you can type **telnet 198.110.75.1**.

2. **Type your user account name where appropriate and press Enter.**

   The system asks you for the server password.

3. **Type your server password where appropriate and press Enter.**

After you log in, you get a prompt on the machine to which you're connected. You can enter commands at that prompt.

ftp: The cybernetic moving van

The `ftp` utility, which is short for *file transfer protocol* utility, is the most common choice for copying files from a Linux machine to other networked machines. For years, `ftp` has been the standard in transferring graphics, text, and other files between machines because of its greater flexibility in communicating with non-Unix machines.

As is `telnet`, `ftp` is a complete program in itself. Activating it actually brings up a new `ftp` command prompt with special `ftp` commands. To start your `ftp` session with a server, follow these steps:

1. **Type** `ftp` *<server name>* **at the command prompt and press Enter.**

   You see a new `ftp` prompt, asking for your user account name.

2. **Type your user account name at the prompt and press Enter.**

   The system asks you for the server password.

3. **Type the server password and press Enter.**

   After you type your user account name and password, they may appear on-screen.

After you log in, you can get any file in the directory that you're logged into. To do so, you use the sensibly named `get` command. To `ftp` a file, complete the following steps:

1. **Type** `ftp` *<server name>* **at the command prompt and press Enter.**

   You get a new `ftp` prompt, asking for your user account name.

2. **Type your user account name at the prompt and press Enter.**

   The system asks you for the server password.

3. **Type the server password and press Enter.**

4. **Type** `get` *<name of file you want to get>* **at the command prompt and press Enter.**

   The file begins transferring. The `ftp` command prompt returns after the job is complete, enabling you to enter new commands.

5. **After you finish with** `ftp`, **type q to quit.**

Similarly, use the `put` command to copy files to the `ftp` server. To put a file on the server, follow these steps:

1. **Type** `ftp` *<server name>* **at the command prompt and press Enter.**

   You get a new `ftp` prompt, asking for your user account name.

2. **Type your user account name at the prompt and press Enter.**

   The system asks you for the server password.

3. **Type the server password at the prompt and press Enter.**

4. **Type** `put` *<name of file you want to get>* **at the command line and press Enter.**

The command places the file on the server. You see the `ftp` command prompt return after the job is complete, enabling you to enter new commands.

5. After you finish with `ftp`, **type** q **to quit.**

Samba: Not just an alternative to the Macarena

People place a lot of emphasis on peaceful coexistence between Unix and Windows. Unfortunately, the two systems come from very different cultures, and they experience difficulty in getting along without mediation. That's Samba's job. Samba runs on Unix platforms, residing on the Unix machine's hard drive (most commonly under the `/etc` directory) but speaks to Windows clients. With Samba, the following becomes possible:

✔ A Unix system can move into a Windows Network Neighborhood without causing a stir.

✔ Windows users can happily access file and print services without knowing or caring that a Unix host is offering those services.

It's a beautiful thing.

A protocol suite known as the *Common Internet File System* (*CIFS*) manages all this cooperation. At the heart of CIFS is the latest spin of the *Server Message Block* (*SMB*) protocol. Samba is an open-source CIFS implementation and is available for free at `http://samba.org/`, the Samba Web site.

Installing Samba onto your Unix system is the first step, and configuring it is the second step. After you install and configure Samba, you can map a network drive from your Windows PC to a shared area on the Unix machine. Samba is free, open-source software.

Samba and Windows aren't the only methods to provide CIFS networking, as the following list reveals:

✔ OS/2 supports SMB file and print sharing.

✔ Commercial CIFS products support Macintosh and other platforms (including several others for Unix).

✔ Samba is ported to a variety of non-Unix operating systems, including the following:

- VMS
- AmigaOS
- NetWare

✔ Dedicated file server platforms from a variety of vendors support CIFS.

For Windows NT and 2000, you can get an add-on client for $149 from Microsoft; it's known as *Services For Unix* (*SFU*). It gives you the following features:

- ✔ Client for NFS
- ✔ Server for NFS
- ✔ Gateway for NFS
- ✔ Server for PCNFS
- ✔ Server for NIS
- ✔ User name mapping
- ✔ Password synchronization
- ✔ telnet client
- ✔ telnet server
- ✔ Server for NFS authentication
- ✔ Remote shell service
- ✔ CRON service
- ✔ ActivePerl
- ✔ Unix shell and utilities

Client Services for NetWare (CSNW)

Client Services for NetWare connects a Windows PC to a NetWare server. It doesn't offer the only method for making this type of connection, but it's the one that Microsoft provides for you.

After you install CSNW on a Windows 2000 Professional-based computer, the computer can function as an *NCP* (*NetWare core protocol*) client and can directly access resources on NetWare networks. CSNW uses *NWLink IPX/SPX* (*Internetwork Packet Exchange/Sequenced Packet Exchange*) as the underlying protocol stack for connectivity to NetWare networks. Installing CSNW automatically installs the NWLink IPX/SPX/NetBIOS Compatible Transport protocol.

Your other choice is the Client for NetWare that Novell provides. See Chapter 6 for details on that client.

Don't become concerned if you lose the preferred server prompt after you log in. Usually, each user first logging in to a workstation sees a prompt for a preferred server, providing that one is already set. After the initial prompt, the user doesn't see the preferred server prompt again.

As you're installing CSNW, make sure that you bind it to the network connection or interface that coincides with the network that the machine is going to use for connecting to the NetWare server(s).

Gateway Services for NetWare (GSNW)

Gateway Services for NetWare is available only for Windows NT and 2000 servers. GSNW performs the following services:

- ✔ Provides basic file and printer connectivity through the CSNW service.
- ✔ Enables an NT or 2000 server to act as a *nondedicated gateway*.

As a nondedicated gateway, your Windows server connects to a NetWare box and shares the NetWare drives that NT shares for all your Microsoft Network (including users accessing your Windows servers coming in via remote access services). This setup means that the Windows server can make additional drives available for users without actually needing the drives physically present in the machine.

After you install GSNW on a Windows 2000 server, the server acts as an NetWare core protocol (NCP) gateway to NetWare networks, giving Microsoft clients access to NetWare resources by using the gateway.

Although GSNW works well, it's likely to cause a bottleneck if you're linking large networks of more than 50 machines through this single gateway.

The NetWare server needs a special group that you must create in the directory tree, which is known as *NTGATEWAY*. You must assign a user account on NetWare to this group and to the gateway service on the NT server.

You can install GSNW or CSNW during Windows 2000 setup.

Client for Microsoft Networks

If you connect any Windows machine to another Windows PC or server, you also install the Client for Microsoft Networks. Just in case you're one of the rare few who hasn't, this section tells you what you need to do through basic steps for installing and configuring this component.

To install Client for Microsoft Networks on a Windows 95/98 machine, perform the following steps:

1. **Click Start and then choose Settings⇨Control Panel from the Start menu.**

2. **Click the Network icon to open the Network dialog box and then click the Add button in the dialog box.**

3. In the Network option in Control Panel, click the Add button.

4. In the Select Network Component Type dialog box that appears, double-click Client.

5. In the Select Network Client dialog box that appears, click Microsoft in the Manufacturers list and then click Client for Microsoft Networks in the Network Clients list.

6. Click OK.

Installing and configuring a Windows NT workstation for access to a Microsoft network is a similar process. After you click the Services tab in the Network dialog box, you see a list of the Windows NT services currently installed. These services enable a Windows NT workstation to access a Microsoft network.

To install Client for Microsoft Networks on a Windows NT machine, perform the following steps:

1. Click Start and choose Settings⇔Control Panel from the Start menu.

2. Click the Network icon to open the Network dialog box.

3. Choose Control Panel⇔Network.

4. Click the Services tab and then click Add.

5. Choose Client for Microsoft Networks and click OK.

FPNW (*F*ile and *P*rint Services for *Net*Ware) does the reverse of CSNW and GSNW: It enables NetWare clients to see an NT server as if it were a NetWare box. FPNW enables an NT server to appear as a NetWare 3.12-compatible server.

Version 5 of FPNW was just released. Check Microsoft's Web site, at www. microsoft.com/ntserver/nts/exec/feature/AddonServices.asp for information.

FPNW isn't free, so make sure that it's the direction that you want to go before you must pay for it.

Chapter 6

Saving the Work That You Do and Printing Those Documents Too . . .

. . . .

In This Chapter

▶ Installing the NetWare Client

▶ Establishing users' accounts

▶ Using NetWare as a print server

. . . .

*I*n your office, you want anyone to get the data he or she needs without needing to run around with a pocket or purse full of floppies. That running-around-the-office scenario is known as *sneakernet*, and it's dead. And it's never going to resurface if your file servers are set up and running correctly. This chapter helps you make sure that your NetWare file servers are doing just that.

Installing the NetWare Client on a Windows PC

For users to access the NetWare file server, you must install the Novell Client on your Windows PC. This client enables users to communicate with the server — to get and store files and to perform print jobs on printers that the NetWare server manages or that queue on the NetWare server.

This section covers the prerequisites, the hardware requirements, and the procedure for installing the client onto Windows 95, 98, NT, or 2000.

Following are the two clients to which these procedures apply:

✔ Novell Client for Windows NT and 2000 Version 4.71.

✔ Novell Client for Windows 95 and 98 Version 3.21.

Various software incompatibilities

The various applications that are incompatible with Windows 95 and 98 are as follows:

✔ Microsoft Client for NetWare Networks

✔ Microsoft File and Printer Sharing for NetWare Networks

✔ Microsoft Service for Novell Directory Services

✔ Novell NetWare Workstation Shell 3.X (NETX)

✔ Novell NetWare Workstation Shell 4.0 and later (VLM TM)

✔ Novell IPX ODI TM Protocol

The software incompatibilities for Windows NT and 2000 you find in the Readme file (WINNT.TXT).

The prerequisites and hardware requirements

Following are the prerequisites for installing the Novell Client:

✔ LONG.NAM installed on NetWare servers for long filenames in Windows 95 or 98 and Windows NT. (NetWare 5 servers automatically support long filenames.)

✔ Connection to a NetWare network.

✔ Applicable server patches installed.

Following are the minimum hardware requirements for Windows 95 or 98:

✔ 486 processor or later.

✔ Minimum 28MB free drive space.

✔ Minimum 16MB RAM.

Windows NT 4.0 (Service Pack 3 or later) or Windows 2000 requires more RAM — at least a minimum of 24MB RAM.

The installation procedure

This section lists the bare-bones installation instructions. Detailed instructions explaining network installation methods are available in the online documentation on the Novell Web site. You can view this documentation at www.novell.com/documentation.

To install the Novell Client, follow these steps:

1. **Insert the Novell CD-ROM into your CD-ROM drive.**

2. **If the Setup utility doesn't start automatically, run** `WINSETUP.EXE` **from the root of the CD-ROM. Do this by starting Windows Explorer, clicking on your CD-ROM drive (usually letter D:) then double-clicking** `winsetup.exe`**.**

   The *root* of the CD-ROM is the default directory that NetWare looks at as you view the contents of a CD-ROM.

   A list of languages appears.

3. **Choose a language, then click Next.**

4. **From the list that appears, click the platform that you want to install.**

5. **Click the button Install Novell Client.**

   NetWare displays the following pair of on-screen messages:

   ```
   If you have a NetWare 4 network or you are using IPX
   TM protocols, click Custom to configure Novell Client
   TM for an IPX network, then select the IPX protocol.

   If you have a NetWare 5 network and you are using IP
   protocols, accept the Typical installation.
   ```

6. **Accept the default installation, which is Typical unless you have previously installed this client.**

   You may want to change some settings, such as the directory where the client is installed, but sticking to the defaults is safest.

7. **Follow the on-screen instructions to finish installing Novell Client.**

Note: Novell Client for DOS and Windows 3.*x* is an IPX-only client. If you're connecting to a NetWare 5 IP-only server, the server must be running Compatibility Mode (SCMD.NLM), and the network must have a Migration Agent on a NetWare 5 server.

Setting Up User Accounts

Each user must have an account on the NetWare server to access and store files and to perform print jobs on printers that the server manages or queues. You set up each user in NetWare by using ConsoleOne, which is a graphical Java application for centrally managing and administering network resources. In setting up a user's account, you can choose from many options. And you can restrict or open up the user's rights to practically anything that the NetWare server controls — printers, directories, files . . . whatever.

Setting up a NetWare user account is traditionally a multistep process, as the following steps describe:

1. Create the user object.

2. Set properties that control the user's login procedure (for example, where log in can occur and what types of information are valid).

3. Set properties to control the user's network computing environment.

In ConsoleOne you can use a *template object* to facilitate this process. A template object defines user-object properties ahead of time, and you can apply it to a large number of users.

The *login script*, a list of commands that executes after a user logs in, is another valuable management feature of ConsoleOne. You can use login scripts to speed user access to frequently used resources. A user doesn't need to request individual access to every vital device or application: He automatically connects to essential files, printers, and network applications.

You can also use ConsoleOne to administer users' rights. Rights are system flags that you assign to network resources that control access to those resources. By using ConsoleOne, you can assign rights explicitly, grant equivalence, block inheritance, and view effective rights.

Typically, administrators use one of the following two methods to get their users set up to use the NetWare server:

✔ **Regional:** You set up users according to their locations if you choose this method. If, for example, your company maintains four offices — say, in Maryland, Florida, Washington, and Minnesota — you may want to set up the users in groups according to these locations. This method works well until someone in Minnesota needs access to files that the Florida users use. Of course, you can grant rights for that one Minnesota person to access the files or directories in the Florida office. But what if two of your accounting people reside in Florida, three in Maryland, and one in Washington? Then you, the administrator, can end up with a management nightmare on your hands.

✔ **Functional:** You set up groups, commonly known as *functional groups*, according to their function. If you choose this method, people's locations aren't as important as what they do. If group members reside all across the country and they all need access to similar data, the functional method is much easier to manage.

NetWare Printing 101

NetWare uses *NDPS — Novell Distributed Print Services* — so that you can use it as a print server for your network printing needs. NDPS is a set of *NetWare Loadable Modules* (*NLM*s), management utilities, and enhanced client software. If you use them in conjunction with NDPS-enabled products, these components enable you to manage network print services more efficiently. And these components also enable your users to use these network print services more easily.

NDPS makes your job easier by enabling you to perform all print configuration and management tasks through the NDPS Printer object instead of using three separate *Novell Directory Services* (*NDS*) objects for each printer. NDPS helps users by enabling them to print without needing to capture printer ports or manually load printer drivers. Users can also check the status and the characteristics of each printer to find the printer that meets their needs. (A user can quickly locate a printer that's not busy, for example, or a printer that can print double-sided pages.) Users can even create customized print configurations. (A user can request notification if a paper tray is empty, for example, or after a print job is complete.)

Printer agents are NLMs that form the core of the NDPS architecture. You install a printer agent on any server that's running NetWare 4.11 or later, and you associate the printer agent with a particular printer. (In the future, companies can embed a printer agent in their printer hardware. You don't need to create printer agents if you use this printer hardware.)

The printer agent stores information about the printer, including the printer's name, network address, features, and status. The printer agent also stores information about the printer's configuration, including the method the printer's to use to schedule print jobs, where these jobs are to spool, and who to notify about particular printer events (such as low toner and paper jams).

You must install an NDPS gateway to ensure that printer agents can communicate with the printers they represent. NDPS comes with three gateways: the Novell Gateway, the Hewlett-Packard Printer Gateway, and the Xerox Printer Gateway. Many companies that make NDPS-enabled products provide their own NDPS gateways. (After companies begin to embed a printer agent in their printer hardware, you don't need to install an NDPS gateway. Printer agents can then communicate directly with printer hardware.)

You must also install the NDPS snap-in module for Novell's NetWare Administrator (NWADMIN) utility. This snap-in module, which comes with

NDPS, extends the NDS schema, adding an NDPS Printer object and other new print-service objects. You can use the snap-in module to create an NDPS Printer object for each printer in your company's network.

Is NDPS right for you?

NDPS isn't necessarily the best way to manage your printers in a small- to medium-sized office setting. NDPS isn't the easiest thing to get working, and unless you're already using it and familiar with it, it may not prove worth the effort.

In a small- to medium-sized office environment, using printers via a Windows domain may prove an easier choice, especially considering that most offices these days use some form of Windows to run their desktops.

Novell recommends using a third-party gateway until NDPS-embedded printers are readily available, if such a gateway supports your environment.

Configuring the printers

In an NDPS environment, you can configure a printer as a controlled-access printer or as a public-access printer.

Controlled access printers

Because objects in your company's NDS tree represent controlled-access printers, you can control users' access to these printers. To configure a printer as a controlled-access printer, follow these steps:

1. **Launch the NetWare Administrator (NWADMIN) utility on your PC by clicking the shortcut on your desktop.**

2. **Click the container object in which you want the NDPS Printer object to reside.**

   This will highlight the container.

3. **From the menu bar in the window, choose Object⇨Create from the menu.**

   The New Object dialog box appears.

4. **Click the NDPS Printer Object option.**

   The Create NDPS Printer dialog box appears.

5. **In the NDPS Printer Name text box, type the name that you want to assign to the NDPS Printer object.**

6. **In the Printer Agent Source list box, click the Create a New Printer Agent option from the list of options.**

   If you already created an NDPS Printer object for the type of printer you're configuring, select the Printer Agent on Existing NDS Object option. If you already configured this type of printer as a public-access printer, select the Public Access Printer Agent option.

7. **Click the Create option from the list.**

   The Create Printer Agent dialog box appears.

8. **In the Printer Agent Name text box, type the name that you want to assign to the Printer Agent.**

9. **Click the Browse button next to the NDPS Manager Name text box and then click the NDPS Manager (NDPSM) object with which you want to associate the printer agent.**

10. **In the Gateway Types list box, click the type of gateway the printer agent is to use to communicate with the printer.**

    Two types of gateways appear in this list: Novell Printer Gateway and HP IPX Printer Gateway.

11. **Click the OK button.**

    The Configure Gateway dialog box appears.

12. **Click on the type of printer you're installing from the printer list and the type of network interface board in this printer from the listing of network interfaces.**

    The Select Printer Drivers dialog box appears.

    Note: This step varies, depending on the type of gateway you select. Some gateways offer more choices than others depending on which features are designed into the gateway that you choose.

13. **Click the Windows 95 and/or Windows 3.1 tab and select the appropriate printer driver from the list.**

14. **Click the Continue button.**

    The new NDPS Printer object appears in your company's NDS tree.

Public access printers

Unlike with controlled-access printers, objects don't represent public-access printers in the NDS tree. As a result, you can't control user access to public-access printers, and all users can see and print to these printers.

To configure a printer as a public-access printer, follow these steps:

1. **Launch the NetWare Administrator (NWADMIN) utility on your PC by clicking the shortcut on your desktop.**

2. **Click the NDPS Manager (NDPSM) object with which you want to associate the printer agent.**

3. **In the Printer Agent Name text box, type the name that you want to assign to the printer agent.**

4. **Click the Browse button next to the NDPS Manager Name text box and click the NDPS Manager (NDPSM) object with which you want to associate the printer agent.**

5. **In the Gateway Types list box, click the type of gateway the printer agent is to use to communicate with the printer.**

   Two types of gateways appear in this list: Novell Printer Gateway and HP IPX Printer Gateway.

6. **Click the OK button.**

   The Configure Gateway dialog box appears.

7. **Click on the type of printer you're installing from the printer list and the type of network interface board in this printer from the listing of network interfaces.**

   The Select Printer Drivers dialog box appears.

8. **Click the Windows 95 and/or Windows 3.1 tab and select the appropriate printer driver from the list.**

   The new NDPS public access printer appears as an available network printer.

Dealing with printing issues

Bindery emulation is something that you may set up on your new NetWare 5 server so that you can access legacy NetWare resources and the older NetWare servers can access the new resources on your NetWare 5 server. You may do so if you have older NetWare 3.*x* servers and are performing a staggered upgrade to your servers. Bindery emulation can become an issue with printing because you create only one thread for all bindery connections; consequently, bindery connections can monopolize a processor. NDPS is the preferred print service for NetWare 5 and is fully compatible with existing queue-based printing resources, which means that you can make the transition from your legacy printing setup gradually.

One server can service no more than 40 printers. More than that number degrades server performance. The optimum number of printers to use, however, depends on the type of printing that you're doing. Printing CAD/CAM designs takes much more processor time than printing text documents. If you have any concerns about utilization problems, we recommend that you set your print devices to do the processing instead of the server. This setup slows down printer output but relieves the utilization on the server.

Adding local printers in Windows

Luckily, for the users of all Microsoft products, the people who brought you Windows 95, 98, and 2000 fully embraced plug-and-play technology, which provides automatic hardware detection and installation for almost all printers on the market today. Simply by plugging in your printer anywhere on your network where the print-server machine can connect (that is, receive a `ping` packet), the server automatically detects the printer after you turn it on.

If your server is having problems seeing the printer, restarting your print server normally does the trick. During the Windows startup process, the computer runs a program to detect new hardware, thus adding the new printer to its list of resources.

You very, very rarely encounter a printer that Windows can't automatically detect and work with. The few that may cause you difficulty include the following:

✔ Printers that connect through a serial (COM) port.

✔ Printers that connect directly to the network via a network adapter.

✔ Parallel (LPT port) printers.

To make these printers available, follow these steps:

1. **Verify that the printer's power is on.**

2. **On the print server, click the Start button and choose Settings⇨ Printers from the Start menu.**

   The Printers window opens.

3. **Click Add Printer.**

   The Add Printer wizard program starts.

4. **Follow the wizard's on-screen instructions to add your printer.**

Adding local printers in Linux

You can add local printers to your network on a Linux machine. To do so, from the GNOME desktop, follow these steps:

1. **Connect your printer to the network and verify that its power is on.**

2. **Log in as the root account.**

3. **On the GNOME desktop, click the Main Menu button.**

4. **From the list of selections that appear, double-click Control Panel.**

5. **Double-click the Print System Manager icon in the Control Panel window.**

   The Print Manager window appears.

6. **Click the Add button.**

   A window appears, asking about the printer that you want to add.

7. **Click OK to add a local printer (the default setting).**

   Linux automatically detects the printer that you plugged in and displays the Info screen.

8. **Type the name that you want to give this printer and click OK.**

   The new printer appears in the Printer System Manager window, ready for use.

If you don't use a version of Linux that enables you to work in GNOME, the process is a little more convoluted. Your best bet is to refer to *Linux Administration For Dummies*, by Michael Bellomo (published by IDG Books Worldwide, Inc.).

Adding local printers in Unix

Unix follows a similar system for adding local printers on the graphic desktop known as CDE (Common Desktop Environment).

To add a local printer in Unix, follow these steps:

1. **Connect your printer to the network and verify that its power is on.**

2. **Log in as root.**

3. **Right-click anywhere on the desktop.**

   The Workspace menu appears.

4. Choose Tools⇨Admintool from the shortcut menu.

The Admintool window appears. Admintool is the Unix equivalent of the Control Panels utility in Windows.

5. From the menu, choose Browse⇨Printers.

The Admintool window displays a listing of printers.

6. From the menu, choose Edit⇨Add⇨Local Printer.

The Add Local Printer screen appears.

7. Type the name of the printer in the Printer Name text box and click OK.

The printer appears in Admintool under Printers, ready for use.

Part III
System Administration Basics

The 5th Wave — By Rich Tennant

"CAREFUL SUNDANCE, THIS ONE'S BEEN LOCKED UP AND FORCED TO BETA-TEST POORLY DOCUMENTED SOFTWARE PRODUCTS ALLLL WEEK AND HE'S ITCHING FOR A FIGHT."

In this part . . .

This part covers the crucial point where machines are physically connected with each other and can therefore exchange data when needed. You use this connectivity to take control and administer your systems.

This part introduces the most important aspects of running your systems every day. Even if you're familiar with two of the three major operating systems, the final one you don't know will be your downfall unless you know its basic quirks and functions. So read on, young administrator!

Chapter 7

Booting Up the Big Boys

· ·

· ·

*W*henever you start up a *networked* operating system, you don't simply flick the power switch to the On position and leave it to run from there. Instead, you interact with the operating system's authentication system first. In every case, the purpose of an operating system's authentication system is to weed out people who don't have a user account on the network, such as *crackers* (hackers who like to break into other people's computers without permission).

In this chapter, we cover the mysterious process known as the *login* (otherwise known as *logging in*). And you discover a distinct difference between logging in to a local machine and to a machine that's part of a network.

We also cover how working with a network of mixed machines can affect the booting up and logging in process. And, finally, we cover the correct way to log out of a machine. (For starters, you don't just flick the power button, pull the plug out of the wall, or play with your fuse box.)

Captain's Log, Stardate Wednesday

To most people (including die-hard fans of *Star Trek*'s Captain Kirk), the word *log* means the official listing of significant data and records of a ship's voyage. But another meaning of *log* is the register of the operation of a machine. Both of these definitions help explain what a log in really is (in stark opposition to the third definition of *log*, which is a really long cylinder of wood).

Some desktop-only operating systems, such as Windows 95 or 98, by default enable you to start up the machine and go right to work. But operating systems that are specifically for networks, such as Unix, Linux, NetWare, and Windows 2000, always ask for a specific login name before you get to the desktop.

The reason is that computers running NOSes (Network Operating Systems) are always on a network for a specific reason or task. Because of this fact (and the fact that a person on the network illegally can do tremendous damage), you need to *restrict* access on a networked machine. So the log-in procedure is the first line — and, in many cases, the last line — of defense for a computer system.

The log-in process is very simple. At one point after you boot up your system, you come to a prompt where you must type your user account name and a password. This prompt can appear in an open graphics field, as in Windows, or it can appear as a simple line of text, as in Linux and Unix. In either case, the answer — the password — is what's all-important.

As you're logging in to a system, the user-account password is your key to success — the equivalent of the magical "Open Sesame!" command. If you don't have the right password, you're out of luck. Setting appropriately difficult passwords and knowing how to store them is the subject of Chapter 9. Turn to that chapter whenever you're ready to tune up your system to prevent hack encounters of the absolute worst kind.

Logging In to Unix

A machine that runs Unix automatically boots up the operating system as you power up your computer. Depending on which type of Unix you're using, you may see a *splash screen*, which is a picture announcing that you're using Unix. (If you're using the Solaris version of Unix, you see an extremely friendly splash screen that welcomes you to the operating system in a number of different languages.)

Nowadays, most of the major brands, or flavors, of Unix use a splash screen — including Solaris, HP-UX, and several others. Most versions of Unix that don't come with a splash screen are older variants.

Unix normally performs tests on your computer to make sure that everything is running correctly from the last time you logged in. You may also see these messages appear on-screen as the machine boots up. All versions of Unix perform similar tasks, such as checking for memory, inserted boot disks, or damaged sectors on your hard drive.

Logging in to Unix without a GUI

You can also log in to Unix without depending on a GUI-style Login screen. (*GUI* stands for *graphical user interface*, and you pronounce it *gooey*. Anytime that a computer screen uses pictures, icons, or any other kinds of graphics to help you access the system or the system tools, you're working with a GUI.)

Whether you get a GUI-style Login screen depends on the type of Unix software you use. You may not see a special Login screen after the machine finishes booting. Instead, you may get a blank screen with a single line of text asking you to log in; that line of text is known as a *login prompt.* To log in from a login prompt, you need to follow similar steps to those you use in logging in from a Login screen: You need to enter your user account name and password.

If your Unix machine doesn't run the X Window System, Motif, the Common Desktop Environment, or any other kind of GUI-based desktop system, you always use this login procedure.

After Unix finishes starting up, you need to log in to start using the computer. Logging in enables Unix to keep track of who's doing what on the machine and also to allocate resources to you as you work.

After your computer finishes booting up, Unix displays a Login screen, where you can enter your user account name and password. Follow these steps to log in:

1. **Type your user account name in the Login text box.**

2. **Press Enter.**

   The cursor moves to the Password text box.

   "Uh-oh. Why don't I move to the next text box after I press Enter?" Because on some GUI-driven Login screens, you must use the Tab key to move among text boxes. Alternatively, you can move from one text box to another by moving the mouse pointer over each text box and clicking to place the cursor there.

3. **Type your password.**

   As you type your password, it appears on-screen as either a row of asterisks (*) or as blank characters. The reason is to prevent someone from stealing your password simply by looking over your shoulder.

4. **Press Enter or click the Login button.**

   If you type your username and password correctly, you get to the command prompt. Unix recognizes you as a user.

Logging In to Linux

As does Unix, Linux automatically starts after you turn on your computer. Unlike with Unix (or Microsoft Windows), however, you probably don't see a splash screen with a pretty picture announcing that you're using Linux. Instead, you see messages appear on-screen as Linux tests your computer to make sure that everything is running correctly since the last time you logged in. These messages vary depending on the version of Linux that's on your computer, but all versions of Linux perform similar tasks, such as checking for memory, inserted boot disks, and damaged sectors on your hard drive.

Note: If you're starting Linux for the very first time, you may not see the graphical GNOME desktop after you turn on your machine. Instead, you may see a black screen with a login prompt asking you to log in. If your Linux machine doesn't run GNOME, you always use this login procedure.

The login procedure for Linux is just like that for Unix. After the boot-up is complete, Linux displays a Login screen where you can enter your user account name and password. Follow these steps to log in:

1. **Type your user account name in the Login text box.**

2. **Press Enter.**

   The cursor moves to the Password text box.

3. **Type your password.**

   As you type your password, it appears on-screen as either a row of asterisks (*) or as blank characters. The reason is to prevent someone from stealing your password simply by looking over your shoulder.

4. **Press Enter or click the Login button.**

   If you typed your username and password correctly, you get to the command prompt. You are now logged in as a Linux user.

If you run GNOME but it doesn't start automatically, follow these steps to get to the GNOME desktop after you log in:

1. **Type** `startx` **at the command prompt.**

2. **Press Enter.**

   GNOME starts up and takes you to the desktop.

 We hear about this Linux log-in problem a lot: "I'm typing the password correctly, but why does Linux tell me the password is incorrect?" Check the Caps Lock key. Linux commands (and passwords) are case-sensitive, which can interfere with your login attempts.

Logging In to NetWare 5 ("Whoa! This One Is Different")

"Oh, now *this* one is strange . . . Is it maybe Linux? It doesn't look like Windows. What *is* it?"

NetWare looks different, feels different, and *is* different. It's always been that way, but as time passes by, it's beginning to look more and more like many other OSes. NetWare is now going GUI (getting a graphical user interface) because the *new* network manager or server manager wants GUI stuff so that things are easier — point-and-click solutions, overall ease of use, universal appearance, and such.

Novell's provided IS organizations with proven NOS solutions for more than 15 years. Novell's NetWare 5 includes technology enhancements that further strengthen its capability to meet enterprise-networking requirements. The key to Novell's acceptance is its extensive directory-based services within its suite of network operating system products that tie together all network-critical technologies — whether NetWare or NT or Unix or OS/390.

Thanks to a more simplified administration and setup front end, you can now manage NetWare 5 and its various complementary optional products from one workstation, known as *ConsoleOne*, from anywhere on the network.

ConsoleOne is a Java-based GUI management console that integrates with NDS. It enables developers to build network management solutions with a common look and feel. ConsoleOne isn't a bolted-down workstation; any PC that the administrator can log in to can run ConsoleOne, including the NetWare server.

The following sections examine the startup process of this NOS.

Starting the server

So you turn on the server, and the screen displays `C:\`, and it looks like . . . a DOS machine?

What — you were expecting whiz-bang NetWare? Well, fret not. To start the server, change to the startup directory (usually, `C:\NWSERVER`) and enter the following at the DOS prompt:

```
SERVER
```

Then press Enter.

After you execute `server.exe`, the splash screen with the Novell logo appears. To prevent the Novell logo (server splash screen) from appearing, you can always load `SERVER` with the `-nl` (no logo) command option, but why bother? Splash screens and corporate logos are just so cool to look at.

If you want, you can place the command to execute `server.exe` in the DOS `autoexec.bat` file. Then, whenever the server computer powers up, the server starts automatically.

If the splash screen is active and you want to see a list of modules as they load, you can still display the system console screen by using the following procedure to toggle between server console screens:

1. **Press Alt + Esc and continue holding Esc until the system console screen appears.**

   A list of modules scrolls up the screen. If you have a color monitor, the color of each module name appears in indicates how the module loads:

   • Cyan (light blue) indicates that `server.exe` loads the module.

   • Red indicates that the startup directory loads the module.

   • White indicates that the `autoexec.ncf` file loads the module.

   • Purple indicates that other modules load the module.

2. **Type** MODULES **at the server console prompt and then press Enter.**

   The loaded module names appear in colors that represent the functional group to which they belong, as we describe in Step 1.

Of course you find that starting NetWare is simple. Why do you think NetWare is such a successful product? Its makers certainly didn't get it there by making something archaic or difficult. (Unlike with Unix/Linux, which come from a world where people seem to take positive *pride* in making something obscure.) NetWare can seem different from other Network OSes, but that's what makes it the workhorse that it is today. So don't disrespect it for what it is.

Understanding NDS and authentication

NDS (*N*ovell *D*irectory *S*ervices) is similar to (if you're a Windows network administrator or support person) the Registry in Windows. Keep in mind, however, that it's only *similar*, because NDS does a lot — and we mean *a lot* — more than the Registry.

NDS is a very powerful technology — so much so that Novell's taken it out of NetWare and packaged it as a technology component that you can buy and integrate into your existing network architecture without ever using NetWare itself.

NDS in NetWare 5 uses objects to create user and resource profiles. Each user object contains information about a person, for example, including access rights, location, and other vital information. Printer objects, for example, contain information on location, type, and speed. Anyone on the network — with the correct authority — can access any other object (such as a printer) on the network without needing to know its location or how it works.

Beyond managing people and devices on the NetWare-based network, various versions of NDS can manage applications on other platforms, including NT Server, SCO Unix, Sun Solaris, and IBM's OS/390.

Keeping it going: NetWare stability

The key to NetWare stability is to keep the latest and greatest CSPs (client support packages) installed on the server. Novell now makes getting these pieces of updated software easier for you by enabling you to sign up for notification of the release of the CSPs. Novell even offers a service that sends the CD right to your door after its release.

This service isn't free, of course, but the convenience factor is very high, considering that you're probably managing several servers — some Windows, some NetWare, some Linux, and some Unix. Getting automatic updates reduces your workload.

New NetWare modules are notorious for their quirky and unstable nature. You'd think that if Novell wrote the OS — NetWare — the modules that are part of it would be stable, right? Yeah, just like the products from those folks up in the state of Washington (the ones who get a paycheck from William Gates) who release no OS before its time.

The new release model for all software these days (masterminded by those folks up in the state of Washington) is to send out the software *knowing* that it includes bugs but also knowing that the bugs are tolerable to some extent. The users can then figure out the bugs, identify them, and maybe even fix them. What a concept: Reduce the release time for products and cut overhead at the same time by using free labor to find the problems.

Understanding ABENDs

An *ABEND* is an *ab*normal *end* of a program; it's also known simply as a *crash*. And it's the most critical problem that a NetWare file server can experience. Sometimes, if errors occur on a NetWare server, they can corrupt vital data in such a way that no one can access it. If a server can no longer access its vital data, NetWare considers that server as in a state of compromise.

If NetWare detects a compromised state, it brings the server's operations to a halt to avoid further data corruption. All code execution stops, and the system preserves the contents of the server's memory as they are. The operating system then calls an ABEND handling routine to take care of the situation from there.

The advantage of the NetWare components known as *NLMs* (*NetWare Loadable Modules*) is that they *are* modules, so they typically don't disturb other NLMs or crash the entire server. That doesn't mean that crashes can't happen, but the design of NLMs compels them to die a simple death. Unix's overall design is similar in that, if a program dies or something kills it, it doesn't usually wipe out the entire server.

The only NLMs that suffer any effects if one NLM does crash, or ABEND, are those that are directly interacting with the ABENDing NLM. So, if the NLM for a mail server ABENDS, for example, it may also cause problems with the Internet gateway NLM — especially if it's receiving or sending mail at the time of the ABEND.

If an ABEND occurs, the server becomes unavailable to handle client requests. Critical processes on the server can't finish. Nothing else can happen on the server until the NetWare auto-recovery process handles the ABEND.

Reboot the server. If the problem persists, reboot with either the recovery disk that comes with your NetWare installation or the boot disk that you create by using the instructions that come with your software (or by using the advice in Appendix D).

Logging In to Windows 2000

Logging in *locally* can mean different things to different people.

If you're from the Unix or Linux world, a *local login* is where you actually log in to the computer that's sitting on the desk in front of you. A *remote login* refers to logging in to any other machine on the network other than the one in front of you. It may lie across the hall, down the street, or even across an entire ocean.

In the Windows world, the terminology is a little different. Only the following three circumstances exist in which you can ever log in locally:

- If your machine's what's known as a stand-alone machine. You can tell whether it is by checking the cables running out the back. If you don't have a network connection or modem line, your machine doesn't connect to any other machine anywhere else in the world; it stands alone.

- If your computer's a member of a Windows workgroup and not a domain.

The difference between logging in locally and logging in to a domain is that, in a local log in, the system checks your user account name and password against a local security database and not against a central one. Similarly, the machine grants you a *local* access token. (An *access token* by the way, isn't something that you use to catch a ride on the San Francisco metro system. It's a unique pass that a computer creates to identify the user for the computers in the granting machine's domain.) In the case of logging in to a single, stand-alone machine or a workgroup, you still receive an access token, although the system uses this token only to identify you on that one machine or group of machines. The computer, using information that it draws from the user's account, creates this token. If the user's settings indicate that the user has permission to view system files, he can do so; by default, however, any user aside from the administrator doesn't get permission to view these files.

To log in to a Windows 2000 machine at either a local or domain level, follow these steps:

1. **Turn the power on (if it's not already on).**

2. **Wait for the machine to finish booting up.**

   After the boot-up is complete, Windows 2000 displays a splash screen that gives you the option to attempt to log in by pressing Ctrl+Alt+Delete.

3. **Press Ctrl+Alt+Delete.**

   Windows 2000 displays a Login screen, which contains a graphics box with two empty text boxes for you to fill in: the User Name text box and the Password text box.

4. **Type your username and password into the appropriate text boxes.**

   If, as the network administrator, you can't remember your administration account password, you're in serious trouble. Flip quickly to Chapter 20, which covers troubleshooting, for some ideas about what to do in this awful circumstance.

   Press the Tab key to move between the User Name and Password text boxes. You can also use the mouse to click each text box where you want to enter information. But don't press the Enter key to move between fields. Pressing Enter incorrectly tells Windows 2000 that you're done entering information and want to begin the authentication process.

5. **Press Enter or click the OK button.**

   If the system verifies your account and password, you go directly to the desktop. If not, Windows 2000 complains and takes you back to the Login screen.

Your domain: Locally mastered

If you log in locally to a domain's grouping of computers, you're essentially telling the computer that you want to access your permissions locally and not on the domain. If you make a change to your account on this machine that the server isn't registering yet, it again refers you *only* to that machine's local security database and not to the machine that controls the log-in process, which is known as the *domain controller*.

That's why you can't log in to a domain locally if you're on the domain controller. A domain controller by its very nature doesn't have a local security database, because it's the keeper of the database that affects the entire system.

To log in locally on a domain, follow these steps:

1. **Turn the power on (if it's not already on).**

2. **Wait for the machine to finish booting up.**

   After the boot-up is complete, Windows 2000 displays a splash screen that gives you the option to attempt to log in by pressing Ctrl+Alt+Delete.

3. **Press Ctrl+Alt+Delete.**

   Windows 2000 displays a Login screen, which contains a graphics box with two empty text boxes for you to fill in: the User Name text box and the Password text box.

4. **The Login screen displays a default domain name in the Domain field. Click once on this field.**

   A drop-down list appears with all of the available domains for you to choose from.

5. **Select a domain from the list by clicking on it. The newly selected domain appears in the Domain field.**

6. **Enter your password to complete your login process.**

So How Does Mixed Networking Affect System Logins?

Okay, how *does* mixed networking affect system logins? Interesting question indeed. If you run a mixed network and you must boot the entire system from scratch, you need to consider a couple things. Although you don't have any magical order to follow to power up machines with specific operating systems on a mixed network, you do want to follow a few rules, as we describe in the following list:

✔ **Boot from the top down.** First, boot up the machines that are the most important (as your network diagram reflects). These machines include file servers, domain controllers, or other mission-critical machines. The reason? You want the client machines to access the servers as the clients first boot; and in some cases, a machine looks for a server on startup and complains if it doesn't see the server already running.

✔ **Boot from the inside out.** This idea is the same as booting from the top down, but it's easier to visualize if you don't use a hierarchical structure on your network.

✔ **Boot peripherals last.** Printers, external CD-ROM drives, and BOSE speaker systems are nice but not critical to starting up an entire system.

✔ **Power up Microsoft operating systems first.** Machines running Windows products are notoriously slow in booting up — particularly Windows 2000 Server and Enterprise Server. NetWare, Unix, and Linux all seem to boot up at about the same pace, which looks like warp speed if you compare it to that of a Windows machine.

In NetWare, NLM instabilities or ABENDS obviously affect other programs, processes, and connections to the NetWare server. By frequently checking the Novell Web site (`www.novell.com`), you can keep abreast of the latest CSPs if you aren't already receiving automatic notification or get the company to ship the new CDs to you on release.

If you're mapping drives to the NetWare server, an ABEND of the server or component that operates and controls the NetWare volumes can cause you to lose your connections to those drives. Utilizing NetWare and its Web server components obviously affects any Web pages or Web sites that are using the Web server if it fails, or ABENDS. So make sure that you keep a close eye on any servers that are giving you problems of this sort.

Logging Out of a Networked Operating System

After you finish working on a networked operating system, you need to consider the following two maxims:

✔ Shutting down and logging out *aren't* the same thing.

✔ You *don't* log out by flicking the power button.

Logging out simply means that you're no longer working on the network. The computer you still do your work on you keep powered up, either to complete work offline or to keep it ready for the next user to log in. Only if you're actually shutting down a system do you go a step beyond logging off by stopping the flow of power to the machine.

Flicking the power button definitely isn't a good way to log off. First, it's a form of overkill, because you don't need to stop the flow of power to the system. Second, by not following the correct logging off procedure, you can lose data in whatever program you're working on or, worse, corrupt the system files that are in use as you work. Your actions can come back to haunt you if part of the system, such as the word processor or the disk drive, refuses to work the next time you log in. Always, therefore, follow the appropriate logout procedure for your operating system, as we describe in the following sections.

Unix and Linux

To log out of a machine running Unix or Linux with a desktop GUI such as GNOME, follow these steps:

1. **Click the Main Menu button.**

2. **Choose the Log Out option from the menu that appears.**

   The Log Out dialog box appears, asking whether you really want to log out.

3. **Click the Yes button to log out.**

If you're not using a desktop GUI, simply type **exit** at the command prompt and press Enter to log out.

Windows 2000

To log out of a machine using Windows 2000, follow these steps:

1. **Click the Start button.**

2. **Select Shut Down from the Start menu.**

   The Shut Down Windows screen appears. Don't select the default option, which is normally Shut Down.

3. **Because you want only to log out, select Log Out from this screen.**

4. **Click the OK button to complete the log-out process.**

NetWare

Because it's the sole exception to the flicking-the-power-button rule, NetWare automatically logs you out if you just turn off your PC.

Chapter 8

Taking Charge

● ●

In This Chapter

▶ Principles for administrative accounts

▶ The root account in Unix/Linux

▶ The NetWare Administration account

▶ The Administration account in Windows 2000

● ●

*I*f you build it, they're sure to complain! And if they complain, they're likely to complain to you. Why? Because you're the master, the chief cook and bottle washer, the designer, the fixer — you name it, you're it. At least that's what the users think after you do some heroic deed such as changing a font.

The point here is that because you're responsible for putting your network together or maintaining the current one, you need certain levels of access and control that others don't (and shouldn't) have. In each case, the OS has an *administrative account*.

In Unix and Linux, this account is known as `root`. In Windows NT and 2000 it's *Administrator*. In NetWare, it's *admin* and *supervisor*. These names basically mean the same thing — you have ultimate power over these servers. You can kill these servers as easily as you fix them, so use your powers wisely, Luke. The force is indeed with you . . . in spades.

In each operating system, you can also assign to additional user accounts the equivalent rights or power on the servers. Treat these accounts as carefully as the actual administrative account. These accounts can fix (and destroy) anything that the real administrative account fixes (or destroys). *Caution* is the operative word in working with these types of accounts.

Rules for Administrative Accounts

Using the force in Luke's case was to do good, not evil. That's exactly what you need to do with your administrative account on the network — use it for good. Because you have these powers, you must always treat them as a loaded gun. *Carefully*.

Tread lightly or not at all: Using your privileges

What can these accounts do that a regular account can't? Surprisingly, in several areas, the administrative accounts bestow very similar privileges, regardless of which operating system you're using. The following list describes these privileges:

- After logging in as the administrator, you can look into all system directories and files.

- You can also look at any user's profile or at any information that users enter into the system about themselves. At the very least, this information includes the users' privileges, the files that they own, and their user names. You may also be privy to their real-world names, phone numbers, and company positions.

- You can change or delete any user's profile or home directory.

- You can disable user accounts so that they're no longer usable.

- You can reconfigure network settings on any given machine.

- You can start or kill any system process.

You get the idea. It's like having the security code for a bank, the combination for the safe, every key for every safe deposit box, and keys for the bathroom, too! What a deal, right?

Well, maybe not. Think about it. You now can do anything to anything or anyone, anytime. Uh, oh. That means that you are *responsible*.

Assign another person to help you and learn the ropes of administrative work on the servers. Doing so serves the following two purposes:

- Someone else can cover your responsibilities during vacations and in case of illness.

- Your users can call someone else at 3 a.m. to fix a problem.

Needless to say — but we really do need to say it — be careful, be smart and always give yourself a back door . . . just in case.

The Root of the Matter — the Administration Account in Unix/Linux

A network has only one administrator account in the Unix/Linux world. This all-powerful account is known as the *root account* (and sometimes as the *super-user* account). As does a more mundane, regular-Joe account, the root account has its own home directory and its own password.

This setup came about because Linux is, like its big brother Unix, an *open system*. Microsoft Windows, on the other hand, is a *closed system*. Unless you're running Windows NT, remotely logging in to another Windows machine from your own is comparatively difficult. Even with NT, most user files remain inaccessible.

If you're using Linux or Unix, keep in mind that, although only one administration account exists, that fact doesn't mean that only one person can log in as that administrator! Anyone who knows the password for the root account can become the root. Anyone who discovers a terminal left open by the root account or overhears the password can cause major havoc. Similarly, anyone with the correct passwords can log in to a Unix or Linux network from around the world and cause a crashing halt. The root account is the first, most basic security measure that prevents users from inadvertently damaging the system.

You can use the cd command, for example, to change directories to the root, or /, directory. This directory is where the root account begins. List the files. You'll see all the directories that handle important information, such as /etc, /usr, and /dev. Executing the ls -l command reveals an interesting pattern, as shown in Figure 8-1. The two middle columns, which indicate the group and user ownership, are all root! This setup isn't accidental. At this juncture of your system, where accidentally deleting any of these directories can bring your system to a crashing halt, only root can edit or otherwise work with these directories.

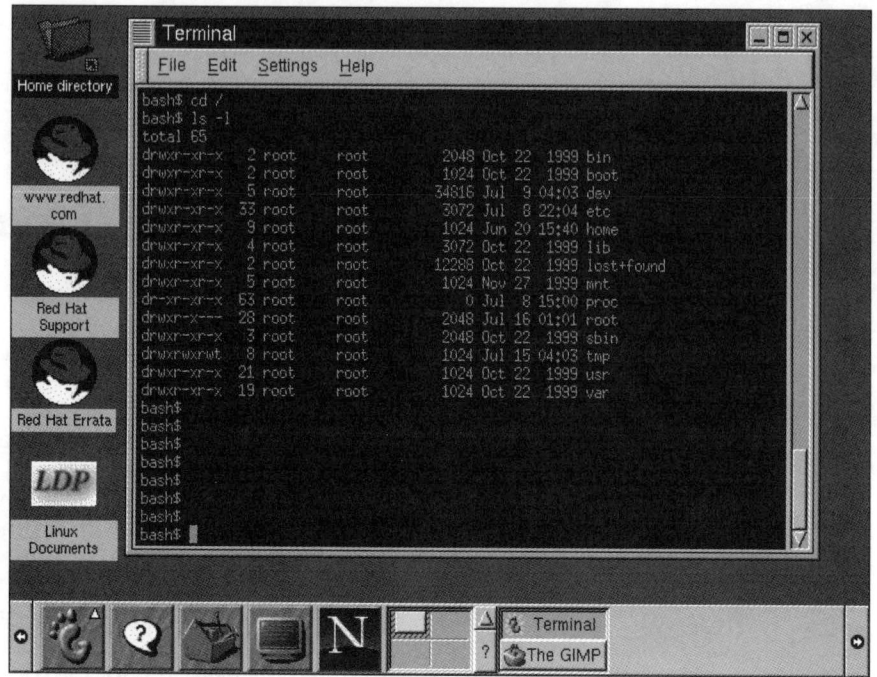

Figure 8-1:
Root owns
the core
directories
in Unix or
Linux.

Becoming the Super-User, Even if You're Sitting on a Crate of Kryptonite

You don't need a telephone booth to change into *Super-user*. Instead, two options tap into your godlike powers, as the following sections describe.

The captain's login

You can simply log in to the system directly as root. On your terminal, after the systems asks for your username, simply type **root**. After it asks for your password, type the password that you selected for root.

Root's screen normally doesn't display a name. Instead, your prompt almost always appears as a simple *hash* mark, as follows:

```
#
```

Only root uses the simple hash sign for a prompt. This prompt distinguishes the root account from that of a regular user, who sees a prompt such as bash$, $, or userman#.

You can also double-check your login name by using the id command. Typing the identify command, id, at the prompt confirms who you are, as the following examples show:

```
# id
# root <gid 0>
```

Su: The new, better way to become root

Another way to become root is through the su command. The su command stands for *super-user*. This designation is really a bit of a misnomer, however, because you can become anyone you want on the system by using su.

The su command morphs you into anyone's account on the system, even if that person is logged in to another machine — or the same machine!

Morphing into the super-user from any user account is even easier. Use id and the su command as before — with su, you don't need a username. Then complete the following steps to use su to become root if you first log in as another account:

1. **If you're using a desktop GUI on your Linux or Unix system, open a terminal window; otherwise, skip to Step 2.**

2. **At the command prompt, type su.**

3. **Press Enter.**

   You see the following prompt, telling you to enter your password:

   ```
   Passwd:
   ```

4. **Type the password for the administrative account and press Enter.**

   The operating system takes a second to verify your password as correct. If it's not, you see an Incorrect Passwd message and return to the command prompt. If the system verifies the password, the root command prompt (normally the hash sign, or #) appears for you to type in your commands as root.

Unless you specify a username, su automatically makes you the root.

To double-check your identity, you can use the id command. Just type id at the command prompt (#). Your current user ID appears, as follows:

```
# root <gid 0>
```

Reducing the amount of time you spend as root if you're not actively administering the system also reduces the chance that you may make a mistake that takes down the system. After you become root, you need to focus more on the task at hand and not, for example, go traipsing through your e-mail.

Call the Supervisor: NetWare Admin Accounts

By default, NetWare names its administrative account *admin*, but you can call it whatever you want. You can both create a backdoor and lock down the security of the system by using a name other than *admin*.

Most administrators stick with the default. It's the easiest username to remember and is often the one constant in an ever-changing computer world. Some other names that you can consider, however, are *leader, super, power, master,* and *guru.* (An administrator who uses the name *MuffinBoy, Sluggo,* or *Bozo,* for example, probably doesn't command as much respect.)

NetWare uses a *schema* (a system) in the form of a tree. The structure of this tree, NDS, enables you to create a group by the name of *admins* and then add users. These users assist you in the administrative tasks of the NetWare environment. After you create this initial group, you can create other groups and users, basing them on whatever your business or network requires.

Within NetWare, thanks to a tool known as *ConsoleOne*, you can use the following items to restrict access and administrative capabilities:

- ✔ Supervisor
- ✔ Create
- ✔ File Scan
- ✔ Read
- ✔ Erase
- ✔ Access Control
- ✔ Write
- ✔ Modify

You can also set *effective rights* on an object (a server, group, user, or other items in the NDS system). Effective rights simplify user administration. They base an object's rights on either of the following:

  ✔ A template

  ✔ A master object that you create as a template

Most users in a group have similar rights for certain servers, directories and files, so effective rights help manage these users.

Additionally, some regions in a company may get special rights for resources that other regions don't need. Planning your NDS tree is hardest, because if you structure the tree a certain way and the organization to which you belong suddenly changes, you must then edit the tree so that users retain the same rights. If you organize by region and suddenly you have HR people in two different regions, for example, you have a problem, because HR folks need similar rights, no matter what their location.

But maybe the HR person in St. Louis is in charge of only St. Louis HR issues and the person in Des Moines is in charge of Des Moines folks. In that case, organizing by regions makes some sense.

No matter how you look at it, make sure that you thoroughly document exactly who gets what rights — and where. Otherwise, you may end up in a heap of trouble.

Built-in Power: The Windows Administrator Account

As you install Windows 2000, the operating system automatically creates several *default* accounts. You use these accounts mostly for system maintenance tasks and Windows 2000 administration. A common characteristic of these accounts is very limited user accessibility. If you're from the Unix side of the operating system universe, you probably know of the standard-system account, nobody, that performs a lot of the dirty work for the root administrative account.

Windows works similarly. To take care of the system administration, Microsoft sets up the default root account, known as *Administrator*. For limited user access if you don't have time to create a new account for a regular system user, it creates the account *Guest*.

The administrative account is responsible for all the system-changing work and maintenance you perform on your system. Of course, you can change file permissions so that other accounts can also change your Windows world, but you want to avoid doing so.

One misinformed user is enough to knock out the right file at the wrong time.

One clever (okay, sort of sneaky) thing that you can do as an administrator is *hide* the administrative account. After all, if someone with criminal intent looks up a list of the system's users, he's probably going for the Administrator account. If that's how you label the account, it's kind of like titling sensitive documents for a warp drive "*TOP-SECRET: WARP-DRIVE INFORMATION.*"

Solution? Change the name of the Administrator account — make it *fred* or any other name that doesn't stick out from the list of user names. (Don't pick something that's a dead giveaway, however, such as *me_root* or *allpowerful-account.*

Chapter 9

Passwords: Pain or Pleasure?

● ●

In This Chapter

▶ Examining strong and weak passwords

▶ Establishing secure password systems

▶ Maintaining password security

● ●

*T*he first and best line of defense for your computer's security is a series of strong user and root passwords. Having secure passwords that are hard to guess, or *crack*, is vitally important for you and every single one of your users. If you're running mixed networks of machines, the principles of keeping passwords strong are the same from platform to platform. The only difference (lucky you!) in running passwords in this kind of environment is that you must know how to set passwords on any machine that you designate as your main server, or the machine that you use to create, edit, and delete your user accounts.

Choosing the Right Password

Because of normal human laziness, most people usually choose passwords from easily remembered sequences of four to eight characters. If people don't know how important password selection is, they gravitate toward choosing passwords such as their name, address, birth date, cat's name, mother's maiden name, or cat's maiden name. Although convenient, this kind of password reduces password security to how clever a cyber-thief is at guessing the obvious.

Typically, the general rule is that, if it's easy to remember, it's easy to guess. If it's hard to guess, it's too hard to remember and you write it down. With so many password-cracking programs available via the Internet, administrators need to increase their odds any way they can by cultivating a happy medium between these two extremes.

In a purely Hobbesian environment (nasty, brutish, and short of cable TV), only the strong survive, right? Absolutely. That goes for passwords, too. If something is weak, it's easy to break. In this case, your *security* is what breaks because of a weakness in your structure.

Buildings fall if you build them with weak wood; bridges fall if you build them with weak steel or rivets; and your security falls if you use weak passwords.

How do you avoid this catastrophe? Strong password security isn't an easy thing to implement — especially if you have an established network with users who've used easy passwords for a long time. You become a marked man or woman if you begin to clamp down on security. So the best place to start is with yourself and your servers. You set the example. Show your users that you're willing to make really cryptic passwords. Follow stringent rules to avoid someone guessing those passwords. And don't write them down in conspicuous places.

Weak passwords

Following are the password types to avoid:

- **Short passwords:** Short passwords are easier to guess, or crack, simply because they're short. Fewer characters in the word means less effort to figure it out.

- **Passwords that follow a pattern:** JULY2000, Monday1, computer9, companyname01 — these are all examples of *patterned passwords*. They're known by that term because you can easily determine them as part of a pattern. Take JULY2000 as a great example. Presumably, the user starts with the month in which he's hired or first logs in to the computer — maybe AUGUST1999. Then, each month, like clockwork, the user changes his password to the current month — say, JULY — and the current year — say, 2000.

- **Passwords that use family or pet names:** James01, Michael12, FidoTheDog, FluffyCat, and the ultimate in saccharine pet names, Sweetums. We bet that we can figure out a person's password simply by asking some questions about his personal life: "Hey, how's your dog, uh, what's his name?" Or "Hi. Isn't your son's birthday, uh — what's his name again? — coming up soon?" Obviously, cracking these kinds of passwords isn't necessarily as easy as cracking the pattern kinds, but certainly if someone wants to try, he has lots more firepower knowing a few things about you.

- **Passwords made of dates:** Birthdays, anniversaries, and the like. Bad. Just plain bad. With a little effort, password crackers can find out these types of things and try them as your passwords.

- **Passwords made of numbers or number sequences that someone can easily pick up:** Phone numbers, Social Security numbers, employee ID numbers, addresses. Password crackers can figure out these types of things pretty easily.

Strong passwords

Now the following types of passwords are the ones that you want to use:

- **Absolutely random passwords:** Ever see the initial password that you get on those AOL CDs that you receive in the mail about once a week? Okay, well, next time that you get one, take a look at the CD cover and check out the password. MatterPatella, SpeakSole, LateralCandor, PartialWrist — these are completely stupid but totally random passwords. You can also use a combination of numbers and letters, making a password even more random and difficult to break. 201MarsChore3, Torn69Ape, and 604Pirate00, for example, are all excellent choices for making a password as random as possible.

- **Long passwords:** 2IUD3WSA56BGI222. *Whew!* Need we say more? Make your password obscure, strange, and with no ties to any personal or company information at all.

Eight Ways to Keep Your Password Security Tight

Password security is your best line of defense against random vandalism, user error, and overall chaos. That's because password security is a relatively easy type of defense to tighten by creating tough passwords to crack, setting high standards for password creation, or even testing your defenses by using password-cracking programs. In this section, we show you the different avenues available for keeping your password protection in ship-shape.

Following is a list of things to keep in mind in establishing passwords:

- **Use all available characters and not just A–Z:** Make sure that A–Z and 0–9 and other available keyboard symbols (< : " { ^ %) are part of the normal password scheme. Doing so is tougher with eight-character limitations, so get creative: Make thieves think outside the box!

  Following are some samples:

  > 2^3=8 (2 cubed equals 8)

  > 4*24<97 (4 times 24 is less than 97)

  > 4+5=nine (Duh!)

- **Make sure that passwords are case-sensitive:** You ideally treat upper- and lowercase letters as separate characters, thereby increasing a password's strength.

✔ **If you can set a default length for passwords, force the default to the longest available minimum value:** Tell your users, "Passwords must be at least X characters long." The shorter, the weaker; the longer, the stronger.

✔ **Get password-cracking tools, such as L0phtcrack and other automatic password dictionary attacks:** Use them to test your users' choices and to eliminate the possibility of using obvious choices (such as *cat, dog, company name, my name,* or any other dictionary-type word).

✔ **Lock out users after two or three failed attempts at typing the correct password:** Don't permit unlimited tries, because that's how attackers blow right through many access-control mechanisms (which, in that case, aren't really controlling access at all, are they?).

✔ **Implement maximum-security controls on password files and directories:** Use audit trails and monitor inappropriate access attempts on these files.

✔ **Implement a secure screen saver in addition to your normal security scheme:** If a user doesn't use the keyboard or mouse for X minutes, the screen blanks and requires a reauthentication of the user. This one technique alone keeps the Wanderers or Friendlies out of where they don't belong.

✔ **Change passwords regularly:** You can set many systems to force the user to change his password on a periodic basis. Don't disable this feature. *Use it.* Every 30 days isn't inappropriate. (Take a look at the nearby sidebar for some tidbits about changing passwords regularly.)

How often do I want to I change my password — and how do I remember it?

The bottom line is that you must change your password frequently. How frequently? Well, some people change their passwords weekly. Others, monthly. And some wait until the system tells them to change their passwords. (Some systems, however, don't make you change them ever. Bad choice, dear friend.)

Say that you decide to change your password weekly. Now the challenge is how to remember it.

If you think writing down your password is a good idea, you're right. Writing it down is a good idea. Where you put it *after* you write it down, however, may be the bad idea. Leaving your password on paper and then taping it to your monitor is bad. Under the keyboard? Bad. In your drawers? Also bad. In one of the many books on your shelf? Bad, particularly if the cyber-thief is a literary sort. In your wallet or purse? Good. But if you leave your purse or wallet near your computer, you're back down to bad.

The idea here is that writing your password down is fine as long as you put that paper someplace where another person isn't likely to find it. That's why wallets and purses are safer: You most likely carry those things around with you most of the time. Even if you leave them at your desk while you're working, you most likely take them with you for lunch and when you're done working for the day.

Setting Up a Secure Unix/Linux Password System

Both Unix and Linux systems come with the passwd program. This program enables you to reset or edit passwords from the command line. In the more recent releases of Linux, such as Red Hat 6.0 and later, the passwd program includes a built-in feature that doesn't permit you to set a password that's easy to guess. The program complains that the password is too short or obvious and refuses to implement it. Don't count on this feature alone, however, to ensure that you have strong passwords. Always set and enforce strong password procedures.

Tales from the encrypt

Both Unix and Linux use an encryption algorithm known as *DES* (which stands for *D*ata *E*ncryption *S*tandard and *not* Does Everything Secretly) to encrypt passwords. Yes, we know that math majors out there are probably howling because DES is a two-way encryption algorithm, but that's not the case with Linux or Unix. The variant of DES that these operating systems use is, by specific design, a one-way algorithm only, because one-way encryption prevents crackers from reversing the encryption to crack your password from the contents of the /etc/passwd password file.

For those of you who aren't particularly mathematically inclined, an *algorithm* isn't something that you can dance to; it's actually a specific kind of computer-based mathematical system that people commonly use to create — or break — coding technology.

On several versions of Unix and Linux, the system stores encrypted passwords in the /etc/passwd file or, on occasion, in the /etc/shadow file. By default, Linux opts to store passwords in the /etc/shadow file, which adds an extra layer of security. (See the following section for details.)

Whenever you create a new password or alter an old one (and both are really the same thing to DES), the /etc/passwd or the /etc/shadow file updates to reflect the change. If you attempt to log in, the system encrypts the password that you enter at the Passwd: prompt and compares it with the encryption pattern that it stores in your /etc/passwd or /etc/shadow file. If the encryption patterns match up, you gain access to the system.

Me and my shadow file

The /etc/shadow file is the same as the /etc/passwd file in that it stores user information — particularly the encrypted passwords that the computer uses to recognize a user after he logs in. The system saves Shadow passwords in the etc/shadow file, which only the root account can access. Although users can still change their own passwords whenever they want, the shadow file is an effective means of keeping your encrypted password field from the view of a curious user or a cracker who looks into your /etc directory.

You may think that using the /etc/shadow file is an odd idea if you already have an encrypted field for the /etc/passwd file. After all, although users can change directories and even use the vi editor on the /etc/passwd file, users can't save any of the changes they make without root permission.

Unfortunately, programs are available on the Internet for the unscrupulous to take advantage of how the passwd file's permissions are set on many systems. Even if a password file is unreadable to a user, for example, that doesn't stop someone from copying the file into his home directory, where he then has full permissions over the file to tinker with at will. If that someone has a program to crack the encryption, he can use the resulting password in the original copy of the passwd file and start coming and going on any of your machines as he pleases, wreaking havoc along the way. Using /etc/shadow enables you to gain a small extra measure of security in this way.

Even if you're not currently using shadow passwords, you can convert your Linux or Unix system to use them immediately. To make your system start using the /etc/shadow file for your passwords, use the pwconv (password conversion) command to convert your system to use shadow passwords. The encrypted fields in /etc/password copy over into the /etc/shadow file, hidden and re-encrypted from all prying eyes except, of course, those of the root account. Just follow these steps:

1. **Log in to your machine as the root account.**
2. **Type** cd /etc **at the command prompt and press Enter.**

   You switch over to the /etc directory.

3. **Type** pwconv **at the command prompt and press Enter.**

   The system creates the /etc/shadow file.

You can confirm that the file exists by using the ls command. Or you can view it in the vi editor by typing **vi /etc/shadow** and pressing Enter. The contents of this file look the same as in /etc/passwd, but the file isn't visible to any user except root.

How to edit the passwords

All your password additions, subtractions, and alterations take place in the /etc/passwd file or, if you're using the default shadow password system, in the /etc/shadow file. So when is the best time to edit this file? Trick question — editing this file is *never* a good idea. You want to touch it only if you really, really need to. Deleting the wrong field in this file can literally lock you out of your computer, perhaps even forcing you to reinstall Linux.

If you want to change a single password and you don't want to edit any other user information, you're best off leaving the /etc/passwd file alone and using the passwd command.

To view the passwd file, type **vi passwd** at the command line and press Enter. The results look similar to what you see in Figure 9-1.

The /etc/passwd file lists each account on one line, with colons separating different parameters into fields. For security purposes, your interest lies only in the second field from the left, which is the user account's password. In Figure 9-1, the password for the first user, root, is TNDrxHsuIcn5I. And, no, that's not really what the password is (talk about obscure!). It's just how the encrypted version looks.

Figure 9-1: The passwd file. Look obscure? That's the whole point.

By the way, Figure 9-1 is noteworthy because it contains the *worst* password of all time. Yes, although you can never have a *best* password, a worst one does exist. See it? It's the password belonging to the `Newuzer` account on the bottom line. Yes, we know you don't see anything in the password field. That's the point. The account *isn't using* a password. This situation is very, *very* bad for security, because without a password for the account, anyone can simply log in as this user *without entering anything*.

Setting Up a Secure Windows Password System

Windows 2000 may be the greatest thing since canned soft drinks to technology people, but that doesn't mean that you can rely on its password system alone for user management and security. You must still establish some kind of password policy to prevent users from granting a cracker easy access to your system.

To create a good, strong password, follow the same rules that we outline in the section, "Choosing the Right Password," earlier in this chapter, about passwords in the Unix or Linux environment.

The ever-helpful folks at Microsoft also provide some guidelines for creating passwords. The best administrators know that Microsoft recommends the following:

- ✔ A password is ideally seven or more characters long.
- ✔ A password ideally contains at least one character from each of the three character groups:
    - Letters (uppercase and lowercase): A, B, C,. . .; a, b, c,. . .
    - Numerals: 0, 1, 2, 3, 4, 5, 6, 7, 8, 9
    - Symbols: ` ~ ! @ # $ % ^ & * ( ) _ + - = { } | [ ] \ : " ; ' < > ? , . /

    Symbols are all keyboard characters that aren't letters or numerals.
- ✔ Ideally, a *new* password is significantly different from the prior one.
- ✔ A password ideally isn't a common word or name or a derivative of a common word or name.
- ✔ Above all, a password ideally doesn't contain the user's real-world name or user name.

Some dialog boxes, such as the one for a telephone-modem connection, give you the option to save or remember your password. Don't select that option because doing so enables someone to easily pull your password from the computer memory.

Pssst! Here's a little-known Windows password quirk. . . .

If you're going to run both Windows 2000 and Windows 95/98 on the same network, know that a little-known password preference differs between the two operating systems. Windows 95 and Windows 98 happily support passwords up to 14 characters in length. A longer password, however, is automatically truncated. So if your favorite password is supercalifragilisticexpialidocious, it gets cut off at supercalifragi.

In comparison, any version of the Windows 2000 generation of operating systems can work with a much larger number of characters — up to 127 as a matter of fact. (And you didn't believe in progress.)

This situation sets up a conflict: You may find that you can't log in to your network from those computers running Windows 95 and 98 if you decide to use the jumbo-sized passwords that the Windows 2000 systems permits. They just get cut off, and the Windows 2000 systems don't recognize them. So consider the upside of brevity in creating passwords on a multi-Microsoft system network.

Changing passwords

To change passwords in Windows, you simply perform what's known in technical circles as the three-fingered nerve pinch. You perform said pinch by pressing the Ctrl+Alt+Delete keys.

Now some among you (particularly the Windows 95 and 98 crowd) may look on in amazement, thinking that you're shutting the system down. Although true in Windows 95/98, the enlightened Windows 2000 actually gives you more choices than that.

Pressing Ctrl+Alt+Delete takes you to a secondary screen that gives you several options, ranging from the aforementioned Shut Down to the milder Change Password. You make your selection by simply clicking the button of the option that you want to take advantage of.

You don't need to be the root account to change passwords by using the Ctrl+Alt+Delete method. In fact, any user can change his password at any time by using this method.

Another option is to insist that all users come to you to change their passwords. To set up your system that way, follow these steps:

1. **Log in as the root account.**

2. **Click Start and choose Settings⇨Control Panel from the Start menu.**

   The Control Panel appears.

3. **Double-click Administrative Tools.**

   The Administative Tools screen appears, which displays several large buttons.

4. **Double-click on the button labeled Computer Management.**

   This opens the Computer Management screen, which is divided into two areas, called panes. The left pane displays the console tree, while the right displays what is under a given section of the console tree when you select an item from the tree. When you initially open the Computer Management screen, this right pane is blank, as you haven't selected anything on the tree yet.

5. **In the console tree that appears, go to Local Users and Groups and click Users.**

6. **Select the user account that you want to change by highlighting it with a single mouse click.**

7. **Click Action.**

   A small Action window appears where you can select the action you wish to take.

8. **Click Set Password.**

   The window displays a text box where you can enter the password.

9. **Type the password that you want in the appropriate text box.**

10. **Click the OK button to complete the task.**

Resetting passwords

You need to work in the Windows 2000 Active Directory to reset a password. To do so, complete the following steps:

1. **Click Start and choose Programs⇨Administrative Tools⇨Active Directory Users and Computers from the Start menu.**

   The AD Users and Computers window appears on the desktop.

2. **In the AD Users and Computers screen's console tree (located in the left pane), click Users.**

   The user accounts on the network appear in the right-hand pane.

3. **In the right details pane, right-click the user whose password you want to reset.**

4. **Choose Reset Password from the pop-up menu that appears, as shown in Figure 9-2.**

   A small Reset Password window appears, containing a text box for you to type and confirm the password.

5. Type and confirm the password in the appropriate text box.

6. Click the OK button to complete the task.

You return to the AD Users and Computers screen.

You can also reset a password by selecting the user account that you want to change (with a single click), and choosing Action⇨Reset Password from the menu bar of the AD Users and Computers screen (see Figure 9-3).

Protecting passwords by using Standby mode

You can protect your password by setting up your computer's Standby mode. After you set this option, whenever you activate Standby mode, the screen saver turns on and effectively locks your computer with your password. Anyone trying to use the computer from that point on must reenter the password of the last person using the machine to get back on the system.

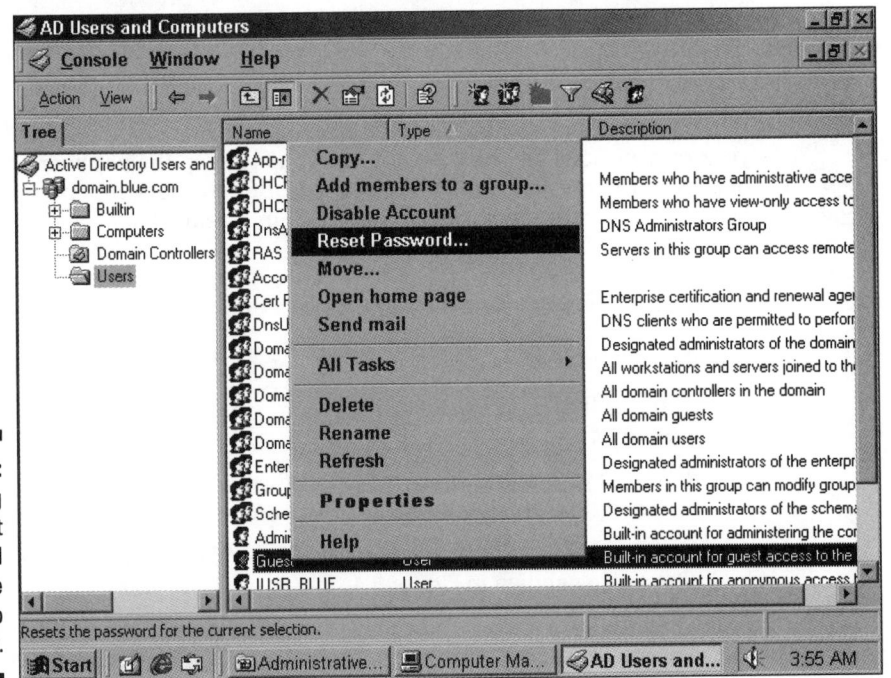

Figure 9-2:
Selecting
Reset
Password
from the
pop-up
menu.

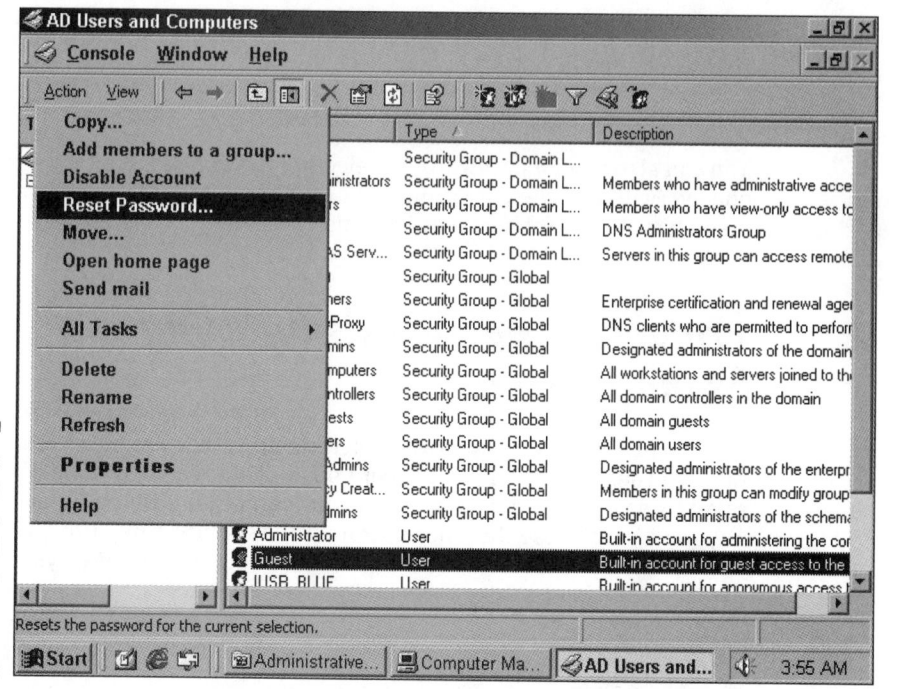

Figure 9-3:
Resetting
the
password
from the
Action
menu.

What if you forget your password while you're in Standby mode? Unfortunately, your only options are locating where you may keep the password on a piece of paper or simply rebooting the machine. But consider rebooting only as a last resort, because it causes you to lose any unsaved information on the computer.

To set up a Standby scheme, follow these steps:

1. **Click Start and choose Settings⇨Control Panel from the Start menu.**

2. **Double-click the Power Options icon, which, appropriately, looks like a battery.**

   Rumor says that the next version's Power Options icon is a Pink Bunny with sunglasses and a drum set, but you never know with Microsoft.

   After you double-click the icon, the Power Options Properties window appears, as shown in Figure 9-4.

3. **Click the down arrow to the right of the Power Schemes drop-down list box and select a power scheme from the list that appears.**

   We suggest that you stick with the default, Always On.

4. **To turn off your monitor before your computer goes on standby, select a time from the Turn Off Monitor drop-down list box.**

5. **To turn off your hard drive before your computer goes on standby, select a time from the Turn Off Hard Disks drop-down list box.**

6. **Click OK to accept your settings.**

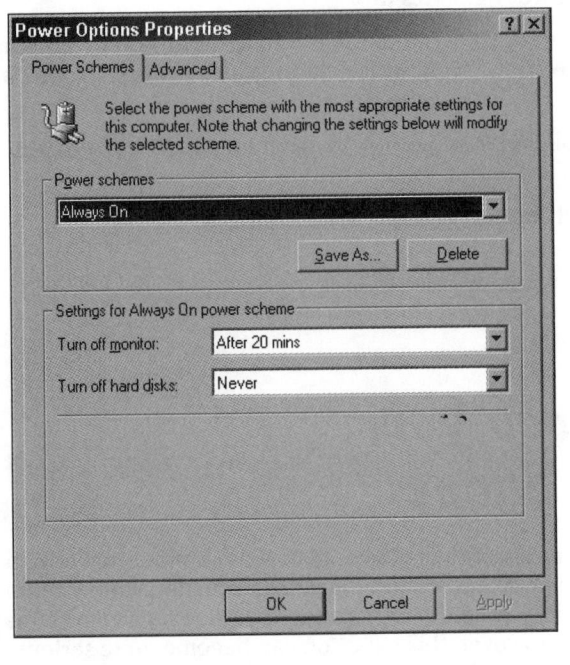

Figure 9-4: The Power Options Properties window, where you can set the turn-off times for your monitor and hard drive.

Protecting passwords by using Hibernation mode

Hibernation mode is a little like Standby, but it takes the password-saving convention to the next level. It also includes a few more built-in safeguards. After a set period of idle time, your computer enters Hibernation mode. Unlike in Standby, a computer going into hibernation saves everything in computer memory to your hard drive. After the save process is complete, the computer goes through its shutdown procedure and switches itself off, thereby preventing anyone from stealing the password of anyone logged in at the time.

You control Hibernation mode via the Power Options icon in the Control Panel. To put your computer into hibernation, follow these steps:

1. **In the Control Panel, double-click the Power Options icon.**

   The Power Options Properties screen appears.

2. **Click the Hibernate tab.**

3. **Select the Enable Hibernate Support check box and click Apply.**

4. **Click the APM tab.**

5. **Select Enable Advanced Power Management Support and click Apply.**

6. **Click the Power Schemes tab.**

7. **Select a time for the system to go into hibernation by clicking the down arrow to the right of the Settings drop-down list box and select a time from the list that appears.**

   The available times will normally be in increments of 1 minute, 5 minutes, 10, 20, and so on.

8. **Click the OK button to apply your changes.**

If the Hibernate tab is unavailable, your computer doesn't support this feature.

Utilities to Keep Your Passwords in Shape

As do an unfortunate number of people in today's modern world, passwords can get out of shape. With an individual, this situation simply requires a trip to the tailor to add a couple inches to the waistline on a favorite pair of jeans. With a password, however, this situation can become quite serious. Of course, out-of-shape passwords don't get flabby around the midsection. Poorly chosen passwords or passwords that people don't change in months, or even years, are a security risk. These situations create a greater chance that someone can crack or steal it. Luckily, today's computers come with a host of utilities that can help you keep your passwords in shape. The following sections list a few of the more popular options.

Advanced Password Generator

The *Advanced Password Generator* is an application that generates passwords of any length and character content. It enables users to use the built-in random number generator, which generates a random seed value, or numerical value, that builds a string of characters to use as a password. Because it's randomly generated, the password is extremely difficult to guess or crack. Of course, the Advanced Password Generator doesn't just create numerical passwords, which many people find cold, impersonal, and difficult to remember. The generator also can create alphabetic, numeric, alphanumeric, or all keyboard characters password of user-defined lengths. It can generate passwords in lowercase or in mixed case (upper- and lowercase). And you can print all passwords.

SFLogin 32

SFLogin 32 is a powerful tool that makes logging in to NetWare networks easier, while enabling the system manager to tighten security and customize login screens.

You can set SFLogin 32 to suggest that a password's unacceptable or force a user to change it. In addition to the usual NetWare limitations controlling password length, you can also insist that the password contain a minimum number of numeric characters, a minimum number of alphabetical characters, a maximum number of consecutively repeated characters, and a maximum number of repeated characters.

Windows NT Password Security Filter

Windows NT 4.0 Service Pack 2 introduces a new password filter, *passfilt.dll*, which implements the following new restrictions:

- Passwords must be at least six characters long.
- Passwords must contain at least three of the following criteria:

  Uppercase letters (A–Z)

  Lowercase letters (a–z)

  Number(s) (0–9)

  Nonalphanumeric character (!, for example)

- Passwords may not contain your user name or any part of your full name.

To enable this filter, perform the following steps on all Personal Domain Controllers (PDCs).

1. **Start the Windows Registry Editor by clicking Start⇨Run.**

2. **The 'Run' window appears on the desktop. In its single open text field, type** regedt32.exe **and press Enter.**

   Use `regedt32.exe`; do *not* use `regedit.exe`.

   When the Windows Registry Editor screen appears on the desktop, several windows inside of it appear in a stack (overlapping in a way where you can read the name of each window).

3. **Select the window named** HKEY_LOCAL_MACHINE\SYSTEM\ CurrentControlSet\Control\Lsa **by clicking on its title bar.**

   This moves it to the foreground so you can work in it.

4. **Double-click the setting Notification Packages, which is listed in the** `HKEY_LOCAL_MACHINE\SYSTEM\CurrentControlSet\Control\Lsa` **window.**

   The Notification Packages screen appears inside the window.

5. **Type** PASSFILT **on a new line in the Notification Packages screen.**

6. **Click OK.**

7. **Close the Registry Editor by clicking the Close button.**

8. **Reboot the machine.**

NetWare Password Management

You manage passwords in NetWare within NDS (Novell Directory Services). After you create a user in NetWare, you can use a few properties to ensure a consistent, high level of security. You can easily manage users (and all other objects, for that matter) by using ConsoleOne or NWADMIN. For a quick review of ConsoleOne and NWADMIN, see Chapter 8.

User accounts have more than 80 properties, so covering all of them would take an entire chapter, but for a complete list of properties, select a User object in NetWare Administrator or ConsoleOne. To display a description for each page of properties, click Help.

The key items to help you ensure security for passwords in NetWare include the following:

- **Account Expiration Date:** This property enables you to limit the life of a user account. After the expiration date, the account locks so that the user can't log in. Great for contractors or consultants who're only there for a short period of time.

- **Force Periodic Password Changes:** This property enables you to enhance security by requiring the user to change passwords after a specified interval — 30 or 60 days is common.

- **Limit Concurrent Connections:** This property enables you to set the maximum number of sessions a user can have on the network at any given time. If you want to restrict each user to one log in to the system at a time, use this property to set that up.

- **Login Time Restrictions:** This property enables you to set times and days when the user can log in. If no one works outside the normal hours of 9 a.m. to 5 p.m., you can set this attribute to restrict after-hours access to the system.

- **Require a Password:** This property enables you to control whether the user needs to use a password. Other related properties enable you to set common password constraints such as password length.

Should you force users to follow password policies?

Touchy subject — especially if you haven't done so from the beginning. People have quit their jobs over these types of policies, so be cautious and seriously evaluate your security needs before forcing anyone to change passwords frequently or to use randomly generated passwords. Carefully assess whether your data and your computers are of such high risk if not secure that you need to implement this type of security.

Obviously, no one right way handles the password issue. Depending on your security requirements or needs, you can use many different schemes to accomplish your security methods and plans.

If you or your company does government work, that work may require you to implement certain levels of security. Usually, the government department you're doing the work for advises you of these specifications ahead of time so that you can get things set up correctly. This situation is one in which you can learn a lot about security and passwords. The governments of the world are pretty good at security and have many ways to ensure that no one breaches or steals their information. If you have the opportunity to work with the government, you're certain to learn a lot about security.

Chapter 10

Utilities, Tools, Help Files —
Your Best Friends

· ·

In This Chapter

▶ Schema, daemons, NLMs

▶ The ps command combination

▶ Windows Registry editors

▶ Using NLMs

▶ Help files and where to find them

· ·

System integration isn't for everyone. In fact, if someone assigns you to integrate a bunch of computers running more than one kind of network operating system, think of yourself as special indeed. People who can even attempt to tackle this highly advanced, technical work are few and far between, and your salary is certain to continue to reflect this fact.

On the other hand, your company may press you into service to carry out this task with little or no expertise. Ah, but things do look brighter at the end of the tunnel . . . namely, the job skill of "system integrator" that you achieve after you get everything on your network running.

You're going to need to know about the most helpful of the various utilities and tools available on your system if you want to extend yourself into areas you currently may not know much about, such as where to find system information or network traffic statistics. Knowing where to go for help if you get into a jam that not even Bill Gates, Steven Bourne, and Linus Torvalds would want to try to help you out of also proves useful in carrying out your duties.

Computer Cardio — Schema, Daemons, NLMs

Time out for a little more terminology. You may have heard that beauty is only skin deep. Well, in some ways that can prove true of an operating system. We grant you that the components of the various systems may be different — not only in appearance, but also in function — but very often, you use the same concepts and ideas to run the show regardless of which system (or systems) you're using.

A case in point is the use of NetWare *NLMs* and *daemons* in the Unix/Linux world. Both fall in the category of helpful utilities that come with your operating system, and until you get down to the code level, the only difference between them may be in the functions or names of the utilities. Other concepts, however, such as the *schema*, transcend operating systems so that you find them on many (or all) systems available to you. A schema is more like a general plan or set of rules that describe your network's structure.

Schema, schmema — what good is it?

As an example of a transcendent computing idea, *schema* is something that's not OS specific. It's more generic, and you can apply the word to many things. But to keep the focus on computer operating systems that you use on servers, you can apply a primary definition for the term.

The schema of a database system makes up the rules of how you actually put the database together. You may, therefore, hear people depicting the schema as the structure of a database system, which you describe in a formal language that the database management system (DBMS) supports. In a relational database, the schema defines the tables, the fields in each table, and the relationships between fields and tables.

You generally store schemas in a data dictionary. Although you define a schema in text-database language, you often use the term to refer to a graphical depiction of the database structure.

Okay, now you know what schemas are — boring — but what do you *use* schemas for? Certainly not just for databases? This book isn't about databases, and if it were, neither of us would be writing it! We're not SQL people.

You use schemas to describe the structure of such things as an *LDAP* (*L*ightweight *D*irectory *A*ccess *P*rotocol), which is what you use to access directory information that you sometimes store in databases. The schema tells the LDAP how you're arranging things, or putting them together, so that you can more easily find them in your database.

Daemons — only their rep is bad

Daemons? You're probably thinking, "Wow, the people who designed Unix can't even *spell* right!" (Personally, we thought the *Demon* was a radical roller coaster at Paramount's Great America in Santa Clara the first time that we heard the term.) You're wrong, of course, but don't just take my word for it. The Encyclopedia Britannica states the following (in its austere tone):

Demon: Also spelled d*aemon*, in religions worldwide, any of numerous malevolent spiritual beings, powers, or principles that mediate between the transcendent and temporal realms.

An alternative definition is as follows:

Daemon: The Greek word for *guardian spirit*. In computing, refers to an auxiliary system program that initiates at startup and executes in the background. Daemons are ready to perform a specific task whenever you need them, such as running a scheduler to start another process automatically at a preestablished time or a routine that checks incoming e-mail messages for addresses that it can't find and then notifies the sender that the message is undeliverable.

Well, after extensive research, you discover that *daemon* is really a word that just means something similar to *program* — but not in the sense of Microsoft Word or CorelDRAW. A daemon is a program or a script in Unix or Linux that may start a process that's continuing to run.

The point is that, as you can see, the traditional definitions of *daemon* aren't exactly what a daemon on a computer system is or does. But these definitions can make some sense if you think of a daemon as a helpful entity that dutifully waits for an event to occur — maybe the arrival of an e-mail or something someone's writing into a log.

After this event occurs, the daemon starts up and kicks into gear and performs its specific set of tasks to accomplish its purpose. Two excellent examples of this type of daemon are `telnetd` and `lpd`. (Notice that Unix and Linux types, ever creative, always seem to tack a d at the end of a process name to remind you that it's a daemon.) Every time that you start a network connection, the system starts a `telnet` daemon that runs until you shut the connection down. Similarly, whenever you send a job to a printer, `lpd`, the *Line Printer D*aemon, starts up and doesn't shut down until it completes the job.

NLMs . . . they melt in your computer, not in your hands . . .

Another type of small programs is the *NLM* (*NetWare Loadable Module*). NLMs are the programs and modules that run on NetWare servers. They're similar to the processes and programs that run on Windows, Unix, and Linux servers. Working with NLMs, however, isn't like working with any of these other OSes in one respect: You need to remain at the console or run RCONSOLE to see the list of NLMs running or to manipulate them in any fashion. By contrast, you can remotely log in to a Linux or Unix server and still start or stop a daemon process.

The Super Combo Command in Unix and Linux

Hands down, the most useful command in both the Unix and Linux worlds is the ps and grep combo, which you connect with a pipe (|). Appearing on-screen as ps | grep, this combination enables you to search for and locate any process on your system that you want. It displays information that enables you to tell the time a process is running and even whether you can stop it. Even better, you don't need to log in as the root to use this command either locally or remotely! The following sections look at each part of this lethal combination one at a time.

Process search

You can search for processes that are currently running on your system by using ps, the *process search* command. The ps command enables you to determine whether a program is running and who's running it. The syntax for process searching is ps <options>.

The process search command enables you to identify the *PID* (or *process ID number*) of processes running on your Linux or Unix box. The process ID number is a number that the Linux operating system generates for the computer to identify a process. The PID is what you use in employing commands, such as kill, to stop a certain process. (The PID identifies the exact process that you want to kill.) The PID appears in the second column from the left on the terminal window where you ran the process search command.

To obtain the PID from a ps command, always use the command options -aef or, on BSD systems, -aux.

Pipes that even Drano can't clean

You transfer the output of one command to another with the help of a Unix shell utility known as pipe. Pipe is a utility that automatically comes with the Linux or Unix operating environment you enter whenever you use the terminal. You don't, therefore, type **pipe** to use the utility. Instead, you type the pipe symbol directly off the keyboard. The pipe symbol looks like a little vertical line (|).

You can normally find the pipe symbol on the Backslash key right above the Enter key on your keyboard. To type this symbol, make sure that you press and hold the Shift key as you press the Backslash key.

Simply using the Caps Lock function doesn't enable you to type a pipe. You must always create it manually by pressing Shift+Backslash to type the symbol.

Groping with grep

The grep command stands for *G*et *R*egular *ExP*ression, which is sort of what the command really does. You find that grep-ing for patterns or words is the easiest, most convenient way to locate a phrase or character pattern in a long text file. You also find that using grep with ps and the pipe shell utility creates one of the most useful combinations that you find in the Linux operating system.

The command format for grep is as follows:

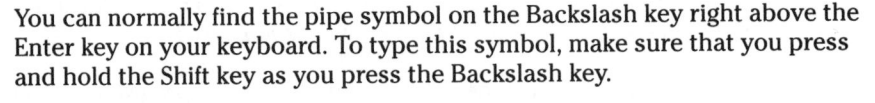

```
grep <pattern you're searching for> <file you're searching
          for>
```

ps, grep, and pipe — they're better together

If you use these three utilities (grep, ps, and pipe) together, you have the equivalent of a cybernetic scalpel. By placing them together, you can search all instances of a given process by name by typing the following at the command prompt and pressing Enter:

```
ps -aef | grep <process you're searching for>
```

The Windows 2000 Registry

The *Registry* is the main Windows repository of all its configuration information. Much like the human brain or a very popular library's card catalog, your system constantly references it as you use the computer. The Registry stores everything from information on interfacing with system hardware to the speed at which your mouse pointer moves across the desktop. The specific divisions within the registry are known as *Registry keys*.

You can view and edit these keys by using special programs known as *Registry editors*. Keep in mind, however, that manually altering the Registry carries the risk of error if you make a typo!

Calling in the editor . . .

A Registry editor enables you to change values within the Registry itself. These editors are either text based or graphics based. If you change a value within the Registry, by definition you change the way the entire computer runs. Of course, if you're working on a server to which many of your computers connect, this change can affect many different machines.

The two current versions of Registry Editor are *Regedt32.exe* and *Regedit.exe*. The Regedt32.exe has the *32* on its name because you install its executable in the systemroot\System32 folder. This version is the default editor that comes with Windows 2000.

Whenever you make a change to a server and users feel the effects across the entire network, that change is known as a *ripple*. In fact, the entire concept of a change at the server spreading out to affect all users is known as the *ripple effect*, because it's akin to tossing a pebble in a still pond and watching the water ripple across the pond's entire surface.

Editing the Registry can assist you in the following areas:

- ✔ Fixing typos in any of the Registry keys.
- ✔ Removing redundant entries in any key.
- ✔ Deleting key values that you alter by uninstalling or deleting programs or applications from the system.

Opening the Registry Editor

Although editing the Registry is a tricky business, opening the Registry Editor isn't. Whether the editor is the standard version or the 32 version, the opening procedure is the same. To open Registry Editor, complete the following steps:

1. **Click the Start button and choose Programs⇨Accessories⇨Command Prompt.**

2. **In the window that opens, type** regedt32, **if you're in Windows 2000, or simply** regedit.

3. **Press Enter.**

   The Registry Editor opens.

The Registry Editor displays five windows, each of which represents a predefined key on the local computer. The Registry Editor stacks these windows in such a way that you can bring any of them to the foreground by clicking that window.

Windows 2000 displays the following keys:

- ✔ **HKEY_LOCAL_MACHINE:** This key contains machine-specific (local) configuration information.

- ✔ **HKEY_USERS:** This key contains settings of all user profiles on the computer that you run the registry editor on.

- ✔ **HKEY_CURRENT_CONFIG:** This key contains hardware profile information that the computer uses at startup.

- ✔ **HKEY_CLASSES_ROOT:** This key is really more of a subkey to the following key: HKEY_LOCAL_MACHINE\Software. We're listing this one because it's listed within regedit or regedt32.

- ✔ **HKEY_CURRENT_USER:** This key contains the root of the configuration information for only the user who's currently logged on.

Because infinite power corrupts absolutely, keep in mind that you can't even start a Registry editor unless you log in as the Administrator account. If you're logging in remotely, Windows further guards the system by enabling you to open only the HKEY_USERS and HKEY_LOCAL_MACHINE keys. This situation is true even if you log in as the Administrator account.

For the truly masochistic, if you really want to read about the Registry editors in-depth, see the book *Windows 2000 Registry For Dummies,* by Glenn Weadock and Emily Sherrill Weadock.

NetWare — Using NLMs

Those little NLMs (*Net*Ware *L*oadable *M*odules) in NetWare are different from what you see in any of the other OSes that we discuss in this book. You need to remain at the server console (that is, at the keyboard and monitor that attaches to the actual server) and run RCONSOLE to see the list of NLMs that NetWare's running.

The RCONSOLE.EXE (*Remote Console*) utility is a DOS-based utility that enables you to access the server's console from a workstation. This utility resides in the SYS:SYSTEM directory of the NetWare 4 server. RCONSOLE transmits

> ✔ Your keystrokes to the server console
>
> ✔ The server console screen to your workstation

The command that you then use to view NLMs is MODULES. The reason that NLMs aren't like what you find in other OSes is that, as you run MODULES, it displays a lot of additional information right off the bat for you, such as the versions of each NLM that is running.

At the server prompt, type **MODULES** and press Enter. You see a list of about four or five NLMs. Pressing any key (other than the Esc key) shows another page of the NLMs.

Even on a default installation of NetWare 5.1, a lot of stuff's running on the machine. You're likely to see a list of 120 to 140 NLMs throughout all the pages of NLMs.

What's cool is that, as you run MODULES, the command also lists other information that you may need in working on and troubleshooting your NetWare servers. You see something similar to the list of modules that's shown in the following section.

NDS troubleshooting

You use the following *NDS* (*N*ovell *D*irectory *S*ervices) utilities for performing NDS tests and checks:

✔ **DSREPAIR.NLM:** A core utility that you use to repair NDS corruption of data. A must have! If you don't use this utility, you're hosed. DSREPAIR is *the* tool for recovering and repairing NDS in the event of a failure or problem. It can help you solve authentication problems, directory-rights issues, file-rights issues, and a plethora of other normally tricky problems.

✔ **DSTRACE.NLM:** Enables an administrator to watch and monitor NDS transactions. DSTRACE is an NLM (a *NetWare Loadable Module*, as we describe in the preceding section) that provides expanded monitoring capabilities. After you load it, you can use DSTRACE (also known as the N*DS Trace* Event Monitor) to monitor synchronization status and errors. You primarily use DSTRACE to determine and track the health of NDS as it communicates with the other NetWare 5 servers in the network.

✔ **NDS Manager:** A Windows-based management utility that comes with NetWare 4.11, NDS Manager is a Windows-based program that replaces Partition Manager (versions 3.*x* of NetWare). It enables you to control the partitioning and replication of the NDS database. It also provides other vital information, such as synchronization and continuity.

✔ **SCANTREE.EXE:** The SCANTREE utility takes a snapshot of the NDS tree. SCANTREE is a DOS application designed to traverse an NDS tree and return a series of statistics. The results help to characterize an NDS tree by describing the width and depth of the tree, as well as the variety and characteristics of leaf objects. Excellent for seeing whether your NDS tree's grown way too big or out of control. You can download this program from the Novell Support Connection Web site at http://support. novell.com. Search for file name SCANDS.EXE. (Novell Technical Services doesn't support SCANTREE.EXE.)

✔ **DSDIAG.NLM:** DSDIAG is a new diagnostic and report tool for NDS. DSDIAG is server-based but provides a client base approach on the server. DSDIAG can run multiple reports in real time without waiting for one report to finish. DSDIAG can also run a report on the tree to display the NDS versions of each server and also modify this report to display only those servers with versions greater, less than, or equal to a given value. This capability enables a quick diagnosis of NDS errors stemming from a single server using an older or newer version of DS.NLM. To download this utility, reference TID (Technical Information Documents) 2928396 for the Novell Web site location. (TIDs are what Novell uses to document their specific technical information.). Go to http://support. novell.com and search for this TID number, and you end up right there at that TID.

You install the preceding utilities as you set up NetWare.

Utilize DS Repair to maintain and repair NDS

You can back up your NDS database for disaster recovery by using `DSREPAIR.NLM`. Just follow these steps:

1. **Load `DSREPAIR.NLM` at the console and then choose Advanced Options from the DSREPAIR menu that appears.**

   See the preceding section for more information about this utility.

2. **Select the Create a Database Dump option.**

   The directory path for the database dump appears on-screen. Of course, you can change this directory to wherever you would like the dump to go to on the server.

3. **Press Enter to save the changes in NDS itself.**

To perform this process from the command line and skip all the menus, type the following at the command prompt:

```
dsrepair /rc
```

You need to keep a couple things in mind as you carry out this procedure. First, the NDS database locks during this process, and any new authentications to this server don't work until the database reopens, so perform this operation after hours, if possible. (The database reopens automatically after the process finishes.) Second, you need to call the people from Novell Support to do the restore. They're the experts, and after you crash, involving them is worth the effort. But unless you experience a total crash, you normally don't need to call them. A repair usually fixes whatever problems you were experiencing in the first place.

Knowledge is Power . . . So Become Powerful

In working with multiple systems, you can never gain too much information. Even a minor bit of understanding of a tricky command or utility may save you lots of downtime as you're making repairs or completing a checkup. So take the time to find out where to find Help on the system in general and on the server itself for each operating system.

Reading it in the man pages

You can get most of your online Linux and Unix system information about topics that you find in the man pages that come with every Unix or Linux installation. Man (short for *manual*) pages provide a listing of all the existing Linux commands, from those of the earliest versions of the Unix operating system to those of the most recent versions of Linux. Rather than a paper manual that comes with the software, man pages are actually text files that come with each Unix or Linux installation.

Man comes automatically with all versions of Unix and Linux. But your version of man may be slightly more out of date than others if your system is six or seven years old. A really old version of the man pages, therefore, may not include some of the newer commands. At the very least, you may not find all the possible command options.

Although man pages are sometimes written in technical terms, they're an invaluable source of information, especially if you're trying to determine what option to use with a given command.

To view the man page on a specific command or concept, type the following at the command prompt:

```
man <topic or concept>
```

Press Enter. Your screen displays the information on the subject. If enough information appears that it scrolls off-screen, press the spacebar to continue. To quit the man pages, either scroll to the end of the entry, or press the *Q* key.

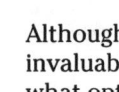

If you need help with the man pages themselves, just type **man –help** at the command prompt and press Enter.

Any user account can access the man pages. Only the root account, however, really finds man helpful, because, as an administrator, you need to rely on information in man from time to time.

Windows help

Help files in Windows are a little sparse — or very abundant, depending on just what you need to know. If you're looking for information strictly about terminology, you may need to consult your documentation or visit Microsoft's Web site at www.microsoft.com. If you're simply looking for a procedure or to troubleshoot one item, however, you can use the built-in Microsoft Troubleshooter programs. We fully detail these programs in Chapter 20.

The Novell support connections

The Novell Support Connection CD contains all the latest files, patches, drivers and technical information that you need to keep your network running smoothly. This service is by subscription, with updated CDs shipping monthly.

Sometimes, however, you simply can't wait for NetWare's update to ship. To bridge this gap, consider visiting some of the helpful sites that NetWare has set up for you to gather more information when you need it.

✔ **KnowledgeBase:** This resource is a Web site that Novell set up specifically to answer many of the more common questions that crop up about the NetWare system. Because this section updates continually with user reports from the field, Novell's decided to call this base of knowledge the *KnowledgeBase* site. You can access it at the following URL:

```
http://support.novell.com/search/kb_index.htm
```

✔ **Minimum Patch List:** NetWare keeps on this site a list of the current, minimum patches that you need for NetWare to run. A software *patch* is a fix that the software designers create to remedy a *bug*, or flaw, in the software that they discover after the software's release. Access this site at the following address:

```
http://support.novell.com/misc/patlst.htm
```

✔ **NetWare 5.1 Support Site** (overall support for Novell products): As its name implies, this site's purpose is to address many of the support issues that administrators face in more complex NetWare environments. If you have questions on networking or printing, you're likely to find it on this site, at the following URL:

```
http://support.novell.com/products/nw51/
```

You can find a wide variety of support-program options for operating systems. Microsoft, for example, offers more than a dozen deals that they can cut with your company. Unix and Linux, on the other hand, don't have a single supplier — so their support programs can vary as much between the vendors (for example, Red Hat versus Sun Microsystems) as they do with the operating systems themselves! We can go into a small amount of detail, however, about the options available from Novell for NetWare. The following list describes three of Novell's support programs:

✔ **Premium Service:** Whether you need occasional access to expert engineers or ongoing access to Novell's dedicated support resources and account management, you can find a Premium Service package to meet your specific needs. Premium service is the top of the line service levels that Novell offers and can include simple phone support or actual on-site engineers to help with complex problems.

✔ **Preferred Service:** Preferred Service offers support packages that you can tailor to meet your business's need. Whether you want immediate access to the latest technical information, occasional assistance from a support engineer, proactive account management, or an ongoing relationship with a technical engineer who's familiar with your company's customers, Preferred Service provides a solution.

✔ **Beta Program:** Put yourself on the bleeding edge of technology with this program, which gives you access to the latest and greatest versions of NetWare and other Novell products. The idea may seem a bit crazy, but beta programs can offer you a great way to discover early on just what's happening in Novell's technology world.

Part IV

Administering Networked Communications and Files

IT'S REALLY QUITE SIMPLE. WITH THE REVISED MAINFRAME PRICING POLICY, YOU'LL BE CHARGED ONE-QUARTER OF THE PREVIOUS PRICE PER CPU BASED ON A 3-TIERED SITE LICENSING AGREEMENT FOR UP TO 12 USERS, AFTER WHICH A 5-TIERED SYSTEM IS EMPLOYED FOR UP TO 64 USERS WITHIN THE ORIGINAL 4-TIERED SYSTEM FOR NEW CUSTOMERS USING OLD SOFTWARE OR OLD CUSTOMERS USING NEW SOFTWARE ON EACH OF THREE CPUs RUNNING A NEW OLD OPERATING SYSTEMS SITE LICENSED UNDER THE OLD NEW AGREEMENT BUT ONLY ON THURSDAYS WITH LESS THAN 10 PEOPLE IN THE ROOM,...

In this part . . .

Now for the heavy-duty portion of the book where you actually start to make use of all the planning, cabling, testing, and so forth. Many of the tasks in this section seem mundane, but they're the bread and butter of the true system integration expert.

This chapter introduces network protocols. Even better, you see how you can shoot packets of information over your network, testing whether your information highway is smoothly paved or full of potholes.

On a more prosaic note, you see how you can ensure that your users can get hard copies of their hard-won work. And you review the utilities you can use to ensure that your centralized style of control doesn't lead to serious server crashes.

Chapter 11

Tawk Amongst Yourselves: UDP, TCP, and IPX/SPX

· ·

In This Chapter

▶ Getting the real scoop on stand-alone vs. client-server computer models

▶ Slogging through the UDP, TCP, and IPX/SPX protocols

▶ Installing and updating protocols

· ·

*I*n this chapter, you're entering a dimension of sight . . . a dimension of sound . . . a dimension of incomprehensible letters strung together in nonsense fashion. You're entering *The Acronym Zone,* the place where you get to know the protocols that allow your machines to talk to each other. If you feel intimidated by large quantities of TLAs (three-letter acronyms), just take a deep breath and don't worry. In this chapter, we help you overcome your fear of acronyms — and at a substantial savings compared to psychotherapy.

A Standard, a Standard, My Kingdom for a Standard!

Along with protocol acronyms comes structure. Structure is critical in designing and implementing a network of systems that aren't similar in their core operating system architecture. Linux and Unix are similar, but Windows NT and 2000 are nothing like NetWare, which is nothing like Linux and Unix. (Got that?)

In order for these guys to all talk and get along, some ground rules, or *standards,* need to be in place. These standards provide the structure required for a smooth operation and a reliable and manageable set of systems.

There's an organization that actually works on these standards, and it's been doing so for a long, long time. The organization is called IEEE (The Institute of Electrical and Electronics Engineers), and it consists of a saintly bunch of souls who help keep things working. Without them, networks would be *not-works* and we'd all still be using the sneakernet to move files around.

No Computer Is an Island: The Old Stand-Alone Model

In the dark ages of computing — long before anyone thought of tying several computers together to share resources — computers were simple, *stand-alone* machines. Computer A had no clue that — and couldn't care less that — there was another computer one desk over called Computer B. Furthermore, these computers were incapable of sharing any information unless it was brought over on a floppy disk via the world-famous *and* still prevalent sneakernet.

Before the client-server model really became the standard for the business and academic worlds, most computer systems worked as stand-alone systems. The stand-alone system allowed everyone to have their own computers, their own hard drives, their own printers, and so on.

Granted, this method appears to have some advantages, which were more pronounced in the early stages of the computer revolution. For example, at first glance, it appears that since this system is so compartmentalized, if one user's machine crashes, it doesn't affect anyone else. And this system appears to be easier to administer; each user is responsible for his or her own system. Finally, this system appears to allow maximum privacy since no user's files can be shared with any other person, unless one person is willing to walk down to the other person's office with a floppy disk in hand.

But each of these assumptions is either wrong or outdated. To begin with, computer operating systems are much more stable than operating systems of a couple decades back. It's also possible to design a network where you can avoid single points of failure by having a backup server on standby.

Also, stand-alone systems are actually harder to administrate. Here's an example that demonstrates this point: Imagine a set of computers in a building that has ten employees — each with a PC. You're the administrator, and you're responsible for maintaining these machines and assisting users with any issues they might have. Suppose that one day a user named John calls you over and tells you that he can't save a file to his hard drive, but the file can be saved to a floppy disk just fine. While you're standing there analyzing this problem, Joanne yells over the cubicle that her floppy disk is stuck in the drive, and it has two important files on it — one of them being your review for a nice raise. Then Shelby walks over and says that her computer can't retrieve any files from her hard drive.

We think you probably understand the advantage of having shared resources for you and all your users, too. This is partly because if each user doesn't have to conform to a single model, each person keeps his or her files in different locations on his or her machine. And, of course, if you're responsible for weekly backups, you have to wander around to each user's office and repeat the same backup procedures on every single machine.

Finally, companies today need to share data between individuals or departments more than ever before. Doing so promotes teamwork, speeds work flow, and prevents unnecessary duplication of effort. In fact, on a stand-alone system, security is a bigger problem because you have absolutely no control over a person's computer if he or she forgets to lock the keyboard or turn the console off when leaving it unattended.

There are several more reasons why networked computers have become the dominant method of computing systems. However, each pales in significance compared to one final reason: The shared-resource, or network, architecture saves companies a *lot* of money.

 If you've ever been intimidated by someone who starts talking about *network architectures*, don't be. When you look at network diagrams, they're simple examples of a network architecture. An *architecture* is a drawing, sketch, painting, or doodle that shows exactly how you have your machines hooked up.

The Future Is Here Now: The Client-Server Model

The client-server model is the electronic equivalent to *outsourcing* tasks from a given company. In this model, the servers provide their resources to multiple client machines. For example, instead of storing large, bulky files on a computer's individual internal hard drive, you can store all files on one large file server that all machines connect to. Here's another example: Instead of having a half-dozen printers serve only six people who happen to have the printers attached to their machines, you can have those half-dozen printers serve 60 people who can send print jobs over the network to those printers.

The idea is that with the client-server model, the clients — your users — don't need to have their own setup for every single item of hardware or software, which ends up saving you administration time and a lot of money. In that last example, try comparing the cost savings of buying only 6 printers instead of 60! (No, a bulk discount won't quite cut it. Nice try, though.)

The popularity of client-server models is also why protocols have become so essential in dealing with computers today. Each computer on your network would run into difficulties if they all used their own methods of talking to a file or print server. In order to avoid this problem, UDP and TCP have quickly become the industry protocol standards to allow widely different computers to communicate on a better level than just exchanging error messages.

UDP: The Connectionless Protocol

UDP stands for User Datagram Protocol. It predates TCP (Transmission Control Protocol) and is correspondingly used less frequently, but you should be aware of what it is and how it differs from TCP. Typically, UDP is not something you even think about or need to *do* something about. UDP is frequently used in applications that take advantage of the features of UDP, and most of the time, the application has some sort of configuration settings, but even then it doesn't state that you're configuring its UDP components.

Datagrams and streams

We want to clarify how TCP and UDP really relate to each other. In modern data networking, it's important to distinguish between *datagrams* and *streams*.

A *stream* is what you typically think of as a communication channel. Remote logins, file transfers, mail delivery — all use streams. A stream appears to be like a pipeline, because pipelines make a connection — just like TCP. A stream has two endpoints. Data is put in one end and comes out the other. None of the data is duplicated or discarded or reorganized in any way. Two streams can be paired together to form a full duplex connection.

A *datagram*, often called a *packet*, is much more atomic in nature. It is a small piece of data, often required to be less than a maximum length (typically in the 256- to 2000-byte range). Datagrams are completely self-contained. They have a source and a destination but *nothing* that could be called a connection, so you could say that datagrams are what are passed through the pipeline, or

TCP connection. They're really like spurts of water that go through the pipes. A single datagram has no relationship to any other datagrams that came before or after them.

Although most networking communication uses streams, all Internet transfers are in the form of datagrams. Internet streams are actually emulated using datagrams by the. To diagnose Internet operation, a packet decoder views individual packets. This, along with knowledge of TCP operation, enables the Internet engineer to assemble a mental picture of network operation.

What a connectionless protocol is good for

A *connectionless protocol* is one that is not targeted at a specific machine. For example, where a TCP packet must be sent to a given machine's host name or IP address, a UDP packet has no such restriction. Instead, a connectionless protocol moves out from its point of origin rather like a ripple in a pool of water, expanding as it moves from machine to machine.

The best-known protocol that works in this manner is UDP. UDP has the advantage of sending smaller chunks of data across the network, thereby using less processing power through the gateway or router. Because of this ability, UDP is an alternative to TCP and, together with IP (Internet Protocol), is sometimes referred to as UDP/IP.

Like TCP, UDP uses the Internet Protocol to actually get a data unit (called a datagram) from one computer to another. Unlike TCP, however, UDP does not provide the service of dividing a message into packets (datagrams) and reassembling it at the other end.

Specifically, UDP doesn't provide sequencing of the packets that the data arrives in. This means that the application program that uses UDP must be able to make sure that the entire message has arrived and is in the right order. Network applications that want to save processing time because they have very small data units to exchange (and therefore very little message reassembling to do) may prefer UDP to TCP. The Trivial File Transfer Protocol (TFTP) uses UDP instead of TCP.

Incidentally, UDP provides two services not provided by the IP layer. It provides port numbers to help distinguish different user requests and, optionally, a *checksum* capability to verify that the data arrived intact. A checksum capability is exactly what it sounds like — the capability to check the data (which to the computer is a bunch of numbers) and make sure that the sum total of the data it received matches what it expected from the packet. Think of it as a microscopic form of quality assurance.

For those who are truly nerdy but also in the know, UDP also stands for U Don't Ping. This is a quick mnemonic phrase to remind you that the `ping` command, discussed in Chapter 13, creates a TCP connection, not a UDP one.

Keep in mind that information sent via a UDP connection can still be lost, or dropped, over a network. If this situation happens, UDP isn't set up to tell you about it. Compare this kind of quality assurance service to the more reliable TCP protocol. If you're sending a packet with the `ping` command, you get:

- ✔ The number of packets transmitted
- ✔ The number of packets received
- ✔ The percentage of the packet loss

Given UDP's lack of reliability at the packet level, UDP is not the best protocol for sending important information. For this reason, UDP's use tends to be restricted to applications where speed is more important than high levels of reliability.

UDP is most commonly used on UNIX or Linux operating systems that run the Network File System server components. When an NFS server is first booted up, it sends out a UDP broadcast that's much like a ripple in a pond. This UDP broadcast enables the machine to gather as many replies as it can within a very short amount of time, telling it whether it should assume its role as a server or bind to another existing server as a client machine.

TCP/IP: Welcome to the Virtual Circuit

TCP stands for Transmission Control Protocol. TCP is frequently talked about as TCP/IP, which is actually two protocols tied closely together. TCP/IP (Transmission Control Protocol/Internet Protocol) is the basic communication language, or protocol, of the Internet. It can also be used as a communications protocol in private networks, called *intranets* and *extranets*. These days, all operating systems come with a copy of the TCP/IP stack, or program, and it is almost always part of the installation to set up a networking scheme.

TCP/IP has inherited the mantle of "most well known, beloved, and universally used" protocol standard of all time. Well, at least it's well known and used. TCP/IP is the result of early pioneering efforts into protocol standardization. This protocol system was developed by the ARPAnet (Advanced Research Projects Agency). ARPAnet needed standardized protocols mostly for compatibility and heavy-duty security reasons. The fact that ARPA was backed by military research projects reflects this.

TCP/IP's design and open-system policy allow any kind of operating system and hardware to make use of it. Although this focus on universal adaptability sacrifices some of its speed, TCP/IP is still considered tops in reliability and overall usefulness.

How TCP improves network reliability

TCP/IP is actually a two-layered program. The higher layer, Transmission Control Protocol, manages the assembling of a message or file into smaller packets that are transmitted over the Internet and received by a TCP layer that reassembles the packets into the original message. The lower layer, Internet Protocol, handles the address part of each packet so that it gets to the right destination.

This setup can be illustrated with a post office analogy: Say you have a whole bunch of documents to send from your house to your Uncle Giovanni in Europe. You could send these documents in one huge packet, but that would be expensive. So, instead, you separate the documents into pieces and mail each one individually in a certain sequence, numbering the outside of the envelopes.

But wait. How does the post office know *where* to send those packets in Europe? It knows by looking at the country, city, street address, and so on, that you wrote on the envelopes. The post office looks at the address, and then it decides whether to put the envelopes on an airplane bound for New Zealand or a truck heading to Ohio. And even though some letters from the same sender are routed differently than others (different trucks may drive down different roads to get the letter delivered), they're all delivered to the destination address. But without an address on the envelope, the packet doesn't go anywhere. Furthermore, if you don't put a return address on the envelope, it's gone forever.

That's like the IP part of the whole system. IP is the part of the equation that handles the addressing of the packets as they travel. Each gateway computer or router on the network checks the address to see where to forward the message.

Now, say that you sent your packages in the correct sequence to your uncle. He receives them in order for the most part. But one or two show up out of sequence or not at all. Uncle Giovanni puts the packets in order and calls you to report that one or two didn't make it. Can you resend them?

You had made copies, of course, so you resend the packets. Uncle Giovanni gets them, reassembles them, and *voila*! The message is now translated in the right order. This scenario is very similar to how TCP gets the bits and bytes in the right order.

The fact that TCP (or Uncle Giovanni) calls you back to notify you to send replacement packets is why TCP/IP is called the *virtual circuit*. A real, *physical* circuit constructed out of batteries and wires must have a complete connection, or the circuit is broken and no power flows through. A *virtual* circuit connection is the same way except that electrical current is replaced with packets of information. Because of this, the vast majority of the communications that take place on a computer network — and almost 100 percent of Internet connections — are taking place thanks to TCP/IP.

The protocol without a state to call its own

TCP/IP is also popular today because it makes use of the client-server model of communication in which a computer user (a client) requests and is provided a service (such as sending a Web page) by another computer (a server) in the network. TCP/IP communication is primarily *point-to-point,* meaning each communication is from one point (or host computer) in the network to another point (or host computer). TCP/IP and the higher-level applications that use it are collectively said to be *stateless* because each client request is considered a new request unrelated to any previous one (unlike ordinary phone conversations that require a dedicated connection for the call duration).

Being stateless frees network paths so that everyone can use them continuously. Note that the TCP layer itself is not stateless as far as any one message is concerned. Its connection remains in place until all packets in a message have been received. So, as you can see, TCP/IP is more sophisticated in keeping its connection until everything gets to its destination. (That would be like keeping a phone call open to Uncle Giovanni over in Europe until he says he got all of the many packets you've sent him. Imagine that phone bill!)

TCP adds to the IP portion of this network protocol in these ways:

- ✔ **Streams.** TCP data is organized as a stream of bytes, much like a file. The datagram nature of the network is concealed.

- ✔ **Reliable delivery.** Sequence numbers coordinate which data has been transmitted and received. TCP arranges for retransmission if it determines that data has been lost.

- ✔ **Network adaptation.** TCP dynamically learns the delay characteristics of a network and adjusts its operation to maximize throughput without overloading the network. This reduces the amount of "the tail before the head" syndrome and alleviates a lot of wasted bandwidth due to unnecessary retransmissions.

- ✔ **Flow control.** TCP manages data buffers and coordinates traffic so its buffers will never overflow. Fast senders are stopped periodically to keep up with slower receivers. These buffers are also what TCP uses to grab a packet that needs to be retransmitted. Naturally, these packets are not kept there for very long, and the packets, or datagrams, are spilling out of the buffers as soon as TCP has verified delivery.

TCP/IP: A family photo album

TCP/IP is not actually a single protocol. Actually, TCP/IP is an entire family of protocols that were designed with the same basic programming structure but perform different tasks on your network. The variants of the TCP/IP family are listed in the following sections, broken down (roughly) by function.

Networking protocols

Networking protocols allow the machines on your network to share information. Therefore, these members of the TCP/IP suite of protocols are often considered the most vital to the operation of a mixed network of systems:

- ✔ **TCP (Transmission Control Protocol).** This protocol provides the reliability aspect of the TCP/IP connection duo.

- ✔ **RPC (Remote Procedure Call).** This protocol enhances the IP protocol by allowing a program to make a subroutine call on a remote machine. RPC is normally used only by advanced programmers and designers.

- ✔ **SMTP (Simple Mail Transfer Protocol).** This protocol is specifically set aside to handle the transfer of the special text files that are sent over a network as electronic mail.

- ✔ **NFS (Network File System).** This protocol allows Linux and Unix machines to make remote directories on a given machine available for users to access.

- ✔ **NIS (Network Information System).** Another Unix/Linux system protocol, NIS helps administer machines running Sun Microsystem's brand of Unix, called SunOS or Solaris.

Transport protocols

Transport protocols are the trucks, tankers, and railways of your network. These protocols assist the network protocols in getting data packets to their destination properly:

- ✔ **IP (Internet Protocol).** This protocol acts to direct a TCP packet to the right network address or host name.

- ✔ **ICMP (Internet Control Message Protocol).** This protocol provides the IP protocol with status messages that it can use for quality assurance — messages like network errors and routing changes that could affect whether the TCP packet is received at its destination.

- ✔ **RIP (Routing Information Protocol).** This protocol is designed to calculate the most efficient routing method for your datagram packets on large networks that use more than one router or bridge between widely spaced networks.

Addressing protocols

Due to the growth of ever more complex networks, specific protocols that ensure proper delivery of information packets have become more common. These are known as addressing protocols, and they can greatly speed up the receipt of information on a large network:

- **ARP (Address Resolution Protocol).** This protocol helps determine the numeric address for each machine on your integrated network.

- **RARP (Reverse Address Resolution Protocol).** This protocol works the same as ARP, but it goes about it in the reverse order.

- **DNS (Domain Name System).** This protocol is a more advanced version of ARP and RARP in that it helps translate numeric addresses into host names for the administrator to work with.

Gateway protocols

A relatively recent development, gateway protocols came into being when routers and networks became more common than stand-alone computers. Gateway protocols work to keep routers and bridges functioning properly by recognizing and processing data as efficiently as possible:

- **EGP (Exterior Gateway Protocol).** This protocol works to keep data transfer information flowing between external networks.

- **IGP (Interior Gateway Protocol).** This protocol works at transferring routing information between internal networks only.

- **GGP (Gateway to Gateway Protocol).** This protocol works on transferring routing data for gateways on the Internet.

User service protocols

The most commonly seen protocols on a network are those that actually transfer large files from one area to another. Using these protocols is different from using the `cp` (copy) command on a machine because these protocols assist in moving jumbo-sized amounts of information from one machine to another without the need for a floppy disk:

- **FTP (File Transfer Protocol).** This protocol is an extremely efficient method of transferring data files, such as text or binaries, between computers at a user's request.

- **TELNET.** The name is derived from the idea of the *telephone* as part of the *network* (*tel-net*). This protocol actually starts up on your machine as a small program, or daemon. Telnet allows you to remotely log in to other machines on your network.

Some common IP questions and solutions

How can I measure the performance of an IP link?

You can get a quick approximation by timing how long it takes to FTP or RCP a large file over the link. But bear in mind that the measurement will be skewed by the time spent dealing with the local and remote file systems, not simply with the network itself.

Also, remember to measure the time it takes to receive a file, not the time it takes to send it; the sender can report completion even though large amounts of data are still buffered locally by TCP and haven't yet been delivered to the destination.

Two well known, open-source programs that measure and report throughput over an IP link without involving the file system are

- ✔ TTCP, which is available for anonymous FTP from the Silicon Graphics FTP archive at `ftp://ftp.sgi.com/sgi/src/ttcp/`

- ✔ Rick Jones' NETPERF, which is available on the Web at `http://www.cup.hp.com/netperf/NetperfPage.html`

If neither of those tools does what you want, then you may find something that meets your needs in CAIDA's measurement tools list at `http://www.caida.org/Tools/meastools.html`.

What IP addresses should I assign to machines on a private Internet?

Your only limitation is that you shouldn't use IP addresses that have been assigned to some other organization because if knowledge of your network ever gets leaked onto the Internet, the IP addresses may disrupt that innocent organization's activity.

Using the following address ranges for internal networks is a safe bet. If you never connect your network to the Internet, you can use this set of addresses for your internal usage instead of registering an IP address set with the Internet Assigned Numbers Authority (IANA)

The Internet Assigned Numbers Authority (IANA) has reserved the following three blocks of the IP address space for private networks:

```
      10.0.0.0        -
  10.255.255.255
      172.16.0.0      -
  172.31.255.255
      192.168.0.0     -
  192.168.255.255
```

If you plan to connect your network to the Internet, then you will not be able to use these addresses in any direct connection to the Internet. Instead, you either register an address range for your connections or use an ISP to make your connections to the Internet. Because IP addresses are running low, an ISP connection is your best bet for simplicity's sake.

Today, your router/outside network administrator should set up all routers so that the predefined private IP addresses (known as standard RFC1597) aren't used. This standard was set up about 20 years ago by the committees that transitioned the old precursor to the Internet, ARPANET, to using the current TCP/IP protocols. The predefined addresses are

```
10.255.255.255
172.31.255.255
192.168.255.255
```

The IPX/SPX Protocol: It's a NetWare Thang

IPX (Internetwork Packet eXchange) is a networking protocol from Novell that interconnects networks that use Novell's NetWare clients and servers. IPX is a datagram, or packet, protocol. It works at the network layer of communication protocols and is connectionless, unlike TCP, which is not connectionless but maintains a connection (that is, it doesn't require that a connection be maintained during an exchange of packets as, for example, a regular voice phone call does).

In a sense, IPX blasts the data out onto the wire with some destination information in the packets, but IPX couldn't care less whether the data gets there or not. IPX's counterpart, SPX (Sequenced Packet eXchange), knows the stuff was sent (because SPX is a nosy busybody of a protocol) and checks to see that the stuff arrived where it was supposed to. Being so nosy can have advantages but not too often. When SPX verifies that the stuff got there, it snoops the wires again for more packets, ensuring that they arrived safely.

SPX is the protocol for handling packet sequencing in a Novell NetWare network. Packet acknowledgment is also managed by SPX. It prepares the sequence of packets that a message is divided into and manages the reassembly of received packets, confirming that all have been received and requesting retransmission when they haven't. SPX works directly with IPX, which manages the forwarding of packets in the network.

Related Novell NetWare protocols include the Routing Information Protocol (RIP), the Service Advertising Protocol (SAP), and the NetWare Link Services Protocol (NLSP).

IPX and SPX are comparable to the basic Internet protocols IP and TCP. NetWare, made by Novell, is the most widely installed network server operating system. Initially very successful in installing its products in large- and small-office local-area networks (LANs), Novell has redesigned (or at least refeatured) NetWare to work successfully as part of larger and heterogeneous networks, including the Internet. How did Novell do this? Can you say *Tee Cee Pee Eye Pee*?

The latest version of NetWare, NetWare 5, comes with support for both Novell's own IPX network protocol and for the Internet's IP protocol.

IPX: The network layer

IPX is the original NetWare network-layer (Layer 3) protocol for routing packets through an internetwork. IPX is a connectionless datagram-based network protocol and, as such, is similar to the Internet Protocol found in TCP/IP networks.

As with other network addresses, Novell IPX network addresses must be unique. Otherwise, how will those little packets get to their destinations? They'd be lost forever. Since IPX doesn't recognize IP addresses, it must use some other scheme to deliver the packets. So it uses a two-piece addressing scheme: a network number and a node number. The IPX network number is assigned by the network administrator within NetWare. The node number is usually the Media Access Control (MAC) address for one of the system's network interface cards (NICs).

SPX: The transport layer

The SPX protocol is the most common NetWare transport protocol at Layer 4 of the Open Systems Interconnection (OSI) model. SPX resides atop IPX in the NetWare protocol suite. SPX is a reliable, connection-oriented protocol that supplements the datagram service provided by IPX.

SPX was derived from the Xerox Networking Systems (XNS) Sequenced Packet Protocol (SPP). Novell also offers Internet Protocol support in the form of the User Datagram Protocol (UDP). IPX datagrams are encapsulated inside UDP/IP headers for transport across an IP-based internetwork.

SAP: The service advertisement protocol

The Service Advertisement Protocol (SAP) is an IPX protocol through which network resources, such as file servers and print servers, advertise their addresses and the services they provide. Advertisements are sent via SAP every 60 seconds. Services are identified by a hexadecimal number, which is called a SAP identifier (for example, 4 = file server and 7 = print server).

Installing and Updating Protocols

Luckily, both of these areas are non-issues for the system integration manager. Thanks to the rigorous universal standards set for protocols, there is no such thing as installing "the Unix version of TCP" or the "Windows 2000 version of IP." Protocols aren't like printer or sound card drivers.

Also, when protocols are tweaked and updated to make them slightly faster or more reliable, don't worry about upgrading. Your best bet is to simply wait until the company that makes your operating system releases a new version of the operating system. When you install or upgrade to the latest version of the operating system, all the new standards, including the updated protocols, are automatically put in place.

Chapter 12

Network Connectivity: Testing and Verifying the Roads

● ●

In This Chapter

▶ Using `ping` to test TCP/IP connections on Unix, Linux, Windows, and NetWare machines

▶ Testing connectivity by using the `netstat` command

▶ Taking a peek at other TCP/IP utilities

▶ Taking a peek at other NetWare utilities

▶ Examining the pros and cons of DHCP

● ●

*A*fter you set up the physical network, you need to see whether your machines can communicate with each other. Some administrators liken network testing to building a boat and then launching it into the water to see whether it floats or sinks. That's not a bad analogy, although if you test networks, you don't get to break a bottle of champagne over the server. (At least not without achieving *electrifying* results.)

Your most basic network test tool is probably the `ping` command. Controversy clouds the origin of the name `ping`, making it the ideal subject for an episode of *20/20*. According to some sources, `ping` stands for *Packet Internet Groper*, although to my knowledge, `ping` has nothing to do with submarine sonar operations or groping anything.

According to Mike Muuss, the programmer who wrote `ping`, however, another side exists to the story. He made the following statement in 1983: "From my point of view, `ping` is *not* an acronym standing for Packet Internet Groper. It's a *sonar analogy*." Various rumors claim that another network pioneer, Dave Mills, offered the groper expansion of the name, so perhaps both explanations are correct. (And you think the *government's* bad about expanding acronyms. *Nothing* beats technology gurus at the acronym game.)

Using ping to Test TCP/IP Connections on Unix, Linux, and Windows

You can use the ping command in either the Unix or Linux operating system to test whether two machines can potentially communicate with each other. The ping command can tell you whether a network connection exists and the speed of the data transmission. But it doesn't verify that you can ftp or Telnet to that same machine. The ping command uses the most simple of techniques to verify only a capability to connect via a special protocol known as *ICMP/TCP* (*Internet Control Message Protocol/Transmission Control Protocol*).

ICMP defines a small number of messages that you use for diagnostic and management purposes. It depends on the IP (Internet Protocol) to move packets around the network on its behalf. (If you need a quickie course on any of the protocols and what they do, check out Chapter 11.)

ICMP is basically IP's internal network management protocol and isn't for use by applications. Two well-known exceptions are the ping and traceroute diagnostic utilities, which function as the following list describes:

- The ping utility sends and receives ICMP *Echo* packets, where you can take the response packet as evidence that the target host is at least minimally active on the network.

- The traceroute utility sends *UDP* (*User Datagram Protocol*) packets and infers the route taken to the target from ICMP Time to Live Exceeded or Port Unreachable packets that the network returns. (Microsoft's tracert sends ICMP Echo packets rather than UDP packets and so receives ICMP Time to Live Exceeded or Echo_Response packets in return.)

Note: Following are some terms you want to remain aware of in testing network connections:

- **Host ID:** The part of an IP address that identifies a specific host on a network.

- **IP Address:** A logical 32-bit address (which divides into four octets) that identifies a TCP/IP host. Each address has two parts: a network ID and a host ID.

- **Network ID:** The part of an IP address that identifies all hosts that are on the same physical network.

Linux/Unix testing

On a Linux or Unix machine, perform the following steps to use `ping` in network testing between two machines:

1. **If your machine uses a desktop interface such as CDE or GNOME, open a terminal window.**

2. **Type the following at the command line:**

```
# ping <host name of the computer where you want to test
        the connection>
```

Time for a little Unix /Linux jargon: The computer you're sending the `ping` packet from is the *request* machine. Sensibly enough, the computer you're trying to contact is the *response* machine. If you can send a packet between the request and response machines, you have a solid network connection. In theory, no matter which different platforms you're integrating, you can make any sort of TCP/IP connection that you need.

Here's an example: Say that you want to see whether one Unix box, Ferrari, can talk to the main Unix server, Jaguar. Because you're typing the command from Ferrari's console, Ferrari is the request machine and Jaguar is the response machine (see Figure 12-1).

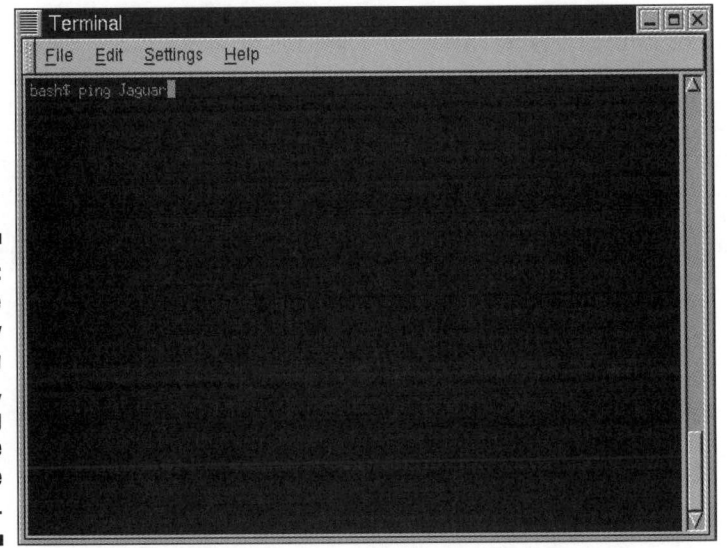

Figure 12-1:
The amazingly useful `ping` command, specifying the response machine.

If Jaguar receives the `ping` packet, it sends back a number of response packets to Ferrari. Back on the request machine, Ferrari, the result prints out on-screen (see Figure 12-2).

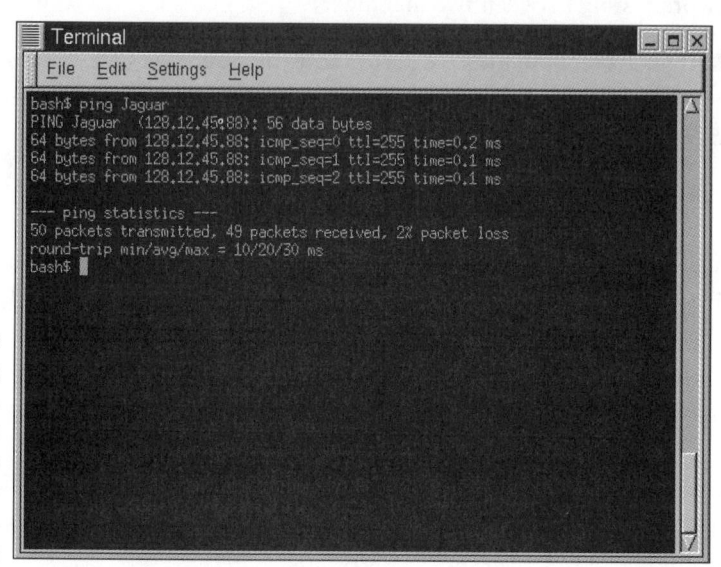

```
Terminal                                                      _ □ ✕
 File   Edit   Settings   Help

bash$ ping Jaguar
PING Jaguar  (128.12.45.88): 56 data bytes
64 bytes from 128.12.45.88: icmp_seq=0 ttl=255 time=0.2 ms
64 bytes from 128.12.45.88: icmp_seq=1 ttl=255 time=0.1 ms
64 bytes from 128.12.45.88: icmp_seq=2 ttl=255 time=0.1 ms

--- ping statistics ---
50 packets transmitted, 49 packets received, 2% packet loss
round-trip min/avg/max = 10/20/30 ms
bash$ █
```

Figure 12-2:
The
response
machine's
response to
ping.

On the other hand, if the `ping` packet doesn't reach the response machine, nothing returns. The request machine usually displays an error message similar to `ERROR: Unknown Host` or `ERROR: Host unreachable`. On some older versions of Unix, the machine *hangs* — doesn't enable you to do anything while it waits — until it eventually *times out* — gives up on waiting for the return `ping`, rather like a person who's stood up for a date. After a machine times out, it returns you to the command prompt.

Continuing with the example, say that you send out a `ping` message from Ferrari to Jaguar and get the reply shown in Figure 12-3.

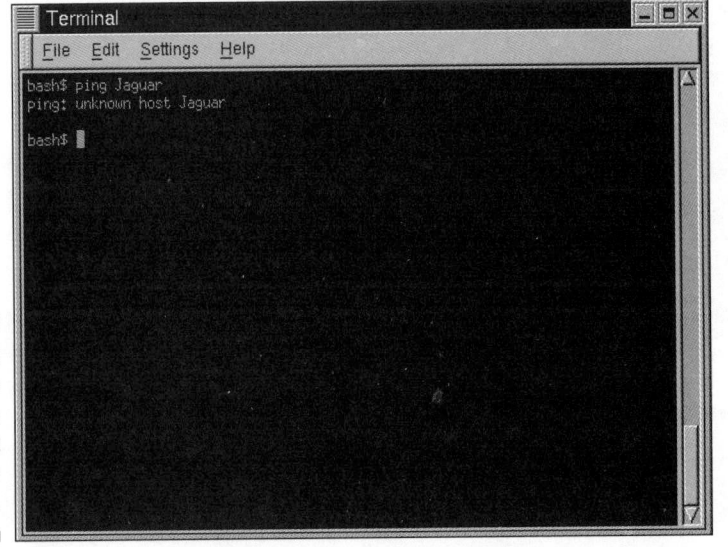

Figure 12-3:
The
response
that you get
if the host is
unknown.

Take a deep breath and start counting the blessings in life. (Yes, if you must, you can count the fact that you're a system integration professional.) This response isn't a great sign, but it doesn't mean that all's lost either. This error at least confirms that your ping packets are getting onto the network. If the packets can't leave your machine (if, for example, you forget to plug the network cable in), you get no reply at all.

On the other hand, this sign also tells you that you're not talking with your specified response machine, Jaguar. Sometimes, the reason is simply a matter of name recognition. If you're busy mixing together machines running multiple operating systems, some computers prefer to respond to the system's IP address instead of the host name. (It's like talking to someone who prefers you to call him General Slawskowski rather than Fred.)

Instead of typing **ping _<host name>_** at the command prompt, try typing **ping _<IP address>_**. This number is the machine's network address, which you normally state in four numeric fields of up to three characters each, such as _128.12.45.88_. If you determine that Jaguar's IP address is 128.12.45.88, try to ping it by typing **ping 128.12.45.88** at the command line and then pressing Enter (see Figure 12-4):

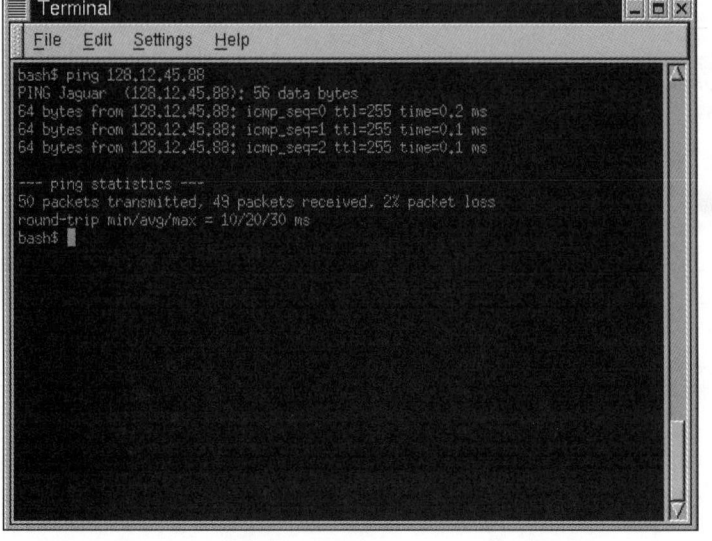

Figure 12-4: ping-ing via the IP address: The response is the same as if you ping by host name.

Windows testing

On a Windows machine, you use ping the exact same way as you do on a Unix or Linux computer. About the only real difference is that, instead of using a command-line terminal window, you use the DOS window, which you can usually access from the Start menu by choosing Start⇨Programs⇨ Accessories⇨MS-DOS Prompt. Perform the following steps to use ping in network testing between two machines:

1. **Open a DOS window.**

2. **Type the following at the command line in the DOS window.**

   # ping *<host name of the computer where you want to test the connection>*

The result of the network test is exactly the same as on a Unix or Linux box: a response detailing packet loss and time spent in transit or a simple host not found message if no connection occurs.

It don't mean a thing if it ain't got that ping

Although ping is very useful at establishing whether two machines on the same network can talk to each other, that's not the only useful aspect of the command. ping can also provide you with information about whether a ping-ed machine responds to its host name as well as its IP address or whether a remote machine's network card is working correctly. One of the most widespread uses of ping is to provide information on how healthy a given network is at any point in time. Following are the last two lines from the network query to machine Jaguar (using the example from the section "Unix/Linux testing," a little earlier in this chapter):

```
50 packets transmitted, 49 packets received, 2% packet loss
Round-trip (ms) min/avg/max = 10/20/30
```

The first line means that, of the 50 ping packets, one was lost out in the electronic Ethernet. The remaining 49 hardy pilgrims of the packet world, however, made the journey unscathed. The server probably didn't receive the lost packet because it was too busy to handle it at the exact moment in time that it arrived.

The odd packet out is known as a *dropped packet,* and you don't want to worry about it individually. (Your machine resends dropped packet messages.) On the other hand, if your machine starts dropping more than five percent of its packets, that's usually a sign of serious network congestion, meaning that your server is working too hard.

In the second line, your round-trip numbers of 10/20/30 are also useful if you want to assess the overall network health. The response time is measured in a quantity useless to humans but quite useful in superfast computers — milliseconds. In this example, response time varied between a minimum of 10 milliseconds to a maximum of 30, making the average about 20 milliseconds.

Depending on your connections to servers, you may see times of 100+ milliseconds. Usually, these slow connections result from very long-distance connections to remote offices using a small bandwidth circuit, such as a 56K circuit to Australia.

If a host can't ping another host, do the following:

- ✔ Ensure that the host you're trying to ping is on and is configured to use TCP/IP.
- ✔ Check the TCP/IP configuration of both hosts by trying to ping the destination host from a third host.
- ✔ If both hosts are on the same LAN segment, ensure that you assigned both hosts an IP address that uses the same network number.
- ✔ If the hosts are on different LAN segments, ensure that you configured TCP/IP routing correctly.

Table 12-1 lists some of the options available to you for use with the ping command on a Windows machine. Table 12-2 lists some ping options available on Unix and Linux machines.

Table 12-1	ping **Options for Windows NT**
Option	*Result*
-t	ping the specified host until interrupted.
-a	Resolve addresses to host names.
-n (count)	Send specified number of echo requests.
-l (size)	Send buffer size.
-f	Set the Don't Fragment flag in packet.
-i TTL	Time to Live. The time to live is the number of seconds that a packet is allowed to exist on the network. After the time has expired, the packet deletes itself. This prevents "old" information packets from clogging up the network by contributing to the network traffic.
-v TOS	Type of Service. The type of service parameter assists the router in categorizing the packet as text information, code, or a simple signal. This helps the router to send the packet to the right machine, whether it is a user's computer, a mail server, or another router.
-r (count)	Record route for count hops.
-s (count)	Timestamp for count hops.
-j (host-list)	Use loose source route along host-list.
-k (host-list)	Use strict source route along host-list.
-w (timeout)	Give up waiting for each reply after this number of milliseconds.

Table 12-2	ping **Options for Unix/Linux**
Option	*Result*
-d	Set the debug option to provide more detail.
-l	Use loose source route. (Use this option in the IP header to send the packet to the given host and back again.)
-n	Show network addresses as numbers. (ping normally displays addresses as host names, such as Jaguar and Ferrari. -n instructs ping to show addresses, such as 160.101.80.10.)

Option	Result
-v	Verbose output. (List *any* ICMP packets, other than Echo_Response, that you receive.)
-l *<interval>*	Specify the interval between successive transmissions. (The default is 1 second.)
-t TTL	Specify the IP time to live for a ping packet. (The default time to live for most packets is 1 hop.)

Using ping to Test TCP/IP Connections on NetWare

After you enable TCP/IP on your server and workstations, you need to test your server and each workstation to ensure that they can communicate by using TCP/IP. The easiest way to test a TCP/IP connection is to use a ping utility, which sends a ping request to the IP host that you want to test. After the destination IP host receives the ping request, the host immediately read-dresses the ping packet and returns it to the host that sent the ping request. After the ping utility receives a response from the destination IP host, the utility reports how long it took for delivery and the return of the message.

NetWare includes the ping utility, which tests to see whether a particular server can communicate with other IP hosts on your network. To test IP hosts on your network, complete the following steps:

1. **Load the ping utility by entering the following command at your NetWare server console and pressing Enter:**

   ```
   LOAD PING
   ```

2. **Enter the IP address of the IP host that you want to test.**

   For this test to work, the host must be on, configured to communicate with TCP/IP, and connected to the network.

3. **Press the Escape key to begin testing the configuration.**

4. **To test other hosts, press the Insert key and repeat Steps 2 and 3.**

If the NetWare server can communicate with the host, the value in the Received column increases. In addition, statistics appear in the High, Low, Last, and Average columns, detailing how long it takes for the host to respond to the ping messages.

Testing by Using the netstat Command in Linux, Unix, or Windows

The `netstat` command is a sort of catchall command in Linux and Unix that does a great job summarizing network statistics and information. It's usually not as machine-specific as `ping`, and it's better at giving you the big picture of your entire web of machines.

`netstat` offers you a whole slew of options from which to choose, as shown in Table 12-3. Your best bet in terms of checking connectivity, however, especially from your main Linux or Unix server, is the `-a` option.

Table 12-3	The netstat Command's Options
Option	**What It Does**
-a	Displays all connections and listening ports. (Server-side connections don't normally appear.)
-e	Displays Ethernet statistics.
-I	Displays information about all of your network interfaces (such as your network or Ethernet cards.)
-n	Displays addresses and port numbers in numerical form. `netstat` normally displays addresses as host names, such as Jaguar and Ferrari. `-n` instructs `netstat` to show addresses such as 160.101.80.10.
-r	Displays the contents of the routing table.
-s	Displays per-protocol statistics. By default, statistics are shown for TCP, UDP, and IP; you may use the `-p` option to specify a subset of the default.

Using the -a option

The `-a` option displays all the network end-point data. In other words, it tells you which machines connect to the network, which protocols they use, and whether the connection is actively in service.

Here's an example: Say that a user is trying to make a TCP connection from box Pinto to server Jaguar. Log in to Jaguar and type **netstat -a**. You get a result that looks as follows:

```
# netstat -a
Active Internet connections
Proto  Recv-Q  Send-Q  Local Address   Foreign Address   (state)
tcp    17      10      tpci.1001       mustang.1201      ESTABL.
udp    1024    0       tpci.1002       Ferrari.2501      LISTENING
tcp    0       0       tpci.1005       quattro.login     ESTABL.
tcp    0       0       tpci.1006       bronco.2477       ESTABL.
tcp    0       0       tpci.1008       porsche.678       CLOSED
tcp    0       0       tpci.1009       pinto.1222        TIME_WAIT
```

This output explains that six machines are contacting or waiting to contact Jaguar. The (state) column shows that mustang, quattro, and bronco are making connections; their connections are *established*. Ferrari is *listening*, which is another form of connection where the connector is just waiting for packets to arrive. A glance at the Recv-Q column shows that machine Ferrari is *receiving* packets.

The bottom line of the output shows that pinto is trying to connect but that the connection is on hold. Now, unless pinto blows up, this problem is most likely to solve itself whenever Jaguar has fewer requests to handle. If Jaguar continues to handle all other requests besides pinto's, pinto itself may have something wrong with it. Rather than hunt for which network daemon may be down, if nothing vital's running on pinto, your best bet is just to reboot the machine.

Using the -i and -e options

If you can think of the ping command as a quick checkup, you can consider the real heavy-duty network tool — the netstat command — as more of a full-body workout. The ping command enables you to check a single connection's availability and speed. But if you use it with the -i command option, netstat shows you the actual behavior of the network interface cards on your machine, as the following example shows:

```
# netstat -i
Name  Mtu   Network Address     Ipkts  Ierrs  Opkts  Oerrs  Collis
lo0   8464  loopback localhost   400    0      400    0      0
lan0  1478  177.0 Ferrari       2399    0      243    0      0
```

The health of the network card appears in several fields of the readout. The Name field is the logical name assignment that your network card gets. The lo0 is a loopback interface that the machine uses in its general feedback check. The outgoing connection normally carries the designation lan0 or le0.

By *health* of the network, we actually mean several things, each appearing as part of the netstat readout. Ierrs refers to the number of incoming traffic errors. Oerrs refers to the number of outgoing traffic errors. Finally, Collis shows how many packet collisions are taking place on the network.

As an example, assume that you're having problems getting information on the machine again. After you run **netstat -i,** you get the following result:

```
Name  Mtu   Network Address       Ipkts  Ierrs  Opkts  Oerrs  Collis
lo0   8464  loopback localhost     400      0    400      0       0
lan0  1478  177.0 Ferrari         2399   2318    243      0       2
```

You can immediately rule out network problems that an overworked server causes. The reason is that the numbers under Collis are very low: Almost no packets are colliding on the network. Because you know that the problem isn't with the network per se, you can begin by checking out any network function that's local to your machine. Consider replacing the network card and checking the conditions of the network cable that attaches to the computer.

But suppose, on the other hand, that you get a different result, as in the following example:

```
Name  Mtu   Network Address       Ipkts  Ierrs  Opkts  Oerrs  Collis
lo0   8464  loopback localhost     400      0    400      0       0
lan0  1478  177.0  Ferrari        2399      0    243      0    2003
```

Here, the high rate of network collisions may signal a network problem. If the problem is persistent, too many machines are sending out too many packets for the network to handle. Consider upgrading the server or expanding your system's bandwidth with higher Mbps cabling.

In Windows, use **netstat -e** to get similar stats on your network interface, as follows:

```
C:\>netstat -e
Interface Statistics
                         Received          Sent
Bytes                  140633653       8878031
Unicast packets           123021         86162
Nonunicast packets         43682          4143
Discards                       0             0
Errors                         0             0
Unknown protocols              0             0
```

Looking at Other TCP/IP Commands and Utilities

You can use any of the commands that you see in Table 12-4 to connect to other TCP/IP-based hosts on Linux, Unix, Windows, or NetWare. Notice that only ftp appears as a server feature; the rest provide only clients to access the services on other servers.

Table 12-4   Additional TCP/IP Connectivity Commands

Connectivity Command	Function
File Transfer Protocol (FTP)	Provides bidirectional file transfers between a Windows NT computer and any TCP/IP host running FTP server software.
Trivial File Transfer Protocol (TFTP)	Provides bidirectional file transfers between a Windows NT computer and a TCP/IP host running TFTP server software.
Telnet	Provides terminal emulation on a TCP/IP host running telnet server software.
Remote Copy Protocol (RCP)	Copies files between a Windows NT computer and a server running the RCP service.
Remote Shell (RSH)	Runs commands on a server running the RSH service.

(continued)

Table 12-4 *(continued)*

Connectivity Command	Function
Remote Execution (REXEC)	Runs a process on a remote computer.
LPR	Prints files to a host running the Lpdsvc service (server side of TCP/IP printing for Unix clients).

The utilities that you see in Table 12-5 come with Microsoft TCP/IP for trouble-shooting TCP/IP problems.

Table 12-5	**Troubleshooting Commands**
Troubleshooting Utility	*Function*
ping	Verifies configurations and tests connectivity.
finger	Retrieves system information from a remote computer that supports the TCP/IP FINGER service.
arp	Displays the cache of locally resolved IP addresses to MAC (Media Access Control) addresses.
ipconfig	Displays the current TCP/IP configuration.
lpq	Obtains the status of a print queue on a host running the LPD service.
nbstat	Displays a list of NetBIOS computer names that resolve to IP addresses.
netstat	Displays the TCP/IP protocol session information.
route	Displays or modifies the local routing table.
hostname	Returns the local computer's host name for authentication by the RCP, RSH, and REXEC utilities.
tracert	Displays the path a packet takes to a destination host.

Some common problems that you may run into

A common configuration problem is that the host doesn't initialize or one of the services doesn't start. Verify your configuration parameters of the host and services, especially of other services on which the failing service may rely.

A common IP addressing problem is that you can't communicate with other hosts or your own host may hang. If either problem occurs, double-check your network diagram (or speak with your local network guru) to make sure that you're using the correct address.

Another common problem involves network IDs that don't match. You can communicate with hosts on the local network only if your network IDs match. If they don't, your host assumes that they're on another network. Again, refer to your network diagram to ensure that you're using the correct IDs.

Finally, you may run into a rare problem that involves host IDs that are the same on the same network. If two hosts on the same network have the same host ID, problems ensue. NT checks before initializing, and if another host is using the same host ID, TCP/IP doesn't initialize and records an error instead. Other operating systems may still initialize despite more than one host using one host ID. They may, however, experience trouble in communicating. The source host may also prove unable to communicate with a remote destination if the destination uses the same host ID as another computer on the remote network.

Does IP protect data on the network?

IP itself doesn't guarantee to deliver data correctly. It leaves all issues of data protection to the transport protocol. Both TCP and UDP, on the other hand, contain mechanisms that guarantee that any data they deliver to an application is correct.

IP does try to protect the packet's *IP header*, which is the relatively small part of each packet that controls how the packet moves through the network. It does so by calculating a *checksum* on the header fields and including that checksum in the packet it's transmitting. The receiver verifies the IP header checksum before processing the packet. Packets with checksums that no longer match are those suffering damage in some way, and the system simply discards them.

How does TCP try to avoid network meltdown?

TCP includes several mechanisms that attempt to sustain good data transfer rates while avoiding placing an excessive load on the network: TCP's Slow Start, Congestion Avoidance, Fast Retransmit, and Fast Recovery algorithms.

You don't really need to know the specifications of all this stuff, but knowing what TCP's doing with the data that's blasting all over those wires in your building is a good thing.

Another cool thing TCP employs is known as *SWS*, or *Silly Window Syndrome*. (we're serious here — that's its real name.) TCP doesn't permit a ton of mini-packets to go out from the sending unit or machine, thereby preventing a flood of packets that are too short (which are also known as *runt packets* in the network nomenclature).

A programmer by the name of Van Jacobson has contributed significant work to this aspect of TCP's behavior. The FAQ (Frequently Asked Question) list at the following Web site contains a couple of historically interesting pieces of Van's e-mail concerning an early implementation of congestion avoidance. You can snag this FAQ from the following address: `ftp://ftp.isi.edu/end2end/end2end-1990.mail`. That directory contains other TCP-related papers, including one at `ftp://ftp.ee.lbl.gov/papers/fastretrans.ps`, written by Sally Floyd, which discusses an algorithm that attempts to give TCP the capability to recover quickly from packet loss in a network.

Looking at Other NetWare Utilities

You can use the following NetWare utilities to check for specific NetWare functionality:

- **Sapcheck:** Checks to make sure that a workstation can identify NetWare file servers on a network. If it can, Sapcheck displays a list of the file servers and a count of all servers that it finds in the broadcast domain. If it can't, an appropriate error message appears, along with possible causes. You don't need to log in to the network to run this utility. You can find more information at the Sapcheck home page at the following URL:

  `www.execpc.com/~keithp/kpfware.htm`

- **Sapprint:** Checks to make sure that a workstation can identify NetWare print servers on a network. If it can, Sapprint displays a list of the print servers and a count of all servers that it finds in the broadcast domain. If it can't, an appropriate error message appears, along with possible causes. You don't need to log in to the network to run this utility. You can find more information about Sapprint (surprisingly enough) at the Sapcheck home page at the following URL:

  `www.execpc.com/~keithp/kpfware.htm`

- **MACView for NetWare:** Displays and searches for network addresses on your NetWare servers. It searches for and displays network connections by a MAC network address. It automatically cross-references network addresses to more than 1,600 vendors, and it displays the network number, object type, tree, last login time, and connection number. You can find more information at the MACView for NetWare home page at the following address:

```
www.wiredred.com/macview.html
```

✔ **QuikTakes for NetWare:** Graphically displays real-time NetWare server statistics. QuikTakes displays real-time core server statistics complete with meters, LEDs, and real-time graphs. It displays the CPU utilization and NCP traffic loads, and it can monitor multiple servers simultaneously. You can find more information at the QuikTakes for NetWare home page at the following address:

```
www.novellshareware.com/
```

Note: Because NetWare IPX/SPX utilizes MAC addresses, this utility helps you if you're administering and troubleshooting NetWare-related problems on your network.

✔ **Ethernet Card ID:** Retrieves network card information from all workstations in a LAN. On Ethernet networks, it also identifies more than 90 board manufacturers. It supports more than 250 workstations. Can redirect output to a file or printer. More information about this topic is available at the following address:

```
ftp://ftp.cdrom.com/pub/novell/card.zip
```

DHCP: Headache or Godsend for the Network Administrator?

The *Dynamic Host Configuration Protocol (DHCP)* provides a means for automating host configuration settings such as the IP address and default gateway. Automatic host configuration settings diametrically oppose everything that you already know about IP addresses. DHCP can be a great thing for administrators and network engineers, or it can prove your worst nightmare — if you don't know what it's really doing and how it does it.

Simple version: You log in to a machine, and it blasts out a request on the wire (UDP) to find a DHCP server. The server hears the query and looks at its table of available addresses not yet issued. It picks one and sends back a special reply to the requesting machine, and then the machine that requested the address receives this special set of packets. In these packets are the IP address for the machine, its default gateway or router, and DNS and WINS information. The machine takes on these attributes and is now ready, willing, and capable to do combat on the information highway.

DHCP, if you use it correctly and plan correctly, removes from techs and engineers the tasks of configuring and managing IP addresses on machines. DHCP is especially useful in networks encompassing thousands of hosts or machines in numerous buildings or even other cities.

DHCP clients send a discovery broadcast-packet request to locate a DHCP server. This DHCP client and server process is a local communication, because a router's job isn't to forward broadcast packets. In response to this broadcast packet, the DHCP server offers an address to the DHCP client.

The DHCP client then requests the following related address parameters:

- **Lease Time (LT):** This parameter determines how long the DHCP client may use the IP address.

- **Renewal Time (T1):** This parameter determines when the DHCP client must request an extension of the lease time (typically, ½ of T1) from the DHCP server that originally grants the IP address lease.

- **Rebind Time (T2):** If the renewal is unsuccessful (because the DHCP server is down, for example), this parameter determines when the DHCP client is to attempt to reacquire an IP address from any DHCP server.

If the DHCP server and the DHCP client are on separate networks, the DHCP address-assignment process becomes a bit more complex. In this case, the DHCP client sends the discovery broadcast packet on the local network. Because the discovery broadcast packet can't route, it uses a special relay-agent process (often known as the *BOOTP* or *DHCP relay-agent process*) to enable communications between a DHCP client and a DHCP server on separate networks.

DHCP communications use the connectionless services of UDP with the following port numbers:

- **UDP Port 67:** DHCP server (the port for BOOTP server processes)
- **UDP Port 68:** DHCP client (the same port for BOOTP client processes)

DHCP communications also define a set of options, or tags, that indicate the information clients use DHCP to locate.

Although people often look at DHCP as the salvation from the manual agony of IP address assignment, DHCP actually offers much more capability. The name — Dynamic Host Configuration Protocol — is an accurate definition.

Chapter 13

Centralizing Control with Auditing Server Resources

In This Chapter

▶ Understanding server auditing

▶ Monitoring your resources

*W*ant to know one of the best methods for ensuring maximum control over how your integrated network works with minimum effort? Keep watch over the resources on your server or servers. By checking that your servers aren't running out of anything critical, such as disk space or processing power, you ensure that your entire network runs smoothly. You can do so through a combination of manual checks or automated programs that perform what's known as *auditing*.

You may or may not be familiar with the concept of auditing. It generally refers to the process of examining a company's assets and procedures to ensure that you can account for all assets and that all procedures correctly protect the assets. Similarly, server auditing ensures that your server assets — both hardware and software — are in adequate supply and that you're correctly implementing your resource distribution policy. This chapter covers the utilities available for you to complete these tasks. The utilities vary from operating system to operating system, but they all keep your users happy, which, of course, makes *you* happy.

Auditing: Knowing Each Nut, Bolt, and Hard Drive

The word *audit* is scary in some circles. What often leaps to mind is a pair of IRS agents coming to your home dressed like Will Smith and Tommy Lee Jones from *Men in Black*. Or perhaps you're used to seeing internal auditors if you work in an accounting firm or department. These people are usually scrutinizing your financial records and maybe making you pay additional taxes. In an integrated network environment, however, *audit* refers to a useful resource measurement, not a method of verifying your tax returns. So you can breathe easier. Auditing doesn't automatically improve or degrade the performance of your network. It's an enabling technology that enables you to protect resources and ensure quality of service to your users.

Actually, we want to qualify that last statement a little, which is true — at least to a point. But remember the following:

You want always to keep in mind that you must use a certain amount of system resources to *monitor* system resources — whether you use processing power or disk space that a log file takes up. So if you're running a space- or processor-strapped network, consider carefully whether you want to expend even more in a quest to monitor what's left.

To perform a server audit, you must either configure your operating system's auditing feature to automatically record certain events or manually run a check on a regular basis. Then you can later generate reports. You can use these reports as evidence that your resource security policy is correctly implemented or to find weaknesses in the policy. As you know, you always can find room for improvement, so make sure that you don't get caught up in trying to show that the policy is right and good. Be fair and look at both sides of the street, so to speak.

Suppose for example, that your policy limits users to a certain quota of disk space in a particular directory. After configuring your server's auditing feature to monitor that directory, you can print a report of all users who're using too much space in that directory and justify your changes accordingly.

Servers are more equal than clients

We have a reason for focusing on server auditing in this chapter and not system or client auditing. Two reasons, as a matter of fact:

First, with a centralized system, you're going for efficiency but with the risk of a single point of failure. (For you hard-core technology types, this situation is known as a *gravity* model.) If a user's machine crashes because it runs of out disk space, therefore, it's just a statistical blip. But if a major server dies for the same reason, it's a tragedy of such scale that you'd need Kate Winslet and Leonardo DiCaprio on casting call to reenact it.

Second, spending your time watching one important machine instead of 40 less-important machines is simply a lot more efficient. If you want to spend your day, every day, running around or remotely logging in to check each and every system on your network, well, we're not about to stop you. But pursuing such a course does make you look a little ridiculous if you can do other, more productive things with your time instead.

Making the Quota with Windows 2000

The helpful folks at Microsoft gave Windows 2000 an extremely useful, automated system to audit and control disk-space usage. This system is known as *Disk Quota*. Disk Quota automatically tracks volume usage for new users from the moment that you activate the system.

Because Microsoft considers the Disk Quota utility an entire *system* running under Windows 2000, some interesting restrictions apply on how you can use it. In essence, you must format the drive for NTFS (NT File System). The version of NTFS that Windows 2000 creates, however, isn't the only version that works; if you format your drive with the version of NTFS that Windows NT 4.0 uses, you can still use the Disk Quota system. The Windows 2000 Setup program automatically upgrades the version of NTFS that NT 4.0 uses to handle the Windows 2000 Disk Quota system.

Enabling the Disk Quota utility

By default, Windows 2000 comes with Disk Quota disabled. The reason is that auditing comes at a price — in system time and resources. But enabling the Disk Quota system is very easy. Just follow these steps:

1. **Double-click the My Computer desktop icon.**

   In the window that appears, you see one or more disk volumes, depending on how many volumes are on your Windows 2000 computer.

2. **Right-click the disk volume where you want to use the Disk Quota system.**

3. **Choose Properties from the pop-up menu that appears.**

4. **Click the Quota tab on the Properties dialog box that appears.**

   Doing so takes you to the Quota panel, as shown in Figure 13-1.

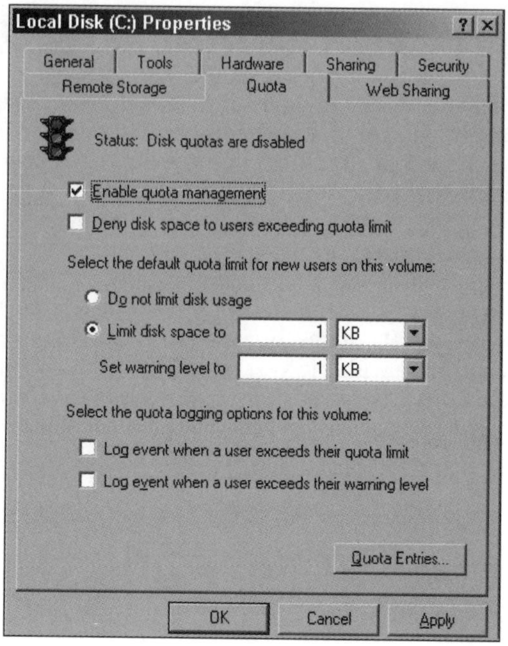

Figure 13-1:
The Quota
panel on the
Windows
2000
Properties
dialog box.

5. **Click the Enable Quota Management check box to select that option.**

   The grayed-out Quota controls darken (become activated) and become fully usable.

   You can accept the defaults that Microsoft supplies, or you can change them. If you want to accept the defaults, skip ahead to Step 7.

6. **If you want to change the default Quota values, click the radio button to the left of the Limit Disk Space To option.**

   Doing so activates the fields so that you can change the disk space limit to whatever setting that you want. Microsoft helpfully enables you to type numeric values into the text fields and to select a disk space limit unit from the drop-down list (see Figure 13-2).

7. **Click OK to complete the enabling process.**

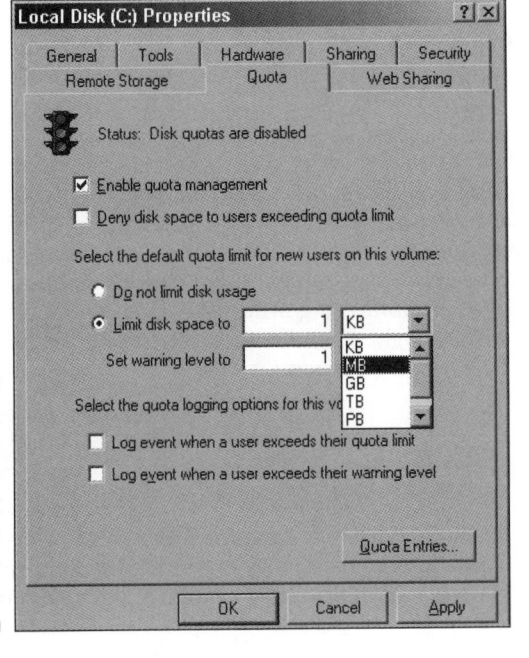

Figure 13-2:
Selecting a
disk space
limit unit
from the
handy drop-
down list.

Keep in mind that Windows 2000 doesn't impose your activated disk quota on existing users. To apply the disk quota to existing users, you must add new quota entries in the Quota Entries panel, which you can access by clicking the Quota Entries button on the Quota panel.

Disabling the Disk Quota utility

If you decide that you don't want to monitor disk usage on your Windows 2000 system because you moved to a standalone system (or for any other reason), you can turn off the Disk Quota system. To do so, follow these steps:

1. **Double-click the My Computer icon on your desktop.**

2. **Right-click the disk volume where you want to disable the Disk Quota system.**

3. **Choose Properties from the pop-up menu that appears.**

4. **In the Properties dialog box that appears, click the Quota tab.**

5. **Click the Enable Quota Management check box.**

   Clicking the check box removes the check mark and disables the feature.

6. **Click OK to complete the task.**

Watching Resources in the Unix/Linux World

Most people think of Unix and its younger cousin, Linux, as anything but lightweights in the networking and server world. Yet, in an odd sense, that's really what they are. The reason is that both Unix and Linux can run efficiently on slower, older machines; require less RAM than other OSes to get tasks done; and take up a whole lot less disk space than other OSes. This philosophy shows up in the orientation of their monitoring processes. Because Unix and Linux are more in the way of lightweight systems, their older auditing functions monitor *processes* rather than disk space.

Here's one off the top

The tool that you use most commonly to monitor processes in Unix and Linux is the top command. The top command acts as a sort of system snapshot, grabbing the current statistics of the running system and displaying them for you on a single screen.

To run top, you simply need to type **top** at the command prompt and press Enter. You see a display similar to the one shown in Figure 13-3.

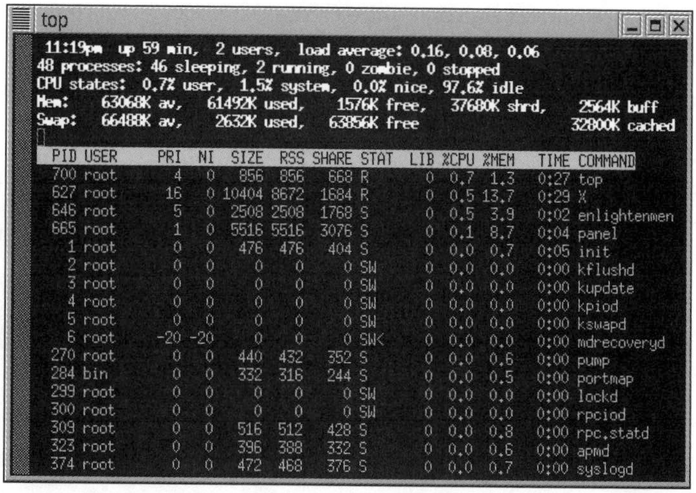

Figure 13-3:
Whichever
flavor of
Unix you
use, the top
command
gives output
similar to
what you
see on this
screen.

```
top                                                          _ □ X
11:19pm  up 59 min,  2 users,  load average: 0.16, 0.08, 0.06
48 processes: 46 sleeping, 2 running, 0 zombie, 0 stopped
CPU states:  0.7% user,  1.5% system,  0.0% nice, 97.6% idle
Mem:    63068K av,   61492K used,    1576K free,   37680K shrd,    2564K buff
Swap:   66488K av,    2632K used,   63856K free                  32800K cached

  PID USER     PRI  NI  SIZE   RSS SHARE STAT LIB %CPU %MEM   TIME COMMAND
  700 root       4   0   856   856   668 R      0  0.7  1.3   0:27 top
  627 root      16   0 10404  8672  1684 R      0  0.5 13.7   0:29 X
  646 root       5   0  2508  2508  1768 S      0  0.5  3.9   0:02 enlightenmen
  665 root       1   0  5516  5516  3076 S      0  0.1  8.7   0:04 panel
    1 root       0   0   476   476   404 S      0  0.0  0.7   0:05 init
    2 root       0   0     0     0     0 SW     0  0.0  0.0   0:00 kflushd
    3 root       0   0     0     0     0 SW     0  0.0  0.0   0:00 kupdate
    4 root       0   0     0     0     0 SW     0  0.0  0.0   0:00 kpiod
    5 root       0   0     0     0     0 SW     0  0.0  0.0   0:00 kswapd
    6 root     -20 -20     0     0     0 SW<    0  0.0  0.0   0:00 mdrecoveryd
  270 root       0   0   440   432   352 S      0  0.0  0.6   0:00 pump
  284 bin        0   0   332   316   244 S      0  0.0  0.5   0:00 portmap
  299 root       0   0     0     0     0 SW     0  0.0  0.0   0:00 lockd
  300 root       0   0     0     0     0 SW     0  0.0  0.0   0:00 rpciod
  309 root       0   0   516   512   428 S      0  0.0  0.8   0:00 rpc.statd
  323 root       0   0   396   388   332 S      0  0.0  0.6   0:00 apmd
  374 root       0   0   472   468   376 S      0  0.0  0.7   0:00 syslogd
```

In Figure 13-3, notice that the top command lists the processes running on the system from top to bottom in order of the CPU percentage that each uses. In other words, the process making the machine work the hardest appears at the top; the process making the machine work the second hardest appears next; and so on, in descending order. The three most important figures for you in each row are the first, third, and fourth from the right.

The fourth and third columns from the right tell you how much CPU and memory each process is using. If the process is out of control, you may see it taking as much as 90 or even 100 percent of available system resources. The first column on the right tells you the name of the process that's responsible for the usage. Notice how the very act of *monitoring* changes the behavior of the system; the most demanding process in Figure 13-3 is actually the top monitoring utility itself.

The GNOME System Monitor

In recent years, both Unix and Linux adopted a graphic desktop and GUI-like functionality for many system aspects, including monitoring tools. The most popular of these tools on the Linux side is the GNOME System Monitor, which is available on any version of Linux that uses GNOME, such as Red Hat, Caldera, and Debian.

Opening the System Monitor is easy. Simply click the Main Menu button on the Linux panel and choose Utilities⇨System monitor (see Figure 13-4).

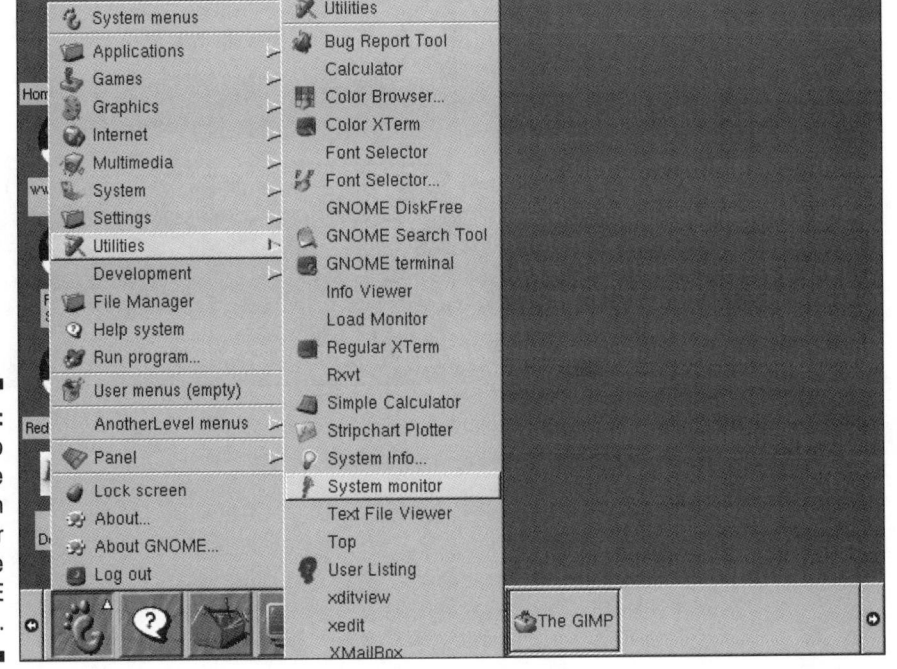

Figure 13-4: Preparing to open the System Monitor utility on the GNOME desktop.

The GNOME System Monitor screen opens, as shown in Figure 13-5. By default, the monitor opens to a `top`-like panel — showing the most system-intensive processes from top to bottom.

Detailing all of System Monitor's functions would take an entire chapter. But for the purposes at hand, you need to be aware of the following two other panels that are very useful in monitoring your system:

- Memory Usage
- Filesystems

While you're on the System Monitor screen, click the Memory Usage tab to access the screen shown in Figure 13-6. This screen shows you in colorful, column-style detail which processes are taking up what slice of the memory pie.

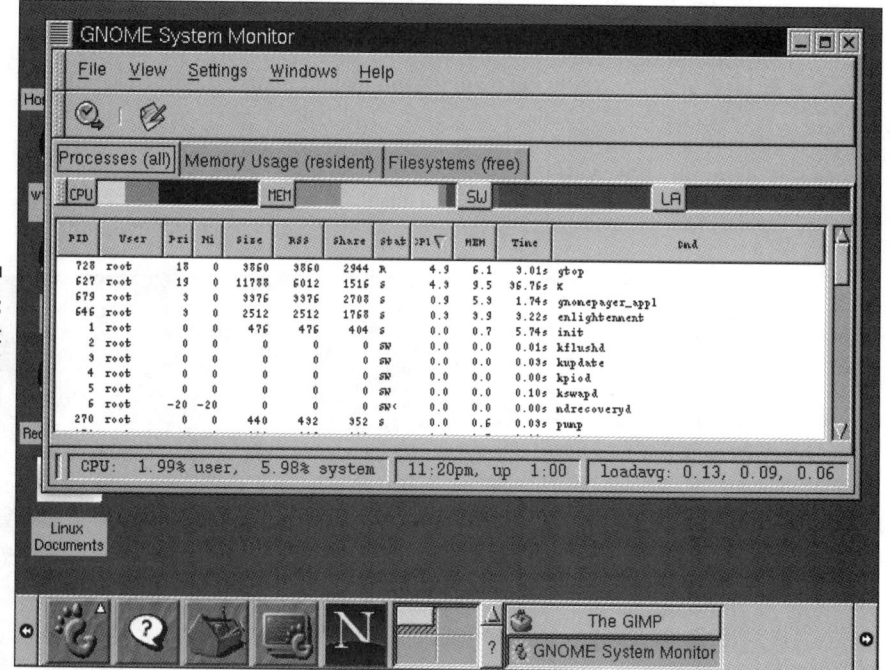

Figure 13-5: The default GNOME System Monitor's display in Linux, similar to the results of the Unix top command.

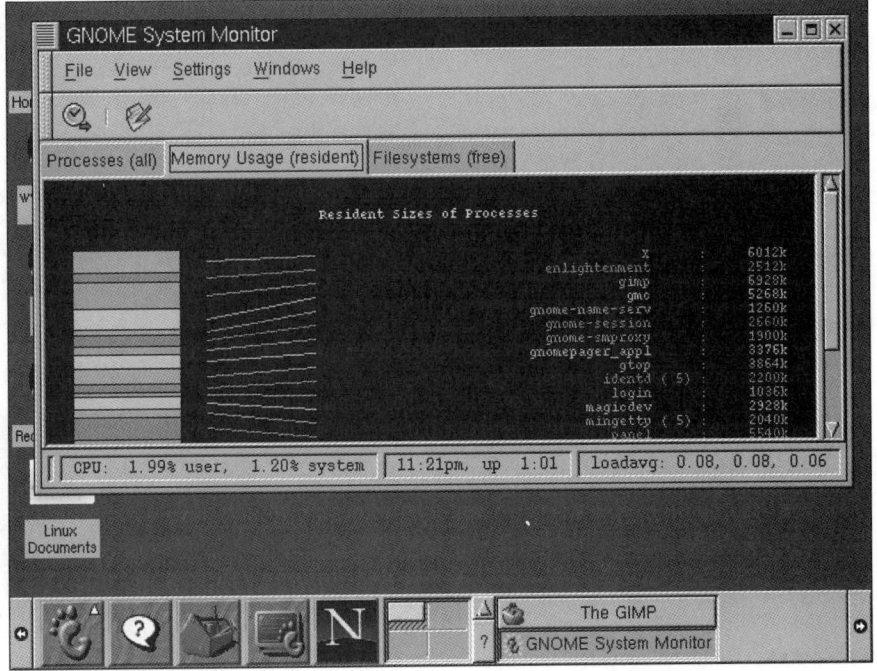

Figure 13-6:
The
Memory
Usage tab of
the System
Monitor
screen.

As a side note, if your processes aren't running out of control and yet a large amount of memory seems taken up, you have a clear sign that you need to install more RAM right away. Otherwise, you may suffer significant system slowdowns, which, on a server, translates to complaining users.

Now click the Filesystems (free) tab to access the screen shown in Figure 13-7. Again, you see a colored, column-like bar that indicates how much space that the drive you're allocating for Linux is using. If this drive fills up, your entire system may crash, so checking the drive every month or so is worthwhile, even on a system that's experiencing no initial space issues.

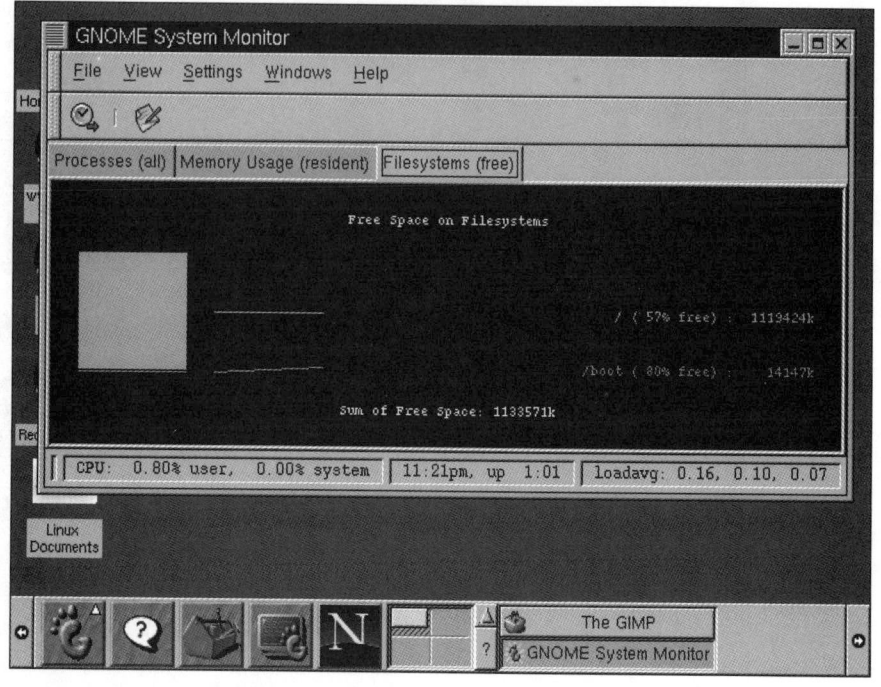

Figure 13-7: The Filesystems (free) tab of the System Monitor screen, showing drive-space usage.

NetWare Auditing with the AUDITCON Utility

NetWare must be the king of the hill for overall auditing flexibility. As a NOS, NetWare applies auditing for functions ranging from system monitoring to security. If you enable Intruder Detection, for example, NetWare automatically locks a user's account after a certain number of incorrect login attempts. Network auditing, on the other hand, provides data to help you investigate security-related events and improve your network security.

The AUDITCON utility, which comes in NetWare, is your prime auditing tool for collecting and managing network auditing data. You can use the AUDITCON utility (which you find in the SYS:\PUBLIC directory) to enable, configure, and manage NetWare's auditing capabilities.

Enabling AUDITCON

To enable NetWare's auditing capabilities, type **AUDITCON** at the console. After it loads, the Available Audit Options menu offers you the following choices: auditing directory services, enabling external auditing, changing the current server or volume, and enabling auditing for the current volume.

The directory-services choice and current-volume choice enable you to audit events that occur on your network server. The external-auditing choice enables you to store auditing events from network clients. With external auditing, network clients record auditing events that occur on these clients. The clients then send this auditing data to a NetWare server, which stores the data. External auditing requires third-party client software, and we don't cover it here.

To enable directory services or volume auditing, you must have Supervisor access to the container or volume that you want NetWare to audit. Whether you enable auditing for a container or for a volume depends on what kind of events you want to record.

The AUDITCON utility enables you to audit almost every directory services, file, and server event that occurs on your network, as the following list describes:

- ✔ To audit directory services events, you enable auditing for the Novell Directory Services (NDS) container that holds the objects that you want to audit.
- ✔ To audit file events, you enable auditing for the volume that you want to audit.
- ✔ To audit server events, you enable auditing for the SYS volume of the server that you want to audit.

Container auditing

To enable NetWare's auditing capabilities, type **AUDITCON** at the console. After it loads, the Available Audit Options menu offers you the following choices: auditing directory services, enabling external auditing, changing the current server or volume, and enabling auditing for the current volume. Choose Audit Directory Services.

After you enable auditing for a container, NetWare collects auditing data only for the objects directly within that container. NetWare doesn't collect auditing data for the following:

- ✔ **The container object itself.** To audit the events that affect a particular container, you must enable auditing for that container's parent object. So, for example, if you want to audit events that affect the US_corp container object (which is under the root container), you don't enable auditing for the US_corp container; instead, you enable auditing for US_corp's parent container, root.

- ✔ **Objects within subcontainers.** The container holds these objects. So, using the preceding bullet's example, if the US_corp container holds the SouthEast organizational unit container, and you enable auditing for the US_corp container, NetWare records any changes that you make to the SouthEast container because that container resides directly within US_corp. NetWare doesn't, however, record any changes that you make to objects that the SouthEast container holds. You must enable auditing for the SouthEast container if you want to record events involving objects within that container.

- ✔ **The file system of volume objects within the container.** If you want NetWare to record file system events, you must enable auditing for the volume that stores the file system that you want to audit.

Volume auditing

If you enable volume auditing for a particular volume, NetWare can record almost any action that a user may take on that volume. NetWare can, for example, record every time that a particular user opens any file on that volume. NetWare can also track events associated with individual files and directories, which means that you can configure NetWare to track a particular file. NetWare then records every user or other NDS object that accesses the file. NetWare can even audit print queue directories that you store on a volume.

If you enable auditing on a server's SYS volume, NetWare can audit server events in addition to auditing file system events. In all, you can audit 150 volume and server events if you enable auditing for NetWare volumes.

Notice that enabling auditing for one volume doesn't affect other volumes. If you want to audit the file system of other volumes, you must enable auditing for each volume that holds the file system that you want to audit. If you want to audit the server events on other servers, you must enable auditing for the SYS volume on each server that you want to audit.

Configuring auditing

After you enable auditing for either a container or a volume, you can select the events that you want NetWare to audit. We recommend that you audit events that help you verify whether your security policy is implemented and executed correctly. If your security policy strictly defines each user's rights, for example, you may want to enable auditing for both NDS container objects and volumes.

You can configure NetWare to record Change Access Control List (ACL) events on containers and Grant Trustee and Remove Trustee events on volumes. This means that anytime an administrator changes the rights to a container, volume or directory, those changes will be recorded. Doing so is very important if you have more than one administrator using your servers. Additionally, you want those administrators to use their *own* IDs rather than the generic admin account. (Otherwise, you have no record of who really makes the changes; admin simply appears to do everything. And then you have a weak policy.) NetWare then records any changes anyone makes to users' rights, and you can print a report of the changes that occur from the time that you enable auditing.

You can use the AUDITCON utility to configure NetWare to track and record events according to the criteria you specify. You can configure NetWare to perform the following tasks:

- ✔ Audit particular network events whenever they occur.
- ✔ Audit the events that particular users initiate.
- ✔ Audit the events that involve a particular file or directory.
- ✔ Perform auditing based on combined file and user-event selections.
- ✔ Restrict auditing to the users you select.
- ✔ Audit users' actions before NDS authenticates the users.

Auditing based on selected events

By using the AUDITCON utility, you can configure NetWare to record every occurrence of any event that you select. Say that you want to track each time anyone renames any NDS objects. You enable auditing for the container that holds the objects that you want to audit and then enable the Rename Entry event on the Audit by DS Events screen. To do this, start AUDITCON, choose Audit Directory Services, then choose Audit by DS Events.

If you want NetWare to record every time that anyone purges a file from a particular volume, you enable auditing for that volume. To get this setup, start AUDITCON, choose Enable Volume Auditing, then select Audit by File Events and choose the File Purge event.

Auditing based on selected users

You can choose to audit a user's actions in both containers and volumes. After you select a user for auditing, NetWare associates an audit flag with the user's NDS User object. It then tracks that user's actions in all containers and volumes for which you enable auditing.

Suppose that your boss or the business owner needs a record of Administrator X's work on the network. Just enable auditing for all events that user Administrator X initiates. If you also enable auditing for both the SouthEast.Admin.US_corp container and the Admin_SYS volume, NetWare records all events initiated by Administrator X on both the container and the volume.

You can't, however, limit this audit to a particular container or volume. By choosing to audit user Administrator X, you automatically choose to audit Administrator X's actions on every container and volume for which you enable auditing.

Auditing users before authentication

Before a user logs in to the network, NetWare enables the user to access files in the LOGIN directory. By default, the server doesn't audit events initiated by unauthenticated users. If you select the Audit NOT_LOGGED_IN option, however, NetWare audits these events.

Auditing files

NetWare stores all online audit data files in protected, hidden directories that network clients can't read by issuing file and directory NetWare Core Protocol (NCP) messages. It stores the audit data files for each volume on that volume. The audit data files for the VOL1 volume, for example, it maintains on the VOL1 volume.

An average event record occupies 30 bytes in an audit data file. If you enable all the auditing events for both directory services and volumes, auditing only one user generates approximately 150 event records during the login process alone. If that user logs out, NetWare records another 130 event records. At 30 bytes per record, recording these events uses 840 bytes.

If each user on a 25-user network logs in and logs out only once each day, NetWare generates 21KB of event records in a single day. If you consider how many times per day an average user accesses the network, you can see how audit data files can balloon.

Be careful. You may find yourself tempted to configure NetWare to record every event that occurs on your network. But this approach is impractical. If you choose to audit all network events, your audit trail grows quickly, potentially consuming all the available space on your volumes.

To help keep audit data files from consuming too much space on your volumes, the AUDITCON utility enables you to copy these files from the hidden directories to a server or workstation. Of course, after you copy an audit data file, the hidden directory no longer protects it. You must then take the appropriate steps to protect the file. The file contains user IDs and what the activities were, so if you use the file in any sort of litigation or legal matter, it's protected just as tightly as CEO's salary records of most companies.

Using AUDITCON as a defense mechanism

By using the AUDITCON utility to enable auditing for your network, you can verify that your company's network security policy is working, thereby ensuring that your confidential data is protected and that it remains that way.

Auditing your network only once and determining that your security policy was correctly implemented during that audit does *not* mean that the security measures in place at that time are maintained. Don't become complacent.

Unfortunately, after you establish network security, the overall level of security tends to deteriorate over time. This breakdown in network security occurs for a number of reasons, including user apathy, temporary security assignments that you never revoke, users who change roles but whose rights you never reassign, and users who find ways around security measures.

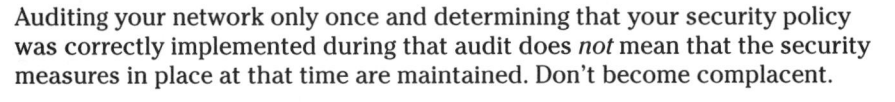

Chapter 14

File System Integration

• •

• •

*M*ost of the business of running servers involves making sure that users can communicate on the network.

Your main network point, or server, is by default a file server — it must make more information available than a regular client machine. In fact, being able to view and edit files on different machines is so important that busy networks subdivide servers by task — one main task being, of course, file serving. Other task-specific servers handle Web functions, database storage, and e-mail. Because making files available for viewing, editing, and printing is so important, we show you in this chapter how to do just that with a minimum of fuss.

Integrating Your Networked Hardware and Software

The majority of work that your users want to accomplish involves files, which can be text files (such as Microsoft Word), graphics files (such as GNOME snapshots), or sound files (such as MP3s). Each networked operating system has a different method to its madness - specifically, Windows 2000, Unix/Linux, and NetWare have different ways that they organize their files. Each method of organization is called a file system. One of your main jobs as an integrator will be to 'hook up' different machines on a network so that they can see files that reside on a completely different file system.

Integrating file systems is far from a science, even today. In fact, it is more of an art, considering that there are so many permutations in today's mélange of different operating system versions and hardware. However, there are a few major rules that you can follow which will make your job easier. As a rule, integrating different file systems on an integrated network fall into the following two major categories:

✔ **Pure networking:** The hardware that makes such things as intercontinental network communications possible. We cover this subject in loving detail in Chapter 6.

✔ **Office-related hardware and equipment:** The most important of these networked resources are the servers and printers that you hook up to your network.

This chapter covers the most common connections that you make.

In true geek-speak, a networked file system can also be called a *networked drive*. Furthermore, the process of connecting file systems is also known as *mapping*.

Connecting Unix/Linux to NetWare

You can seamlessly integrate environments supporting both NetWare and NFS by using Novell NetWare NFS. This product mounts file systems on NetWare servers and accesses NetWare files as if they're NFS files. It includes authentication, authorization, and file locking features.

NFS, which stands for *Network File System*, is an old standby for distributing files across Unix and Linux networks. You can find entire books about NFS, which is beyond the scope of this book. You find a very good introduction to the whos, whats, and whys of NFS in *Linux Administration For Dummies*, by Michael Bellomo (published by IDG Books Worldwide, Inc.).

Mapping a Windows network drive to a Unix/Linux server

Samba, which we discuss in Chapter 5 on the client side of the Client-Server equation, connects the Windows and the Unix/Linux universes. You can rely on it for most simple network connections. To get Samba running, perform the following steps:

1. **Right-click the My Computer icon and choose Map Network Drive from the pop-up menu that appears.**

2. **In the Map Network Drive window that appears, select any available drive.**

3. **In the Path: window, type the following:**

   *<the name of your server>**<your Unix/Linux username>*

   The result looks like \\YOURSERVERNAME\UserBob.

4. **Make sure that the check box next to Reconnect at login is selected and then click OK.**

   This last step ensures that the connection re-establishes the next time that you boot your computer.

5. **Enter your Unix/Linux password after the system prompts you for it and then click OK.**

6. **Double-click the My Computer icon to open it.**

   You should now see a drive that shows a connection to your Unix/Linux server, such as Marchetti on SERVER001(Z:).

   If you don't see this connection to the Unix/Linux server, then refer to Chapter 6 on testing the network connection between the two machines.

For more information, the Samba Web site (at www.samba.org) explains all the nuts and bolts of Samba. That site also provides detailed configuration notes.

Mapping Windows to NetWare

In Windows, you use the Network Neighborhood as the primary way to browse the network for machines to connect. If you open Network Neighbor-hood on a computer running a NetWare-compatible networking client, all the NetWare NDS servers your computer sees appear. All computers running File and Printer Sharing for NetWare Networks that use Workgroup Advertising also appear in Network Neighborhood.

Clicking the Entire Network icon displays a list of all NetWare servers on the network. This list also contains a list of workgroups that include computers running File and Printer Sharing for NetWare Networks. You can view the contents of any server without mapping a network drive.

If your computer has both Client for Microsoft Networks and Client for NetWare Networks installed, you also see a list of computers running Windows for Workgroups, Windows 95, and Windows NT. The list of NetWare servers is at the beginning of the list of workgroups or domains in the Entire Network window.

If the computer is running Client for NetWare Networks, drive mappings are limited to the available drive letters. If you want to connect to a NetWare server in the Network Neighborhood, follow these steps:

1. **In Network Neighborhood window, right-click a NetWare server.**

2. **From the pop-up menu that appears, choose Attach As.**

   The Attach As window appears on the desktop. You'll see two open text fields that direct you to type in the name and password for a user account.

3. **Type the name and password of one of your user accounts.**

4. **Click OK.**

To map a directory on this server, follow these steps:

1. **Double-click the server icon in the Neighborhood Network window.**

   A window appears displaying the available directories.

2. **Right-click the directory that you want to map.**

   The directories you select are highlighted.

3. **Click Map Network Drive in the pop-up menu that appears.**

4. **Fill in the necessary information in the Map Network Drive dialog box that appears.**

5. **Click OK.**

The toolbar on every window includes the Map Network Drive button, which you can use to specify the name of a NetWare server and volume (or directory) that you want to map to a drive letter.

Connecting to a directory as the root of the drive

You can connect to a directory as the root of the drive if you want to enter the directory where you can easily see all the available directories in the drive. If you connect to a drive from the /example1 directory, for example, you can see the entire contents of that directory. On the other hand, if you enter the drive as simply **C:**, you can see the directories /example1, / example2, and /example3. If you want to connect to a directory as the root of the drive, you need to follow these slightly different steps:

1. **Double-click the Network Neighborhood icon.**

2. **Double-click one of the NetWare server icons in the window that appears.**

3. **Right-click the directory that you want to map your drive to and choose Map Network Drive from the pop-up menu that appears.**

   A Map Network Drive dialog box opens. Make sure that the Connect As Root Of The Drive check box is selected so that directory appears to your Windows machine as a root of the drive you're mapping.

   With this option enabled, if you switch to this mapped directory in Windows, you see the prompt as `drive:\>` and not as `drive:\directory>`. You can't go farther up the directory tree from the command prompt.

4. **Click OK.**

A Tricky Part . . . Accessing the NetWare File Server

After the NetWare client is installed, as described in Chapter 6, users can access the NetWare servers within your organization. This client makes it easy for your users to

  ✔ Communicate to the servers in order to retrieve and save files

  ✔ Print via your NetWare servers

Each user, therefore, must have an account on the server to perform any of these tasks. Each user is set up in NetWare using ConsoleOne. In setting up a user's account, you can choose from many options, and you can restrict or open up the user's rights to practically anything that the NetWare server controls.

Typically, in setting up users, an administrator uses one of the following two methods:

  ✔ **Regional:** If your company has regional offices, you can put the users into groups based on their locations. This method works well until someone in Minnesota needs files for Florida users. Of course, you can grant access rights for that one person to that file or that directory in the Florida folks' directories. But if two of your accounting people reside in Florida, three in Maryland, and one in Washington, this setup can become a management nightmare for you, the administrator.

  ✔ **Functional groups:** Using this method makes *what* people do more important than where they are. With accounting people located all over the country and all needing access to similar data, the functional method is much easier to manage. This streamlines your design of grouping users. In this day of global and worldwide companies, functional groups are an easier method for managing users.

Part V
E-Mail and News

In this part . . .

In several recent surveys of computer use in the office, sending, receiving, and replying to e-mail were found to take a significant amount of time in a worker's day. Therefore, it's a good idea to familiarize yourself with connecting your intranet to the Internet and know which pieces are part of the e-mail puzzle on your network.

You get a solid introduction to the background processes that power your e-mail system, setting up e-mail on the different servers you'll have available on your network, and Usenet news.

Chapter 15

Message Transport Agents (MTAs) — Superfast Delivery Without Stamps

· ·

In This Chapter

▶ User versus transport agents

▶ How transport agents do their work

▶ Delivery never carries a 100 percent guarantee

▶ Agents with Unix/Linux

▶ The workings of Windows 2000

▶ NetWare's GroupWise utility

· ·

*C*ontrary to popular belief, electronic mail doesn't simply teleport from the sender to the recipients. Nor does it go down the wire, get someone to sprinkle magic pixie dust on it, and magically go where it wants to. In fact, the complex programs and serpentine configurations of most e-mail systems are among the most daunting aspects of setting up any network — let alone a network with mixed operating systems.

An in-depth analysis on all the permutations of each operating system's mail setup isn't the idea here — in fact, each one takes up a separate book. You do need to know, however, about all the pieces of the e-mail puzzle, what options are available to you, and some ideas about how to hook them up!

The Dynamic Duo — User Agents and Transport Agents

At the most basic level, you can break all e-mail systems down into the following two components:

- ✔ User agents
- ✔ Transport agents

Although it sounds like you're working on a throwback to the Cold War, with two teams of agents working at odds to uncover secrets, assassinate each other, and ordering martinis shaken, not stirred, this isn't the case. As a matter of fact, these agents cooperate so messages go from a sender to a waiting recipient.

User agents

The term *user agent* is a bit of a misnomer, one that carries over from the dark days of DOS and Unix. In fact, user *agents* actually is a broad definition encompassing all sorts of programs that users access to write, read, reply, and carbon-copy e-mail. If you're from the old school of Unix or Linux, you're probably familiar with `mail`, `mailx`, `elm`, and `pine`.

On the other hand, if you're working (as many of us poor integrators do) with a GUI-based system, you're likely using Netscape. Long-term GUI users from Windows are probably more familiar with Internet Explorer or Microsoft Outlook. (We cover the user-agent side thoroughly in Chapter 16.)

Transport agents

Transport agents are what you can call behind-the-scenes operators, as they involve the actual mechanics of breaking down and moving electronic mail. You run the danger of turning any chapter about transport agents into strongly diluted alphabet soup, with abbreviations such as POA, MTA, MUA, and the like, but they're what get the job done without your user community being the wiser for it.

Because of their behind-the-scene nature, transport agents are a classic *back end* program, as we describe in Chapter 13, while user agents are *front end*.

Some argue that *delivery agents* and *spooling systems* are a third and fourth piece of the e-mail puzzle. Delivery agents are programs that work by placing incoming e-mail into a given directory or space on the hard drive that you allocate as a user account's *mailbox*. Spooling *systems* are the allocated space set aside to hold unread user e-mail. (In Unix, for example, this space is /var/mail or /var/spool/mail). In today's world of software, however, these definitions are more of a semantic distinction. Delivery agents and spooling systems are part of the user-agent or operating-system software.

How Transport Agents Do Their Work

Whenever you send an e-mail message, your *MUA* (*M*ail *U*ser *A*gent) follows this set of predesignated steps:

1. First, the MUA establishes a connection with your default mail server or MTA.

2. Next, it sends a sequence of commands to the server or MTA. (Your MTA is often the same as your DNS server.)

3. After the MTA receives a message, it acts on it, basing its action on the destination address or addresses within the message.

4. If a destination address is local to the MTA, the MTA stores the message and waits for an MUA to retrieve it.

5. The MUA checks for stored messages depending on how the network operating system is set up.

In most Windows 2000 installations, for example, the system automatically checks the mail of any user who logs on and sweeps it into the user's account, along with a recorded announcement ("You've got mail!"). On the other hand, most Linux and Unix systems check only after the user activates the e-mail program or specifies a check while online. You can, however, initiate automatic checking here as well. Instead of a friendly voice, most systems use the biff program to announce when e-mail arrives.

A Unix software programmer who wanted a program to beep as e-mail arrives developed biff. In fact, he named the program itself after his dog, Biff, who always barked whenever the mailman came up the driveway to the mailbox outside the door.

If a destination address isn't local to the MTA, the MTA either forwards the mail message to the destination MTA (if known), sends it to the Internet gateway, or relays it to another MTA server that may lie closer to the final destination. After the mail message finally arrives at the destination MTA, the system again stores the message until the MUA of the destination host retrieves it.

Guaranteeing Delivery — Not Your Normal Postmaster, Indeed

Local delivery agents are nothing more than your e-mail clients. Several different types or brands deliver your e-mail fast.

E-mail systems are highly efficient ways of moving messages back and forth. They rarely lose mail, but nothing in this world carries an absolute guarantee, especially if you take into consideration that you're dealing with an electronic format of messaging. If you lose one bit, the message may not get to the destination, which is why all e-mail systems today utilize variants on the TCP/IP protocol family.

As we describe in Chapter 11, TCP acts as a sort of electronic circuit. If it loses part of a message, it reports that the message didn't go through. Luckily, you don't need to manually configure any transport or user agents — it's automatic. And at the very least, if a message doesn't go through, you normally get an alert to that effect — and far more quickly than you do if the Post Office misplaces your letter.

Another automatic function beyond your control is nationwide e-mail routing. Even if you control a large domain with hundreds of users, your network alone is unlikely to span the entire continent. Whenever you send an e-mail any significant distance, it usually travels across the Internet via multiple routers set up by ISPs (Internet Service Providers) with connections and transport agreements. If a downed server blocks the path, these intelligent machines route your message to its destination. The best part of the system? If you must detour through two or three states, you don't even notice the delay at the speeds that computers work.

Transport Agents That Work With Unix and Linux

Many different transport agents work with both Unix and Linux. Most, however, are obscure. The following two agents are the most common in Unix/Linux:

- ✔ In the Unix world, the *sendmail* transport system is predominant.
- ✔ On the newer systems, particularly in Linux, the *smail* system is now the standard.

Both systems use the *UUCP* (*Unix to Unix Copy Protocol*) and *SMTP* (*Simple Mail Transfer Protocol*) standards.

Sendmail

Sendmail predates smail, which explains its larger installation base and its widespread use among Unix systems. This fact doesn't mean that it's antiquated, however. In fact, sendmail comes with both the Slackware and Red Hat versions of Linux. Sendmail is more stable, particularly in Unix and Linux environments.

Sendmail's workings are the subject of entire courses and book series, so you may want to consider consulting some additional material if you want to become a sendmail guru. Configuring sendmail, however, is pretty basic. Go to the location of the configuration files in the /etc directory and open sendmail.cf. The latest versions of this configuration file are designed in such a way that you get information on what to type and where. The file itself, for example, tells you where to replace the default values with your own computers' hostnames and aliases.

Smail

Smail, often thought of as sendmail's cousin, is more common on Linux systems than on Unix. In essence, you must perform minor edits on the following two files:

```
/usr/local/lib/smail/config
/usr/local/lib/smail/paths
```

In each file, find the text for the entries *Hostname* and *Subdomain*. You want to make the following three changes:

- ✔ Replace the default setting of myhostname with the hostname you decide on for server.
- ✔ Replace the default setting of subdomain.domain with your own domain name.
- ✔ Replace the default setting of my_uucp_neighbor with the UUCP name of your upstream site.

Edit files such as sendmail.cf only if you're familiar with the vi editor in Unix or Linux.

You can get a good overview of how to use this editor from several different books, including *Debian/GNU Linux For Dummies*, *Linux Administration For Dummies*, and *Mastering Red Hat Linux*.

Transport Agents with Windows 2000

Microsoft's made some interesting design choices by moving mail transport and receipt out of the operating system proper and into a separate application such as Explorer, Eudora, or, more recently, Outlook.

Microsoft still uses the TCP/IP protocol family as the strategic enterprise network transport for its platforms. In fact, you must give the company some serious credit for upgrading the variation of the TCP/IP stack that its systems use into a *high-performance, portable 32-bit implementation of the industry-standard TCP/IP protocol*. Reportedly, this upgrade provides greater speed and stability on the system. As far as you're concerned, this newer form of TCP/IP is still recognizable by other operating systems and shouldn't cause you any sleepless nights.

Message Transport Agents with the GroupWise NetWare Utility

A basic *GroupWise* system consists of a single domain with one post office, a document library, and one or more users. Each GroupWise user has a mailbox in the post office; users run the GroupWise client to access their mailboxes and to send mail to and receive mail from other users. GroupWise includes an Installation Advisor and Setup Advisor to step you through the installation and setup of your basic system.

GroupWise uses the following two major parts of the server system to move messages:

- Message Transfer Agent (MTA)
- Post Office Agent (POA)

The MTA (Message Transfer Agent)

The MTA runs at the domain level, which means that you need to run one instance of the MTA for each domain that you create. In addition to routing user messages between post offices and other domains, the MTA routes administration messages from the domain to the post office.

The POA (Post Office Agent)

The POA runs at the post office level, which means that you need to run one instance of the POA for each post office that you create. The POA performs the following tasks:

- ✔ Routes messages within the post office.
- ✔ Updates the post office database as it receives administration messages from the MTA.
- ✔ Performs other maintenance tasks on the post office.

Chapter 16

E-Mail in a Mixed-Network Environment

• •

• •

*A*t the dawn of the Information Age, e-mail was heralded as a way to move information at a speed a quantum leap faster than anything seen before. It was to revolutionize business, bring the world together, and even help prevent cavities. At least, that's what its promoters wanted you to think.

Fast forward to today. If you spend any time connected to the Internet or working in an office environment with an intranet, you know what people really use the bulk of e-mail for. Besides a few office memos, they use it to set up meeting times for polka night at six, offers to join the latest diet fad, or semihumorous jokes that have been around the Internet a half-million times in the last year.

Still, e-mail does hold a tremendous amount of power in relationship to your job. Why? Because if you don't keep it up and running, your user community complains like nobody's business! Becoming reasonably familiar with what you need to do to ensure that your clients are getting their share of office memoranda and knock-knock jokes, therefore, is certainly a worthwhile endeavor.

Use the Force, Luke! Choose Your Mail System Carefully!

E-mail in a mixed environment isn't nearly as tough as it can be as long as you understand the basics. Consider the following three elements, therefore, as much as you may the ten or so commandments (in other words, ignore them at your own peril!):

✔ In planning an e-mail system, choose a mature system, such as GroupWise, Exchange, or Sendmail.

A *mature* system of any sort is one that's been around for a while and enjoys a reputation for being relatively stable. A piece of software that's still undergoing testing (known as a *beta version*) isn't a good choice for a system that needs stability. In addition, always consider the company behind the product. Choosing a product that's ready for prime time does you little good if your supplier is a fly-by-night company that may leave you high and dry when you need emergency services.

✔ Think carefully about using a separate server for your e-mail. E-mail is the toughest part of a server environment to keep up, running, and stable. If the mail server crashes and it's also the file server or Web server, you may get quite a few nasty phone calls from your users.

✔ Ensure that whatever system you choose is both *POP3* and *IMAP* compliant. POP3 and IMAP are the current standards for e-mail sending/receiving protocols, and anything that you use must at least have the capability to use these two standards.

Setting Up E-Mail on an Integrated Network

Setting up e-mail in a mixed environment can prove a long, tedious project unless you follow those three magic words, plan, plan, and *plan*. Do your homework; get advice at the local computer software exposition; visit vendor Web sites; get another system administrator to show you how he did it. Lots of resources and places on the Internet give sound advice for tons of different platforms.

A budget for stampless mailing

One major consideration for small and mid-sized network environments is cost. Up-front costs for many of these systems can run into the thousands, and that can prove a big pill to swallow if you're talking about e-mail. You may find that you can easily convince the decision-maker that you can justify the cost. But if you can't? *Go free!*

Yes, you read right: *free.* Although you can buy Linux products from a given vendor, such as Red Hat or Caldera, you can still download Linux software — and even versions of Linux itself — directly from the Internet at *no* cost to you. If you already run a Linux machine, you know that you need to do a bit of digging to get something going right, but it's usually worth the effort and it saves some cash.

The trick is to get e-mail from everyone to everyone with little or no consideration to the platform you're using. To accomplish this feat, you need to follow standards. If you stick to the standard delivery protocols, all you must do is create a specific standard for your environment with regard to your client software. Doing so makes both your decision and your workload a good deal easier.

The most popular commercial e-mail systems for these NOSes that we discuss in this book include the following:

- Microsoft Exchange
- Novell GroupWise
- Netscape Messaging Server
- Lotus Notes
- Eudora World Mail Server

Buy none, get one free

If you decide to go the free software route, you have (surprisingly) even more choices. Notice that you have many free e-mail clients but not nearly as many servers. Following are some that are worth looking into:

- Sendmail (Unix and Linux and now NT!)
- Mercury (NetWare and now NT!)
- SmartServer3 (NT)
- EMWAC Internet Mail Services for Windows NT
- Eudora Internet Mail Server 1.2 (NT)
- Exim (Unix/Linux)
- Vintra Systems Mail Server (NT)

Two excellent (and free!) IMAP4 servers that you can use are as follows:

- The Cyrus IMAP server (Unix/Linux)
- University of Washington (U.W.) IMAP Server (Unix/Linux)

Consider, too, the following popular, free e-mail client programs:

- **Pegasus Mail for Windows:** Pegasus Mail is a free, standards-based electronic mail client suitable for use by single or multiple users on single computers or on local area networks. A proven product, it's served millions of users since 1990. It's extremely feature-rich and powerful, yet remains small and fast.

- **Eudora Light (Windows):** Eudora Light has been around as long as the hills and is one of the premier free e-mail programs. It's a stripped-down version of the company's commercial application, Eudora Pro, but if all you need is simple e-mail, this free program is a good way to go.

- **Microsoft Outlook Express (Windows):** Outlook Express is the Internet standards-based e-mail client and newsreader shipping with Microsoft Internet Explorer 5.0. Built on open Internet standards, Outlook Express is designed for use with any Internet standard system (POP3, SMTP, and IMAP). New migration tools that automatically import existing mail settings, address-book entries, and e-mail messages from Eudora, Netscape, Microsoft Exchange Server, the Windows Inbox, and Microsoft Outlook enable users to easily get up and running quickly.

Getting the Postman to Visit All Your Machines

Getting e-mail to all your users is where the standards become utterly important. If you choose a server that isn't at least POP3 compliant, you're in for weeks of grief. Ensure that it at least exhibits the following characteristics:

- It's POP3 compliant.
- It's IMAP compliant.

  Note: IMAP is a newer mail protocol and many of the e-mail systems are capable of this protocol.

POP3 and IMAP each have advantages and quirks, as the following sections describe.

POP3 goes the weasel

POP3 is *post-office protocol.* You can do the following with it:

- Keep your mail at a server.
- Download headers.
- Choose which messages you want to download, delete, or read.

Most POP3 clients don't take full advantage of the capabilities of the POP3 protocol and make POP3 a client-centered approach to e-mail.

Lost? Get out the IMAP

IMAP stands for *I*nternet *M*essage *A*ccess *P*rotocol. It's a method of accessing electronic mail or bulletin-board messages that you keep on a (possibly shared) mail server. In other words, it permits a "client" e-mail program to access remote message stores as if they are local. E-mail that you store on an IMAP server, for example, users can manipulate from a desktop computer at home, a workstation at the office, and a notebook computer while traveling, without the need to transfer messages or files back and forth between these computers.

Mail in Windows 2000

You have a couple different methods of setting up mail in Windows 2000, depending on your needs, whether you connect a trio of machines to the Internet or create a self-supporting bank of machines that run an entire company. Setting up connections to stand-alone machines is usually either automated or a task that you can find in the documentation that comes with the machine's purchase.

Doing justice to the larger networks would require a full book on the Enterprise Server. Here, we cover a sort of *middle ground* architecture that's ideal for a small business or group of integrated machines that can use a single server-type connection to the Internet, which enables an ISP's machine to fulfill most mail transactions. The advantage to this methodology is that it's extremely inexpensive, easy to set up and maintain, and results in less network traffic for your machines to handle.

The core of this setup system is the *ICS*, or *Internet Connection Sharing*, feature built into Windows 2000. Designate your fastest Windows 2000 machine as the connection-sharing computer. This machine provides the Internet connection as a sort of *proxy* for the rest of the network. Make sure that the machine you select has two connections: one for the Internet and one to connect it to the rest of the network.

You can have only one ICS host on the network.

You can use a modem or network adapter for the Internet-side connection. For the connection to the rest of the network, you use a secondary NIC (Network Interface Card). To complete the ICS host setup, follow the steps:

1. **Log on as the Administrator account.**

2. **Click Start⇨Settings⇨Network⇨Dial-up Connections.**

3. **Right-click the connection that you want to share.**

4. **Choose Properties from the pop-up menu that appears.**

5. **Click the Internet connection-sharing tab of the Properties dialog box that appears.**

6. **Select the Enable Internet Connection Sharing for this Connection option.**

7. **Click the Enable On-Demand Dialing check box and click OK.**

This setting enables anyone on the network to connect to the Internet via the ISP for either surfing the Web, downloading mail from an off-site server, or sending mail out via the same way.

Configuring your client computers to handle most network connections and e-mail by using this method is also fairly straightforward. You require no special software for any computer running Windows 95, Windows 98, Windows NT, or Windows 2000 Professional. Complete the configuration on each machine by following these steps:

1. **Click Start⇨Settings⇨Network Dial-Up Connections.**

2. **Right-click Local Area Connection.**

3. **Select Properties from the pop-up menu that appears.**

4. **Select the TCP/IP Properties tab from the Properties dialog box.**

5. **Check to make sure that the TCP/IP properties for the NIC are configured to obtain an IP address and DNS server automatically.**

6. **Make sure that the check box showing that you're using DHCP is selected; if not, click to select it.**

7. **Click OK.**

8. **If you need to make any changes in Steps 6 and 7, reboot the machine.**

As a side note on e-mail, the quickest way to pop off an e-mail in Windows 2000 is to click the Start button, choose Run and type in the text box of the Run dialog box that appears **mailto:**. This action automatically opens the New Message screen in Outlook Express — or even in Netscape!

Mail in Unix/Linux

Not to be too terse about it, but we actually have as little to say about configuring the non-GUI forms of e-mail in Unix or Linux here as we do about making server-type changes to Windows 2000 in Chapter 15. That's because both Unix and Linux are more heavily server-based. Changing the `sendmail.conf` file suffices for what you need to edit for the e-mail system.

You may want to do more e-mail setup work if you use Netscape as your e-mail center. Doing so is an increasingly popular notion, because Netscape's settings are roughly the same whether run on a Windows or even a Netscape platform.

For your clients to send and receive e-mail, you need to set up their Netscape Web browsers to connect to a mail server. This server normally is a POP server because of the specific kinds of protocols that hold and send e-mail in Unix and Linux.

To set up a Netscape Web browser to handle e-mail, perform the following tasks:

1. **Open Netscape.**

2. **Choose Edit➪Preferences from the menu bar.**

3. **In the Preferences dialog box that appears, click Mail and Newsgroup Settings.**

4. **Click Mail Servers.**

5. **If you don't see an incoming mail server allocated to you in the Incoming Mail Servers field, click Add to the right of the field.**

    This action enables you to type the name of your mail-server machine in the text box.

6. **Press Enter.**

    You return to Preferences.

Mail in NetWare: Mercury and Mercury/32

Mercury/32 can provide an Internet mail gateway for Novell NetWare file servers or for a non-NetWare network or multiuser installation.

The cool thing about Mercury is that it's free, and you can use different clients to access the e-mail server. (Pegasus is also free and written by the same folks who write Mercury. If you want to do it for free, this route is the way to go!)

Mercury exists in the following two versions:

- A set of Novell NLMs to run on Novell NetWare 3.*x*, 4.*x* or 5.*x* file servers.
- A Win32 application to run on Windows 95, 98, NT4 or 2000.

Both versions have similar feature sets, and both offer special support for Novell NetWare local area networks — the Win32 version can act as a mail server for either NetWare or non-NetWare LANs.

Chapter 17

Configuring News Clients in a Sensible Manner

*T*o talk about configuring news, you first must take a step back and consider what news really is all about in the Information Age. In fact, configuring a computer to handle incoming news is different than any other topic in
the book in one important way: News originates entirely off your integrated
network and so is beyond your control. Essentially, you need an Internet
hookup to even consider it as an option for you.

Whether you want to go to the trouble of configuring news is really up to you.
(More specifically, it's up to the demands of your user community.) News isn't
so much an integral, absolutely necessary part of your network as it is a nice
add-on option. If enough people request news service, see what you can do to
accommodate them. In fact, the majority of ISPs (Internet Service Providers)
send out news content as well as mail, so getting news on your system is usually relatively easy.

WARNING!

If you or your users want to download the entire day's news for several dozen
topics, or newsgroups, prepare to run into system or network slowdown!
News isn't a recommended option if your system has resource shortfalls or
speed issues because of extremely heavy network traffic. In these cases, you
can end up with an extremely slow network response time as the information
from news servers contributes to the large amount of network traffic.

. . . And Now, the News

News itself is rarely the same thing as what you see on *Nightline, 20/20,* or in your local newspaper. More often, it's rather like a section of an electronic bulletin board set up to cater to a particular audience who wants to hear about only one subject — the one to which the newsgroup is dedicated. It's often more about expressing opinion than reading a day's events without getting ink smudges on your fingertips!

Usenet news, often known simply as *Usenet* by frequent readers, is a service that you get solely from the Internet. At last count, more than 11,000 newsgroups were out there dedicated to pursuits as varied as photography (`alt.photography`), games (`misc.games`), and discussions about how cool Captain Jean-Luc Picard of the U.S.S. *Enterprise* is (`alt.sexy.bald.captains`). To get news on any of these groundbreaking topics, you need to configure your news-transport software, which varies from operating system to operating system.

News-transport software is a broad category that denotes any program that you design to carry the news from a news server on the Internet to your system.

News in Windows 2000

Microsoft handles news very much the same as it handles electronic mail — with a conscious effort to move away from handling configuration files directly in the operating system and, instead, to use a specific component of the Microsoft suite of products to handle the work.

Informally, this choice is known as the *Microsoft Exchange* model of doing things, probably because Exchange was the first major front-end component to handle such disparate functions as news, e-mail, and even faxes from the operating system.

The separate application that Microsoft allocates to handle news is the Outlook part of Internet Explorer. As of this writing, Outlook Express is the *de facto* standard program for handling news reading in Microsoft Internet Explorer 5.0. This configuration procedure is, in essence, the same no matter which member of the Windows 2000 Suite you're working with, as the configuration files depend on the version of Outlook that comes with your operating system.

NNTP News for Unix and Linux

NNTP, which stands for *Network News Transport Protocol*, comes built into all current news-handling software for Unix and Linux today. NNTP's success comes from the fact that it was one of the first news programs using the TCP/IP-style protocol in its connection between a news client and a news server. This setup gives the news server several advantages.

First, any Unix or Linux host that keeps Net news in its disk storage stores only complete news articles. TCP/IP's *virtual circuit* error protection re-requests, resends, or drops in their entirety any news messages that cut off, get corrupted, or get out of order while in transit.

You may hear some people referring to news *messages* as *articles*. This reference is part of the newsgroup nomenclature. It's a little misleading, because the *news* in *newsgroups* really consists of postings of advice and opinions by subscribers and not of factual reporting by journalists.

Second, the NNTP's setup enables faster downloading of messages, cutting turnaround delay to an absolute minimum. This faster turnaround, in turn, reduces the number of duplicate articles.

The NNTP server works as either a program that the all-important Internet daemon manages (one controlling all Internet connections on a Unix or Linux box,) or as a standalone server that starts at system boot time. If you decide to run NNTP at boot time, you need to edit the /etc/rc.inet2 file. On the other hand, if you want to start it from the Internet daemon, you can complete the following steps. Make sure that you're familiar with the vi editor before attempting to edit these files or you may end up with a typing error that disables your news system. (For more about daemons, see Chapter 10.)

Unix and Linux both use the same convention for naming their daemons, which is to add a d to the end of the program's or utility's name. The daemon that controls the NNTP process, therefore, is nntpd, and the Internet daemon is inetd.

To start the NNTP server from the Internet daemon, follow these steps:

1. **Turn on your Linux or Unix machine and wait for it to finish booting.**

   After the machine completes the booting process, it displays a Login field in which you enter your user account name.

2. **Type** root **for the account name in the Login field and press Enter.**

   The cursor moves to the Password field.

3. **Type your password and press Enter or click the Login button.**

   As you type your password, it appears on-screen as either a row of asterisks (*) or just blank characters.

   If you type your username and password correctly, you can log in as the administrative account. After you log in, you go to the desktop.

4. **If you're running Linux, open a terminal window by clicking the Terminal button on the toolbar, which displays a computer screen; if you're running Unix, right-click the desktop and choose Tools⇨ Terminal from the pop-up menu that appears.**

   A terminal window appears on the desktop.

5. **In the terminal window, open the Internet daemon file by typing** vi/ etc/inetd.conf **at the command prompt and pressing Enter.**

   The document appears in the terminal window.

6. **Use the up or down arrow keys to scroll through the document to find the following line:**

   ```
   #nntp  stream  tcp  nowait  news  /usr/etc/in.nntpd
          nntpd
   ```

   You must *uncomment* the line to get your news working. A *commented* line in a Unix or Linux file is one that displays a hash mark (#) in front of it, which tells the operating system to ignore the line as if it isn't really there.

7. **Delete the hash mark in front of the line by moving your cursor on top of the # and typing the letter** X **once.**

8. **Save and quit the file by typing** :wq **and pressing Enter.**

   You return to the command prompt.

If you can't find the line to uncomment, it may not exist in the file at all! In that case, you must either use Netscape for your news (available if you have a graphic desktop such as CDE or GNOME — see the following section for information) or type the line yourself. Make sure that you omit the hash mark if you choose the latter course.

9. **Next, open the Internet services file by typing** vi/etc/services **at the command prompt and pressing Enter.**

   The document appears in the terminal window.

10. **Use the up or down arrow keys to scroll through the document to find the following line:**

    ```
    #nntp    119/tcp    readnews  untp    # Network News
             Transfer Protocol
    ```

11. **Uncomment this line by removing the hash mark (#) from in front of it; if the file is missing, type it in the file without the hash mark.**

12. **Create a directory in which to store (or *spool*) your news by typing the following line at the command prompt and pressing Enter:**

```
mkdir /var/spool/news/tmp
```

Doing so creates a news-storage direction in the /tmp directory so that a reboot of the system removes it (your best bet).

13. **Use the chown command to change the ownership of the file to the news system account by typing the following line at the command prompt:**

```
chown news.news /var/spool/news/tmp
```

Netscape: From the GUI Side of Doing Things in Unix and Linux

You can also configure Netscape to handle your news as well as your electronic mail for you. Because of its GUI nature, Netscape news is a lot more user-friendly for many system integrators. This option is the one that we recommend if you're using a recent release of Linux, such as Red Hat 6.2. To configure Netscape to handle news, perform the following steps:

1. **Start Netscape Communicator.**

2. **Choose Edit⇨Preferences from the menu bar.**

   The Preferences screen appears. You see a list of Categories on the left side of the Preference screen. Midway down the list of choices, you see Mail & Newsgroups.

3. **Click the arrow immediately to the left of the Mail & Newsgroups setting.**

   The arrow flips down and you see a list of different categories under the Mail & Newsgroups listing, as shown in Figure 17-1.

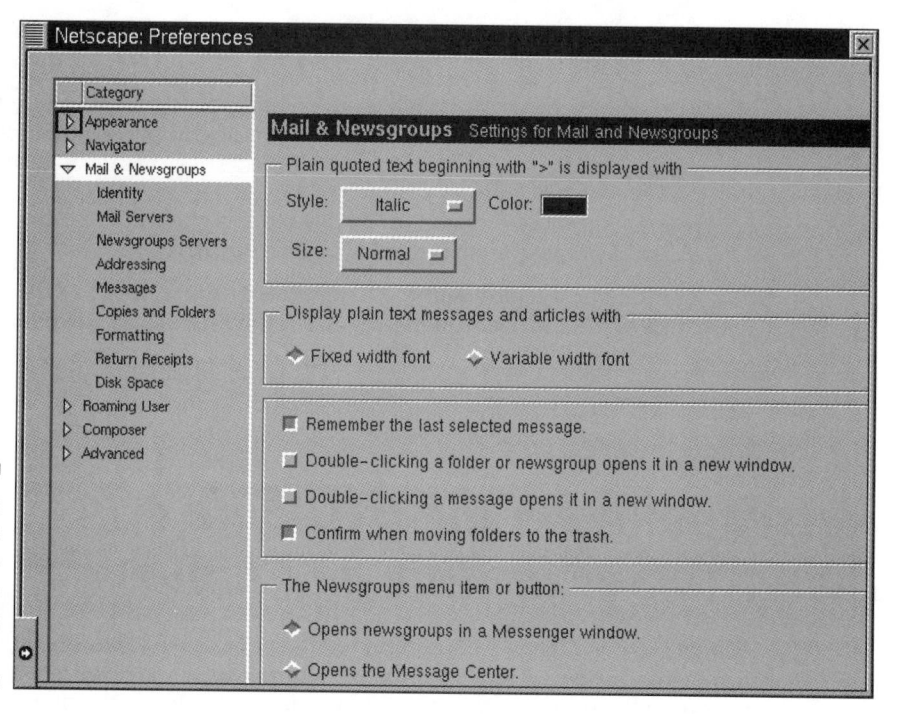

Figure 17-1:
The
Netscape
Preferences
default
screen.

4. Click Newsgroups Servers.

The screen to the right lists your current news server settings, which currently includes only the default News, because you haven't set anything yet. The Newsgroups Servers screen is similar to that shown in Figure 17-2.

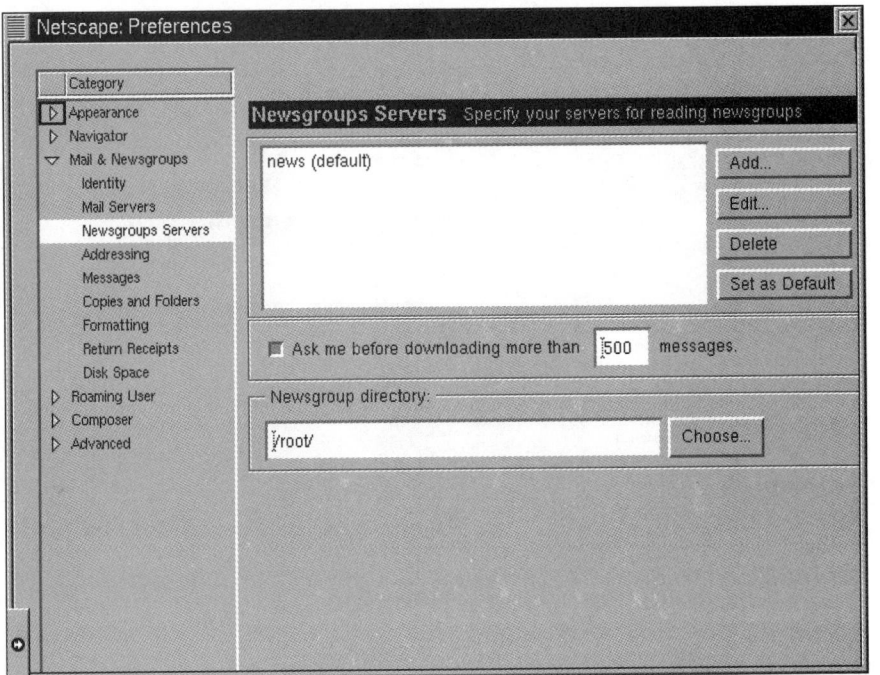

Figure 17-2:
The
Newsgroup
Servers
area on the
Preferences
screen.

5. **If you decide to use the default setting, you can exit the window by clicking the Close button, marked with an X in the upper-right corner.**

   If your ISP uses a news server with a different machine name, however, you need to specify the server's name in this screen.

6. **If necessary, click the Add button and type the appropriate machine name.**

7. **Type the server's name in the blank text box of the new screen that appears, as shown in Figure 17-3, and click OK.**

   You return to the Preferences screen.

8. **To exit the Preferences screen and return to Netscape, click the Close button (marked with an X) in the upper-right corner.**

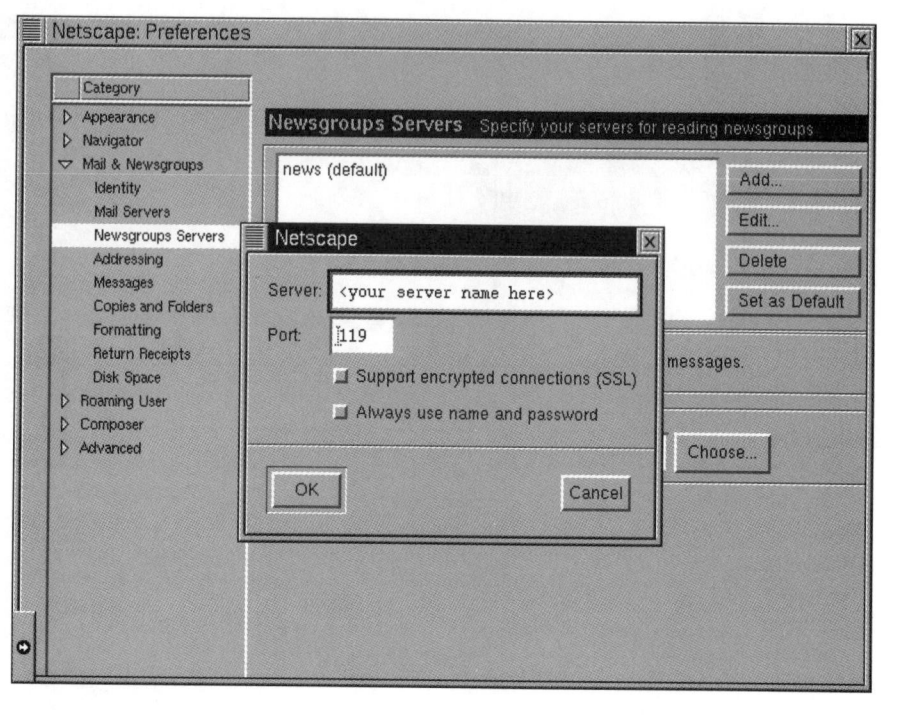

Figure 17-3:
Adding a
new news
server in
Netscape.

Getting News with the NetWare News Server

NetWare's News Server enables you to provide newsgroup and discussion group functionality on your NetWare network. You can provide discussion groups for all your users on the Internet, on your internal network, or on both. You access and read newsgroups by using a standard Web browser, such as Netscape Navigator or Internet Explorer.

Much like the current day versions of Linux, NetWare comes with the best freebie package of them all, the Netscape Web browser. If you recently bought or upgraded your version of NetWare, you have the browser. If, by chance, you lack this marvelous utility or are stuck with an older version of NetWare, you can install NetWare News Server *during* the NetWare 5.1 server installation if you haven't yet completed your NetWare installation. To do so, just follow these steps:

1. **During the start of the NetWare installation, select the Custom button from the Installation Options screen.**

2. **In the Custom window that appears, select Components.**

   The Components screen appears.

3. **Click to select the check box for NetWare News Server.**

4. **Follow the on-screen instructions to complete the installation.**

Installing After the Fact

If you're one of the unfortunate souls who already have NetWare installed without the wonderful Netscape utility, don't despair. Put down the keyboard, take a few deep breaths, and come back whenever you're ready to continue. Remember that we're here to help you. You can install Netscape afterward just as easily (well, almost as easily) as you can during the initial NetWare installation.

To install NetWare News Server *after* the NetWare 5.1 server installation, perform the following steps:

1. **At the NetWare server console, access the servertop by typing the command** STARTX **at the command prompt.**

   A menu appears.

2. **Choose Novell⇨Install⇨Add from the menu.**

   A dialog box appears.

3. **Type the appropriate path into the dialog box to the NetWare News Server files.**

   NetWare News Server files reside on the NetWare 5.1 Operating System CD in the PRODUCTS\NOVONYX directory. To access the CD, you may need to type CDROM at the server console.

4. **Follow the on-screen instructions to complete the installation.**

After you install the News Server, you can complete the set up and configuration NetWare News Server by using the NetWare Web Manager program.

Part VI
Security and Troubleshooting

The 5th Wave   By Rich Tennant

"You the guy having trouble staying connected to the network?"

In this part . . .

Throughout this book, you see how to connect machines that seem to have very little in common with each other besides the fact that they use monitors and keyboards. This is because no matter what, computers must be able to talk with each other, or you have a heap of powered silicon, not an integrated network! Putting all the pieces together is an impressive job, akin to completing a large jigsaw puzzle without knowing what the completed picture is really supposed to look like.

After you've completed the puzzle, ensure that no one and nothing will take it apart again! You have to contend with unscrupulous individuals who will try to crack your security, events that will wipe out your hard drives, and natural disasters like electrical storms, random blackouts, or the comeback of disco music and platform shoes.

By the way, we're kidding about the disco music and platform shoes.

Really.

Chapter 18

File and Network Security — Building Your Silicon Fort Knox

*Y*ou really have two kinds of security in an integrated environment: nonexistent security and vulnerable security. Unfortunately, you must live with the fact that anything that a human being can put together, another human being can take apart. The same goes for cracking passwords, picking locks, or sneaking onto a network. In this chapter, we take a look at some of the methods you can use to secure your environment physically (to prevent theft or vandalism) and electronically (to prevent the misuse of a person's user account).

Vulnerable security is much, much better than nonexistent security, because the people who actually can hack onto a secure network are generally few and far between. If your network really does contain valuable information that others may go to great lengths to despoil, make sure that you augment any instructions that we provide in this chapter with a good vendor security product.

In addition, some operating systems are more prone to network cracking than are others. Unix and Linux, for example, were designed from the start as open systems in that they're extremely network-friendly. The flip side is that they're easier to get into if you know how to crack a password or sneak by a firewall. If you need information on higher level security to protect Unix- or Linux-based Web servers and databases, see the book *Linux Security Toolkit*, by David A. Bandel (also published by IDG Books Worldwide).

Real System Integrators Use . . . the Club!

Ironically, the most overlooked part of any security scheme is also the simplest, on average, to cure — the physical component. Industrial and technological sabotage, not to mention just plain, old-fashioned thievery, is unfortunately not an unknown thing these days. And if you work in a setting where dozens of users come in and out the doors every day, your security situation is tenuous indeed if you don't attend to physical locks as well as screen-saver locks.

Physical locks can include everything from a sophisticated keypad and magnetic pass to a humble iron padlock. Today, most bulk-rate computer vendors include a kind of case-lock system for little or no additional cost if you buy computers by the dozen. A *case lock* is essentially a locking case that prevents someone from accessing a computer unless they have a key.

The most common kind of physical lock that you find today is a *cable lock*. This component is sort of like a bicycle lock in that it's simply a steel cable that connects the keyboard, CPU, and monitor and chains the entire combo to a fixed object or base in the wall.

If you lock a piece of hardware to another object, use your common sense. Make sure that someone can't simply steal the object along with the hardware, or just break it off to get to the hardware.

Screen Locks — A Way of Life

Screen locks are the absolute beginning of network security for any operating system with a *GUI* (*Graphic User Interface*). Such systems include Windows 2000, GNOME and KDE in Linux, and CDE or OpenWindows in Unix. Essentially, if you leave a machine alone for a period of time, the screen saver appears, blocking out the view of the desktop, and it doesn't permit you to return to the desktop until you type your password.

Although they don't help against a determined hacker, screen locks do ensure that, if you leave your machine unattended, no one can tamper with or look at your work. Each of the GUI-based (or -capable) systems uses its own method of activating this feature. Because screen locks aren't an integrated or networked function, you generally must go to each monitor on your network and manually enter the settings that we describe in the following sections, depending on the operating system in question, to activate them.

Locking the screen in Linux

You can most easily implement the screen-locking feature in Linux from the GNOME desktop, which is the default setting for some of the most popular brands of Linux today, such as Red Hat. To configure your screen saver to use the screen-lock feature, follow these steps:

1. **Click the Main Menu button on the GNOME panel.**

   A pop-up menu appears on-screen.

2. **Choose Settings⇨Desktop⇨Screensaver, as shown in Figure 18-1.**

   The Screensaver window appears.

3. **Select the Require Password check box, which you can see in Figure 18-2.**

   You don't need to make up a new password, as the screen saver simply requires your current user-account password.

4. **Click OK to exit.**

   The next time that you leave your computer idle, the screen saver turns on. After you move the mouse or touch the keyboard, the screen saver displays a small window asking you to type your user name and password.

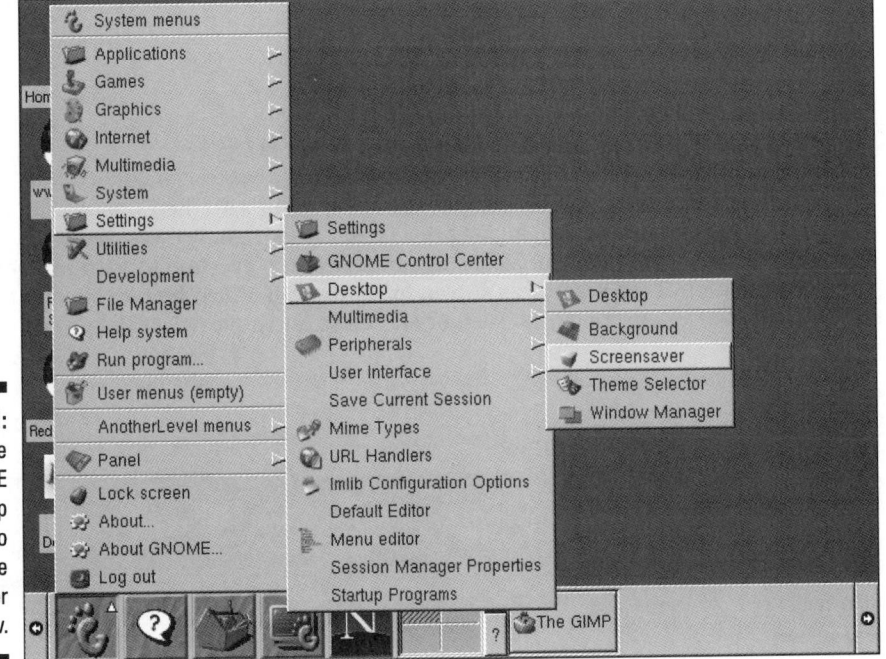

Figure 18-1:
Use the GNOME pop-up menus to access the Screensaver window.

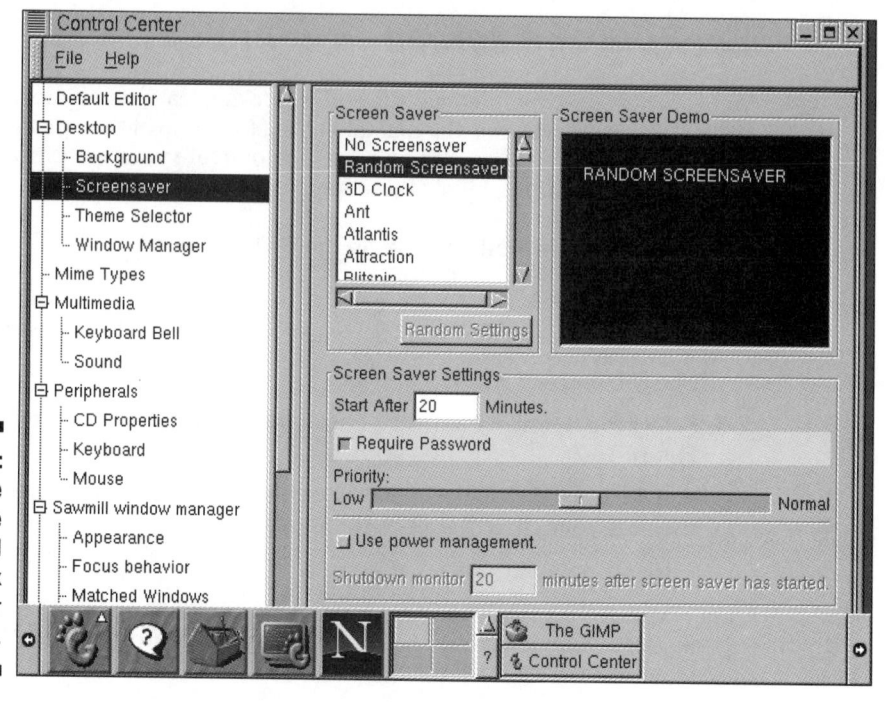

5. **Type your user account name and password and press Enter.**

You return to your desktop.

Locking the screen in Unix

If you're using a standard installation of Unix with the Common Desktop
Environment (CDE), locking the screen is extremely easy. Simply locate the
small button that looks like a padlock, which you find toward the bottom
center of the screen, as shown in Figure 18-3. Click the button, and the computer opens a blank screen or screen saver to block out the desktop.

Figure 18-3:
The basic
CDE screen
and the
padlock
button in
the center.

The next time that you leave your computer idle, the screen saver turns on. After you move the mouse or touch the keyboard, the screen saver displays a small window asking you to type your user name and password.

You can unlock the computer by typing your user-account password. The desktop reappears, and you can continue working where you left off.

The Windows 2000 screen — standing by

If you set your Windows 2000 computer to enter standby mode, the screen saver turns on and locks your computer until you enter your password. Be aware, however, that while the computer's in standby mode, it doesn't place on the hard disk information that you haven't yet saved to the computer's hard drive. If an interruption in power occurs, you lose any unsaved information!

Configure the standby mode by following these steps:

1. **Click the Start button and choose Settings⇨Control Panel.**

   The Control Panel appears on-screen.

2. **Double-click the Power Options icon, which, appropriately, appears in the shape of a battery.**

   The Power Options Properties window appears on the desktop.

3. **Click the downward-pointing arrow at the right of the Power Schemes drop-down list box and select a power scheme from the list, as shown in Figure 18-4.**

   A _Power Scheme_ tells the computer what to do to reduce power usage if you leave the computer idle. Because you're leaving a running machine idle, including password settings is useful so that no one can enter the system.

4. **Click OK to accept your settings.**

   The next time that you leave your computer idle, the screen saver turns on. After you move the mouse or touch the keyboard, the screen saver displays a small window asking you to type your user name and password.

5. **Type your user account name and password on the indicated lines and press Enter.**

   You return to your desktop.

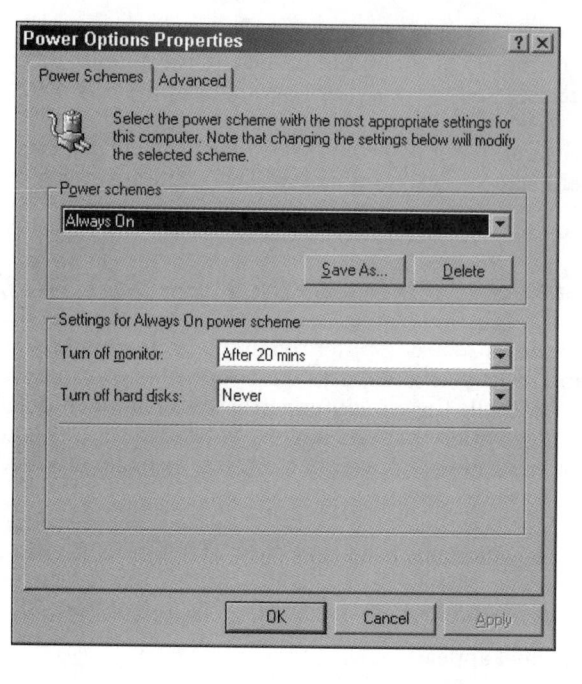

Figure 18-4:
The Power
Options
Properties
window
with sample
settings.

The Shadow File in Unix and Linux

The /etc/shadow *file* stores user and password information in the same manner as the /etc/passwd file does. What sets the shadow file apart is that no user account (except for the administrative root account) can read the shadow file at all. Many administrators like to use this feature to keep the password file private from curious users or crackers searching for passwords to get into the system or attain privileges that aren't due them.

By default, Linux and Unix systems provide the option to use shadow passwords, but this capability isn't automatically active. You can activate the shadow file for your passwords by using the pwconv command, which is short for *password conversion*. This command copies the fields in the /etc/passwd file into the shadow file and hides them from all users except the root account.

To activate shadow passwords, complete the following steps:

1. **Log in to your machine as the root account.**

   If you need a refresher on this process, see Chapter 8.

2. **Type** cd/etc **at the command prompt and press Enter.**

3. **Type** `pwconv` **at the command prompt and press Enter.**

This procedure creates the shadow file and hides it from all prying eyes (except yours, of course, whenever you log in as root)!

Viewing the Security Log in Windows 2000

An additional utility available to you in Windows 2000 is the *Security Log*. You can check the Windows 2000 Security Log whenever you suspect a breach of security, such as a pilfered password. To open and view the security log, follow these steps:

1. **Click the Start button and choose Computer Management from the Start menu.**

The Computer Management screen appears on the desktop displaying two sections or panes.

2. **In the console tree in the lefthand pane, click the Event Viewer icon.**

A list of subheadings appear below it in the left pane.

3. **Double-click the icon in the Security Log subheading.**

The Security Log appears in the right pane.

In the right details pane, examine the list of events for suspicious events, such as multiple logins from the Administrator account when the administrator wasn't scheduled to perform maintenance or upgrades to the machine.

Security in NetWare

To grant permissions in NetWare, we suggest that you use the ConsoleOne utility. Of course, using NetWare Admin from a PC is just as good, but if you're truly security conscious, you want to do all your work from the console and not remotely. This practice prevents an unscrupulous hacker from listening in on the information you're sending in from your remote location.

ConsoleOne comes with Novell Directory Services (NDS) to manage NDS objects and the NetWare file systems. You can also use NetWare Administrator to manage these same objects. ConsoleOne provides most of the functionality of NetWare Administrator, but you still need NetWare Administrator to perform certain management functions. NDS Manager provides management of NDS partitions and replicas.

To read more about ConsoleOne and the latest on its limitations and capabilities, visit the following location on Novell's Web site:

```
www.novell.com/documentation/lg/consol13/docui/index.html#../
                 cl_enu/data/h4cs7lt9.html
```

The NetWare Permission Checker

Within the Novell Script for NetWare components, you find the *Permission Checker* utility. This utility is specifically designed to check user rights for Web pages. The Permission Checker component works with *Novell Directory Services (NDS)* and the Web server to determine whether a Web user has access permissions to a particular file in a Web server.

If a Web page contains hyperlinks, you can also use the permission checker to see whether a user has permissions for the target Web pages. If the user doesn't have the necessary permissions, you can remove or change the hyperlinks to target those pages that the user may not access.

Check Novell's Script for NetWare site for the location of the current Permission Checker that they're supporting by visiting the following address:

```
www.novell.com/documentation/lg/nscript/nscr_enu/data/hie8qzz
                 6.html
```

NetWare Authentication Services

Unlike the other networked operating systems that we discuss in this book, NetWare doesn't automatically integrate authentication systems to the same degree. That doesn't mean to say, however, that authentication doesn't exist! Novell actually offers a really strong security product that it specifically makes for remote-access solutions, the *BorderManager Authentication Services* utility. It provides security for the network manager who wants to grant dial-in access.

Border Manager provides security, manageability, and confidence for remote network access. It's a standards-based solution and uses *RADIUS* (*R*emote *A*uthentication *D*ial-*I*n *U*ser *S*ervice) server data along with user authentication rights and dial-in configuration information. It's also capable of stronger authentication by using token-based technologies within NDS. It provides a single point of administration and consolidates the management of remote services.

The following list describes some features of the Border Manager:

- **Support for ActivCard and SecurID strong-token authentication technologies:** These are third-party technologies that you use for user authentication via dial-in and Virtual Private Network access to your NetWare servers.

- **Audit logging to enhance user support:** This feature enables you to log activities so that you can troubleshoot and isolate problems for users.

- **Accounting features for departmental billing:** This feature enables you to provide reports of usage if your organization bills its departments for network or resource usage.

- **Implementation of user callback for extra security:** This feature requires a dial-in user to dial into the system, hang up, and wait for a callback from the NetWare server itself.

- **Capability to choose virtually any dial-in software:** This feature simply means that NetWare doesn't care what software you use to dial in with.

- **Administration through NDS:** Best of all, you can administer all these features within NDS — a single point of administration.

NetWare Intrusion Detection

NetWare makes intruder detection available within its *containers*, or *objects*, for users. This feature is off by default, but you can easily turn it on for multiple users if you need to. You can, therefore, turn on Intrusion Detection for one user, five users, or as many as you want. The feature even enables you to set Intrusion Detection on within a specific container for a specific user. This capability is handy for catching folks who try to hack or access certain sensitive data areas, such as HR records or payroll data.

In NWADMIN, you can change the properties for multiple users by manually selecting a group of users (by pressing and holding the Shift or Ctrl key while clicking different user names) or by selecting a group object and then going to the Object drop-down list and selecting Details on Multiple Users. From there, you modify the properties for multiple users.

You currently have no way to set the Intruder Detection from the root for the entire tree. You must make changes to existing users within each individual container and by selecting Details on Multiple Users. By using a standard user template (known as User Template in the NDS tree of your system), you can accomplish the desired result of having the same Intruder Detection values for all containers in the tree as you're adding new users.

If you're going to enable Intruder Detection on everyone anyway, consider creating a user template with Intruder Detection on so that, every time you add a new user, this template applies to that user and is automatically on. (For more information on how to create a user template, see *Networking With NetWare For Dummies,* by Ed Tittel, Earl Follis, and James E. Gaskin, published by IDG Books Worldwide, Inc.)

You can use the following command to stop someone that you determine is a threat from logging in:

```
DISABLE LOGIN
```

Note: This command stops *all* users from logging in. If someone just got fired, however, it may be useful to implement it until that person leaves the building . . . .

Use this command to prevent users from logging in whenever you're making repairs, backing up files, or loading software. This command doesn't affect users who are already logged in. A user who logs out, however, can't log in again until you execute the ENABLE LOGIN command.

NetWare Auditing

Where the other network operating systems use security logs and use auditing only for user-account space and processes, NetWare uses auditing in a security role. This feature is especially useful if you suspect tampering or poking around in areas where people don't belong. Whether such an incident is by accident or otherwise, you may need to produce proof that someone did (or didn't) do something on a NetWare system.

AUDITCON is your friend in this case, and you must stay on friendly terms with AUDITCON so that it gives you the correct information when you need it. In other words, don't abuse your friend by turning on auditing on every little thing and event on your server. If you do that, AUDITCON becomes a bad utility and eventually slows your system and fills your disks with logs.

To get AUDITCON, follow these steps:

1. **Log in to the network.**

2. **Run AUDITCON from a network drive (for example, Z) by entering the following command at the command prompt:**

   ```
   Z:\PUBLIC\AUDITCON
   ```

3. **Press Enter.**

   AUDITCON displays a screen that includes a header, a menu area, and a footer line, which indicates that it's running normally.

In AUDITCON, you see a list of the following items:

- Audit directory services
- External auditing
- Audit files maintenance
- Auditing configuration
- Auditing reports
- Reports from old offline file
- Change current server
- Display audit status

Those are the main things that you can do in and view with the utility; if you need a quick review on any of these functions, see Chapter 13.

NetWare also provides the following two general methods of performing surveillance of users' accesses to protected resources:

- *Post-processing* is a method of filtering an existing audit trail to present only the events that are of interest. AUDITCON provides menus to define post-processing filters for volume, container, and external auditing.

- *Preselection* is a method of causing the server to record selected event types (such as opening files), specific users, or specific resources (such as files or directories) to the current volume trail. For volume auditing, you can preselect by event types, users, and files.

A final word: Why to become paranoid enough to care about security

The simple answer is that, concerning security issues, paranoia is a *good* thing. You know friends that you can trust, neighbors to whom you may give the keys to your house to pick up your mail while you're on vacation, and so on. But in dealing with corporate documentation and records, you need to take a page from the *X-Files* and trust no one.

What's funny, really, is that people get really irrational about secrets, and that's essentially what these types of documents are — secrets of the company or organization. Do you recall the Walker case, where an entire family of Navy and former Navy personnel stole secrets from the US Navy for more than 15 years and accumulated a meager $250,000 collectively for their efforts? Now *that* was rather shortsighted for what they gave away.

But the moral that you want to take away from this tale is that, if you have any connections with organizational sections, being paranoid is often worth your while.

Chapter 19

Crash and Burn? Not if You Prepare and Plan

● ●

In This Chapter

▶ Looking at your backup options

▶ Creating a plan — your backup policy

▶ Backing up in Unix, Linux, NetWare, and Windows 2000

● ●

*A*ll great things come to an end eventually. The Roman Empire. The horse-drawn carriage. The original *Star Trek* series. And, yes, even the smooth running of your integrated network. And this end often comes in the form of a system crash that causes the loss of countless bytes of data as well as countless hours of sleep for the careless administrator — and the arrival of untold spam e-mails.

This fate, however, isn't what awaits you. Not if you take the advice that this chapter contains. Whether you select one method of preparation or many is irrelevant. What matters is that you choose one and follow through by regularly updating your personal insurance policy known as a *backup*.

Backup Options: CDs and Floppies and Tapes, Oh My!

A long time ago, back when bell-bottom pants and platform shoes were actually (cringe) in style (well, the first time anyway), you had only one choice for backing up your system: nine-track tape. Today, you face a proliferation of different media for use in backing up your system. Which medium you decide to use depends mostly on your budget, your needs, and your patience to wait.

The following list describes your choices:

- ✔ **Floppies:** Still the most ubiquitous storage device around, a typical floppy disk is a cost-effective method of storing files for a short period of time. The drawbacks to floppies are that they hold very limited amounts of data (1.4MB) and that they're physically quite fragile. You're best off if you stick to using floppies only for storing personal files or system configuration files, which at least assist you in returning a crashed system back to normal.

- ✔ **Removable disks, or *zip* drives:** Removable disks are fully enclosed disk units that you insert into a drive as you need them. These disks, similar to floppies, are very portable, but they're slightly more durable. The most prolific vendors of these drives are SyQuest and Iomega. The main disadvantage of this type of storage was, at one time, the price per megabyte that you could save, but this situation is drastically changing as the marketplace begins to embrace zip drives more heartily.

  One final limitation that's rapidly coming down is the need for well-written zip-drive device drivers for Linux and Unix. Make sure that you check the vendor's Web site to see whether a driver exists yet for your machine — particularly if it's an older Sun box or an ancient flavor of Linux.

- ✔ **Writable CD-ROMs:** Another relatively new technology to consider is the CD-ROM. Buying a stack of CD-ROMs and a jukebox-style CD-ROM *burner* (so known because it literally burns the data into the disk) is a very cost-effective solution for large networks. With most systems, however, you can't wipe the CD-ROM and reuse it, which makes this option more attractive for systems that you don't need to back up regularly (so that you don't end up awash in CD-ROMs).

- ✔ **Hard drives:** Whether internal or external, a separate hard drive is in many ways the cheapest and simplest way of copying files for backup. Always keep in mind, however, that this system faces the following two large problems:

  Lack of portability. If your building burnsdown, gets hit by a tornado, or gets stomped on by Godzilla, everything in the building gets burned/blown/stomped as well. Yes, you *can* carry around a hard drive, but don't try jamming one into the pockets of your jeans.

  File-system incompatibility. Often, files from different operating systems just don't mix. You may face serious problems storing, say, Windows files on a Linux hard drive because the file-allocation tables are completely different.

- ✔ **Tape drives:** The old standby of the backup guru, magnetic tape is still a very popular option. On today's systems, 8mm and 4mm drives are the most common. Because this area is also changing very rapidly (new storage benchmarks seem to come out literally every other week), make sure that you pick the vendor and price point that you're most comfortable with.

Although many tout magnetic tapes as more durable than other forms of media, always remember that magnetic tapes have one major weakness: vulnerability to heat. Nothing's quite like a couple hours on a hot dashboard to reduce a billion bytes to magnetic slag.

Eight- and 4mm tapes come in two grades. The grading refers to the placement and grain of the magnetic particles on the tape. You use a *rough grade* in audio or video recording. What you want is the *data-quality grade* that reliably stores your text, graphics, and binary files, no matter which machine (Unix, NetWare, Windows, whatever) you use.

The What and When of Saving

What you need to do *before* a system crash occurs is to save the all-important files on your system. You must understand this key point as a system integration person. Computers, floppy drives, programs, and operating systems come and go. You can, at worst, replace them with a quick jog down to the local Silicon Toys Emporium. What makes your network unique (at least to your users) are the files that your users store on the machines. The company payroll. The R&D lab reports. The autographed e-mail from Steve Jobs.

To this end, you need to do some planning about what kind of backups you're going to make and what kind of backup media you intend to use. You must decide when and how often you want to schedule your backups. All this stuff is known as a *backup policy*.

In deciding how to set up a backup policy, always use the KISS system: Keep It Short and Simple. Never, *ever* base a backup policy on budgetary flukes, such as "I can use whatever money is left at the end of the quarter to buy backup equipment." Similarly, don't base backups on perceived company policies, such as "Well, marketing traditionally doesn't do much in June, so I can skip their backup."

Instead, you want to base a backup policy on different, less subjective elements. These elements include available resources, how busy your system is, how often users update files, and the importance of the files in question. Keep in mind that you may need to gather some of this information discreetly. After all, if you start asking "Whose data is most important?" you get the same answer from each and every department: "*Ours* is the most important!"

With that fact in mind, consider using one of the following proposed models for your backup policy. Use the suggested guidelines as a way of gauging what level of backup you need.

The quarterly backup

Not surprisingly, quarterly backups are popular in corporate America because corporations conduct many things, such as company finances, on a quarterly system. Unfortunately for you, the hapless integrator/administrator, no one ever thinks that backups can affect the company's stock price. This line of thinking changes, however, immediately after a system crash occurs, and you don't want to be in the hot seat.

Consider performing a quarterly backup if the files that you need to save are mostly personal in nature. Losing a company payroll is very poor form, but losing a company's daily memo is a minor annoyance. In addition, if your users store minimal amounts of data, and you rely on a relatively decentralized system, you don't need to do serious backups. The reason is that, on a decentralized system, most people store data on their personal hard drives or on floppies and not on the central server.

The monthly backup

The monthly backup plan is often more appropriate for the majority of faster-paced businesses in the technology world. In these companies, computer information is more network-based. In other words, although you set up the system to hand users their e-mail, the e-mail itself resides on a central server. This server is more efficient, but it's also a vulnerable point of failure.

The pace of the company is more important as well. If the company keeps departmental or financial files that change on a monthly basis, such as in the case of a mortgage loan office that pegs its rates to monthly changes in the Prime Rate, you need to do backups every 30 days.

The weekly backup

Plan on doing a weekly backup if your situation requires you to continuously run a bank of servers to support your user community. In this case, your users are continuously storing most of their daily product on the servers.

Adding to the equation is the fact that your community is constantly using the network as the backbone of its communication and storage system. If your company is storing valuable financial or technical information, you want to consider a weekly backup to prevent serious failures from crippling how the company conducts its business.

The daily backup

Daily backups are a troubling solution to recommend. In the first place, working at a company that needs backups every day is rare unless you work on a stock-trading floor or at the U.S. military's subterranean Missile Command Center. Daily backups take up system resources and a lot of system time, so consider doing them only if you work in a heavy research environment where daily changes in the data are unique, financially valuable, or completely irreplaceable.

If you work for a company that makes, say, pencil sharpeners, and the company insists that its work is so important that you must do backups every day, consider talking to an employment agency. Organizations that insist on this level of insane backups tend to be poor long-term employers because they don't restrict such demands to one area.

Backing Up in Unix and Linux

Both the Unix and Linux systems use a command-line utility known as tar to back up and restore files on a system as a regular part of system maintenance. tar started out in the distant past (as far as Unix and Linux are go, that is) as a very reliable and effective way to compress and store many large files on a magnetic tape unit. In fact, tar actually stands for *tape archive resource*.

Because of its intrinsic reliability, tar's role has since expanded, and you can now use it to compress all kinds of files to either a magnetic tape, zip drive, hard drive, or floppy disk. Although some of the variables that work with tar seem obscure at first, they're actually pretty easy to work with. Refer to Table 19-1 for a list of the more popular command options in tar.

Table 19-1	tar **Command Options**
Command Option	*What It Does*
-c	Creates a new tar file.
-f	Uses an archive file or a device F (default /dev/rmt0).
-r	Appends the new tar files to the end of an archive.
-t	Lists the contents of a tar archive.
-x	Extracts a tar file.
-v	Replies verbosely while processing files.

A sample `tar` operation

Follow these steps to run a backup operation by using `tar`:

1. **Open a Linux or Unix terminal.**

2. **Type the following at the command prompt:**

   `tar -cvf` *<file to backup> <location to store the backup>*

3. **Press Enter.**

   You get a listing of the files that `tar`'s compressing as it happens. The reason is that you're selecting the `-v`, or verbose, option with the preceding `tar` command. Using this option is always best, even if it's a little slower, because it enables you to monitor the progress of the job.

   After the backup is complete, you return to the command prompt.

4. **Type `ls` *<location to store the backup>* and press Enter to list the files in that location.**

   Your new `tar` file is complete.

Without exception, all files that you compress by using `tar` the system appends with the letters *tar*.

A sample restore operation

To restore the file in your current location, follow these steps:

1. **Type the following at the command prompt:**

   `tar -xvf` *<backed up file>*

   Notice that if you're un-`tar`-ing a file in a *different* location, you need to type the full pathname of the file or `tar` refuses to work.

   To un-`tar` a file to /root, for example, you type the following at the prompt:

   `tar -xvf` *<backed up file>* /root

2. **Press Enter.**

   You see a list of the entire contents as `tar` uncompresses the file. (The reason is that you again use the `-v`, or verbose, option in the preceding command.)

For more help with `tar`, type **tar –help** at the command prompt and press Enter.

The double-whammy compression technique: gzip **and** tar

You can also use a different utility built into the vast majority of Unix and Linux systems: gzip. gzip stands for *Gnu-zip*, and you can use it alone or in conjunction with tar. In benchmark testing, gzip's proved slightly than tar faster and compresses more space out of one kind of file — the text file.

You most commonly use it alongside tar to get an extra 10 percent or so out of a compression job. To do so, first tar a file; then gzip the tar file by typing the following at the command line and pressing Enter:

gzip <file to compress>

In such cases, the resulting file has two suffixes, such as *file*.tar.gz. To restore the file, first type the following at the command line and then press Enter:

gunzip <file that's compressed>

Next, un-tar the file. You can undo the compression commands only in the reverse order from how you initiate them.

Backing Up in NetWare

NetWare comes with a service option known as *SMS* (*Storage Management Services*). SMS enables you to back up targets such as the NDS, binderies, the file system, or hard drives on individual workstations to media such as a tape drive for off-site storage. And SMS gives you a periodic view (daily, weekly, or monthly) of your data. Then, if you experience a hardware failure, a natural catastrophe, corrupted data, or an incorrect deletion of (or change in) data, you can retrieve a previous version of the data.

The primary backup parts of SMS

The following SMS components are the primary parts that you use for backups and restores with SMS:

- ✔ *Storage Management Engine* (*SME*), which you use for backup and restore operations.
- ✔ *Storage Management Data Requester* (*SMDR*) passes communication between the backup program and the Target Service Agents (TSAs) software.
- ✔ The *storage device interface* passes information between the SME and the storage device.
- ✔ *Device drivers* control the behavior of the storage devices.

✔ *Target Service Agents* (*TSAs*) pass requests and commands between the SME and server or NDS database, and they prepare the data for the SME. You must load the TSA500 on the server where you're going to back up the file system data.

✔ *TSAProxy* (*TSADOS* for a DOS workstation) registers the workstation with the host server. TSAProxy also identifies and keeps track of the stations waiting for backups. It receives I am here messages from workstations available for a backup. The TSAProxy keeps the names of these workstations in an internal list and displays the list, enabling you to select a target for a backup or restore procedure.

Tidbits about the restore session

A restore session restores data from a backup. The restore session produces the requested data, which it retrieves from the storage media and restores to the location you specify. If an error occurs during the restore session, it appends an error message to the error file on the host server.

The error file carries the same description that you give the backup session (such as *Friday's Full Backup*), and you access it through the Log/Error File Administration option of the Enhanced SBACKUP Main Menu.

The error file may reside in the default directory (sys:system/tsa/log) or in another directory that you specify during the backup or restore session.

During a restore session, *Enhanced SBACKUP* reads the backup storage media, and the TSA compares the media data set to the existing hard drive data set. The TSA evaluates each data set.

For details on backing up and restoring your NetWare files, consult your system manual or check out the appropriate page on Novell's Web site (at www.novell.com).

Backing Up in Windows 2000

As long as you have administrative privileges on your local group, you can back up any files on machines belonging to a local group. If you want to back up files on any given computer in the domain, you need to be the administrator on the domain controller machine. (Turn to Chapter 8 for more information on the characteristics and limitations of the administrative account.)

Using the Windows 2000 Backup utility

You can use the Backup utility in Windows 2000 to back up data on either
FAT or NTFS volumes. This versatility is useful because you can back up files
from any kind of Windows machine — from Windows 2000 Professional to
Windows 3.1. The Backup utility limits you, however, from saving Unix, Linux,
or NetWare files, which you must store in their own file formats. To handle
backups for those machines, consider using a separate tape, zip, or floppy
drive.

To use the Windows 2000 Backup utility, follow these steps:

1. **Click the Start button.**

2. **Click Programs⇨Accessories⇨System Tools⇨Backup.**

   The Backup utility screen appears (see Figure 19-1).

3. **Click the Job menu and then select the New option from it.**

4. **Click the check box next to any drive, folder, or file that you want to
   back up.**

   Clicking the box puts an *X* in it, which selects that item. Notice that if
   you select a folder, you save everything in the folder; if you select a
   drive, you save everything on the entire drive.

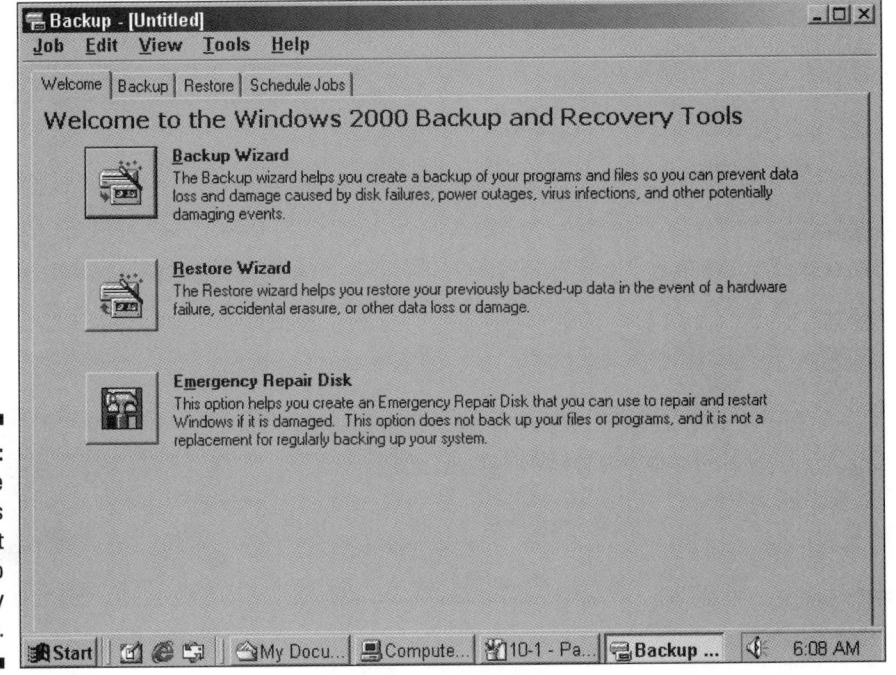

Figure 19-1:
The
Windows
2000 default
Backup
utility
screen.

5. **Select the backup destination.**

   You do so by choosing either a storage device (whichever installed backup equipment Windows detects) or a file location. (If Windows 2000 doesn't detect an installed tape drive, it selects this second option by default).

6. **Click the Backup tab.**

   You return to the Backup utility's main screen.

7. **Click the Start Backup button (see Figure 19-2).**

Restoring files in Windows 2000

To restore your files in Windows 2000, follow these steps:

1. **Click the Start button.**

2. **Click Programs⇨Accessories⇨System Tools⇨Backup.**

   The Backup utility screen appears.

3. **Click the Restore tab.**

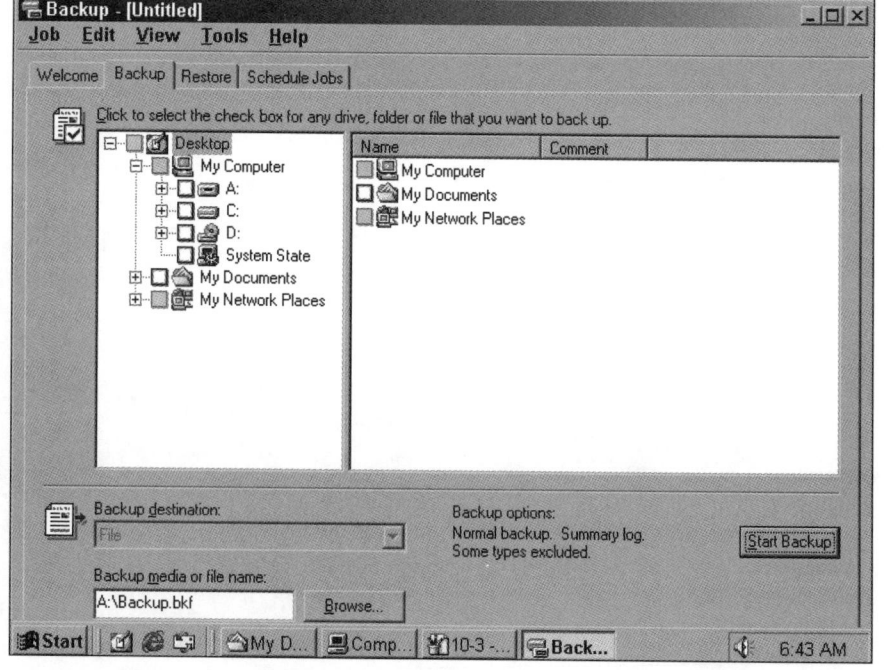

Figure 19-2:
To start the backup session, click the Start Backup button from the Backup utility's main screen.

4. **Select the files that you want to restore by clicking them.**

5. **Select the restoration location for your backed-up files.**

The Restore function in the Backup utility provides you with the following three choices for the location of your restoration (see Figure 19-3):

The original folder where the data was located. If you're trying to restore a system from scratch, this option is your best bet.

An alternative location. This option is the best to use if you don't want to overwrite any of the files that currently exist on your drive.

A single folder. Because the restore dumps all files are unceremoniously into this location, this option is useful only if you don't want to return to the old file structure.

Next, the Backup utility automatically opens the Options dialog box, which enables you to select how you want to go about restoring old files.

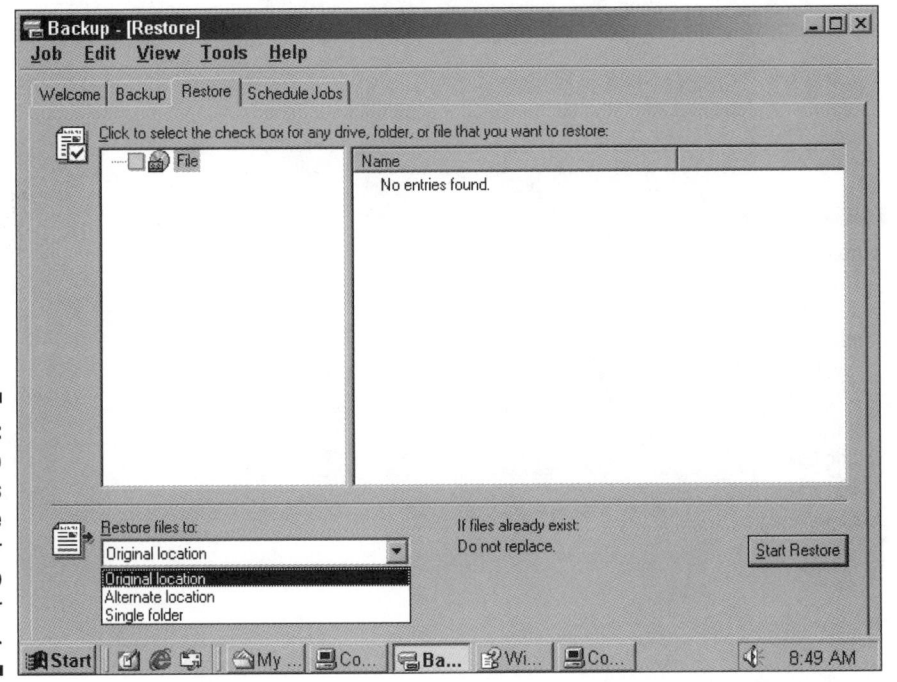

Figure 19-3:
The Backup utility gives you three options for where to restore your files.

6. **Click the Restore Tab to view the available options (see Figure 19-4).**

7. **Set the restore options.**

   Your options are as follows:

   Do not replace the file on my computer.

   Replace the file on disk only if the file on disk is older.

   Always replace the file on my computer.

   The first option, which is the default, is the recommended one.

8. **Click OK to Start the restore operation.**

   The Backup utility prompts you with a dialog box to confirm that you're ready to restore data.

9. **Click Yes to complete the operation.**

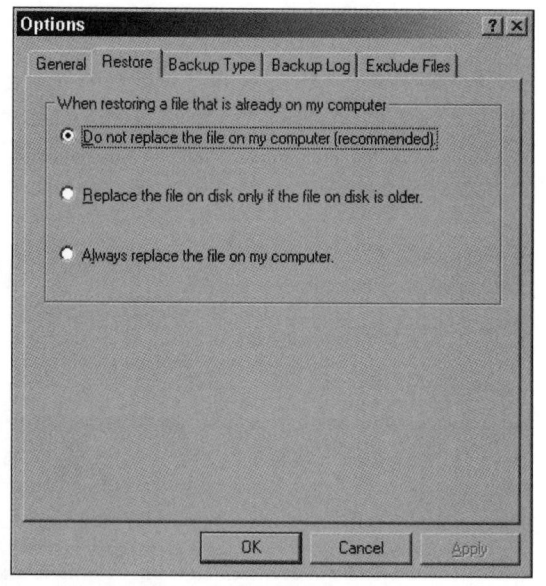

Figure 19-4:
Three
restore
options are
available
from the
Options
dialog box's
Restore tab.

Chapter 20

Troubleshooting

• •

• •

*M*uch as we may want to tell you that you're never, ever likely to run into problems on an integrated network, that's just not the case. You may ask, "Why can't I just build a 100-percent foolproof system, with triple-redundancies and minimal usage for the resources?" Well, even if you're cousins with the CEO for that big operating-system company in Seattle, your unlimited budget itself is not proof against the one thing that can bring a system down and over which you have no control: natural entropy.

Entropy isn't, as some people may think, an expensive dish that you can find only at finer restaurants. The term actually means that the natural state of the universe tends toward disorder. If your network is working correctly, just give it time. A connection's sure to come loose. An upgrade doesn't install correctly. Or a network card goes on strike for no reason. All of which is why you need to understand the basics of troubleshooting, from working on the cabling to the operating systems themselves.

General Troubleshooting Principles

If you're sure to discover one thing as you work on integrating systems, it's that so-called network "cowboys" aren't going to get very far if something breaks. Instead of trying to finagle your way out of a problem, you're best off taking a slow, methodical approach to what you're doing. This rule applies to any problem, whether it's a user who can't log in anymore or a machine that can't talk to the server. The following sections provide you with a series of methodical steps to follow as you attempt to fix almost any problem that plagues your system.

Step 1: Assess the problem, not the symptom

Always take a step back and consider whether you're treating a problem or a symptom of a deeper concern. If you keep getting complaints that users are running out of space, for example, you may cure the symptom by deleting unwanted files on that slice of the hard drive. But you may be ignoring the real underlying problem, which may be that you need a bigger hard drive!

Step 2: Consult documentation

Although this step goes against the grain of many "fly-by-the-seat-of-your-pants" operators, consulting your documentation is actually very helpful. And in consulting documentation, don't just dig out the software user manuals. Look instead at the documentation that you or your administration predecessor created. Wasting hours and hours on a problem that's already been solved is ridiculous.

Step 3: Triangulate the problem

If you're working on an integrated network, making use of your TCP/IP connections often helps you pinpoint the trouble spot. Say, for example, that machine A can't connect to the network. Try using the ping command from machines A, B, and C. If you can ping one machine but not another, you may have a failure on only one subnet or on one cable.

Step 4: Remove the troublesome machine from the network

Another method that you can use to isolate a problem is to remove the machine causing the problem from the network and see whether the problem continues. This action tells you immediately whether the problem is network-related or isolated to that one machine.

If the machine is a server on your network and, in other respects, seems to be operating normally, don't take this step unless you can work after hours when usage is at a low point.

Step 5: Change one system or network variable at a time

If you still need to continue troubleshooting, change only one aspect of the machine or network at a time and take note of the results. You don't want to accidentally bypass the answer as you try 17 things at once.

Step 6: Document, document, document

After you solve the problem, don't assume that it's never coming back. The moment that you turn your head, up it crops again (like a horror movie monster)! Always make sure that you document the procedure that fixes the problem or you may waste time groping for a fix if the same problem returns.

A Final Warning: Always Suspect the Cable

If you needed to pick a problem that was bedeviling your integrated network from a police lineup, you'd see a lot of the usual suspects. With nothing else to go on, your most promising usual suspect is the *cabling*. Although some operating systems (the older versions of the Microsoft Windows family, for example) truly are less than sterling examples of stability, cabling always takes the cake.

Cabling is simultaneously your most important and vulnerable asset. Nothing else must you drag under desks, through skylights, and under carpet. Nothing else do you (and others) trip over, step on, or run over with steamrollers. And no matter how durable it is, it's still only as strong as the telephone-jack connection where it plugs into the back of your computer.

The following list describes some tips to keep in mind as you first encounter a network-based problem:

- ✔ Check connections from the cable to the back of the computer that's causing problems.

- ✔ *Physically* check the connection. Don't just stare at it; give it a gentle but firm tug or push to make sure that it's not just sitting in the socket gathering dust.

- ✔ Check for missing or bad terminators if you're using them on your network.

- ✔ Make sure that the machines on your network backbone — whether modems, bridges, or routers — are showing healthy, green monitoring lights.

If the cable checks out but you still suspect a network problem, always check the network card on the machine by replacing it with a spare one.

You want to develop a plan for routing the external data cables. Such a plan may include the following procedures:

- ✔ Running data cables under a raised floor.
- ✔ Running data cables through a dropped ceiling.
- ✔ Placing the system in a low-traffic area where people are less likely to disturb cables.

Windows' Little Helpers: Troubleshooting from the Mind of Bill Gates

The ever-helpful folks at Microsoft actually loaded Windows 2000 with some very helpful troubleshooting tools. In a burst of originality, the project leader decided to call these tools *Troubleshooters*. In Windows 2000, these Troubleshooters are actually small programs that Microsoft bases on its *Wizard* model. By leading you through a series of questions, these Troubleshooters can help you solve the majority of your problems.

Microsoft currently offers Troubleshooting programs for the following components of your Windows 2000 system:

- ✔ Internet connections and modem settings
- ✔ Monitor setup
- ✔ MS-DOS
- ✔ Multimedia
- ✔ NetWare client services
- ✔ Networking in TCP/IP
- ✔ Peripherals
- ✔ Printing
- ✔ Remote access
- ✔ System setup
- ✔ Windows 3.*x* programs

One for the money, two for the show . . .

The best way to get your Troubleshooter going is to kick it off from the Start menu. Running the Windows 2000 Help command from here gives you access to all the wonderful worlds of Troubleshooting programs that come by default with Windows 2000 Professional or Server. To start the Troubleshooter, complete the following commands:

1. **Click the Start button and choose Help from the Start menu.**

   The Help Topics window appears.

2. **Click the Index tab.**

3. **Type** `troubleshooters` **in the text box at the top of the tab and you jump directly to the correct section of Help.**

   The Index is type-sensitive and takes you to the correct section of the alphabet automatically as you begin to type the term. A list of Troubleshooter programs appears in the right-hand pane, as shown in Figure 20-1.

4. **Double-click the name of the Troubleshooter program that you want to start.**

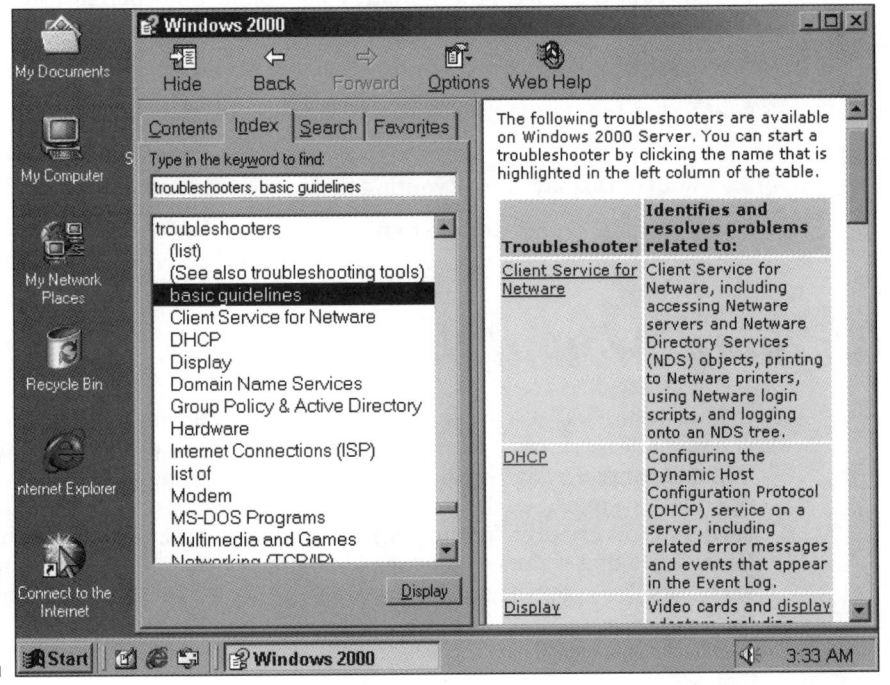

Figure 20-1:
The Windows 2000 list of Troubleshooters.

Troubleshooters aren't cure-alls. They can solve roughly about two-thirds of your problems. Until you prove a particular Troubleshooter useless, however, go ahead and follow the Troubleshooter's steps as closely to verbatim as you can. No matter how cynical you are about Microsoft's capability to solve problems, remember that its designers built this software and may actually know more about a given area than you do. Give them the chance, at least.

Additional Windows tools

In addition to its Troubleshooters, Microsoft provides some very useful command-prompt tools to help you troubleshoot network problems. You can turn to these tools after you exhaust the Troubleshooter resources. The following command-prompt tools are available by default in the Windows 2000 family:

- ✔ Arp: Displays the ARP (*Address Resolution Protocol*) cache and adds and removes MAC (*Medium Access Control*) addresses from the cache.

- ✔ Hostname: Displays the host name of the local computer.

- ✔ Ipconfig: Displays the TCP/IP configuration, renews the DHCP (*Dynamic Host Configuration Protocol*) lease, purges the DNS (*Domain Name System*) cache, and so on.

- ✔ Nbtstat: Displays the statistics and connections of NetBIOS over TCP/IP (NBT) and troubleshoots NetBIOS name-resolution problems.

- ✔ Netdiag: Performs some simple network tests.

- ✔ Pathping: Route-tracing tool that combines the features of ping and tracert.

- ✔ Route: Displays the IP routing table and adds and deletes IP routes.

- ✔ Tracert: Traces a route to remote systems.

Working Around the NetWare File Server

By and large, NetWare is such a solid system on the networking level that you generally don't run into many snags. In fact, a higher percentage of NetWare difficulties arise from the prime suspect — bad cabling — than from any other operating system. (See the section "A Final Warning: Always Suspect the Cable," earlier in this chapter, for details.) The flip side of this high system reliability, however, is that if something does happen to the main point of failure — the server itself — you very rarely can do more than reboot the machine.

The most serious damage that can affect your system occurs if a NetWare server crash results in a corrupted server database. The server database on a NetWare server is also known as the *Directory*, or (if you're working on an older version of NetWare) the *Bindery*. Unfortunately, the sophisticated diagnostics tools that you need to work with such a problem don't generally come with a standard NetWare installation.

Your best bet if you're running a 4.*x* version of NetWare is to simply refer to the NetWare manuals or online Help regarding either of the following:

- ✔ Your NDS Administration manual.
- ✔ The BINDFIX general repair and recovery program.

Another option if you're running a later version of NetWare is to purchase the Server Protection Kit from Alexander LAN, Inc. This Kit is an all-in-one diagnostic and fix-it piece of software that comes with its own documentation that you can refer to. You can locate this company on the Web at `www.networkbuyersguide.com/search/166000.htm` or contact it by telephone at (603) 880-8800.

Shooting Intruders in the NetWare World

NetWare makes Intruder Detection available for users within its *containers*, or *objects*. By default, the feature is inactive, but you can easily turn it on for multiple users if necessary.

In NWADMIN, you can change the properties for multiple users by manually selecting a group of users (pressing and holding the Shift or Ctrl key while clicking different users' names) or by selecting a group object and then choosing Object⇨Details on Multiple Users from the menu bar. From the Properties dialog box that appears, you can modify the properties for multiple users. You currently have no way to set Intruder Detection from the root account for the entire tree. You must make changes to existing users by container and by choosing Details on Multiple Users from the Objects menu. By using a standard *user template*, you can accomplish the desired result of setting the same Intruder Detection values for all containers in the tree as you're adding new users.

If you're going to enable Intruder Detection on everyone anyway, consider making a user template that features Intruder Detection on so that, every time that you make a new user, this template applies to the new user, and Intruder Detection is automatically on.

Another simple way to stop someone you determine to be a threat from logging in is to use the following command, making sure that you use all upper-case letters:

```
DISABLE LOGIN
```

Use this command to prevent users from logging in as you're making repairs, backing up files, or loading software. The command doesn't affect users already logged in. A user who logs out however, can't log in again until you execute the ENABLE LOGIN command.

Taking Pot Shots at Trouble in the Linux and Unix World

First off, disregard any rumors you hear from rabid Linux and Unix fanatics that their operating system of choice cause you so few problems that you're left wondering whether to spend an extra week at the beach on your vacation. Stable does not mean infallible. Although in several cases, Unix and Linux systems run happily for months without a peep, you still need to be aware of potential problems.

One of the main commands you need to know for working on locked-up or "hung" systems in either Unix or Linux is the kill command. Kill shuts down hung processes with either a gentle but firm touch or a slap from a .44 Magnum. (A *hung process* is one that refuses to exit, thereby slowing down or stalling your system.)

If you start a process in a terminal window, you can tell that the process if hung if you don't return to the command prompt after it's supposed to exit.

Kill works by sending to a process a special signal that the program understands as *shut down now*. This signal is also known as *SIGHUP*, for *signal - hang up*, which indicates that a process is to exit as soon as it can. This method is the "gentle" way of killing a program.

If the kill command doesn't shut the process down, you need to pull out the heavy artillery. In that case, you use the variant of kill known as kill -9. The option -9 tells kill to send out a signal to the process that tells it to quit *NOW*, without delay. It's the equivalent of a Force Quit command in the Windows world.

To use the kill -9 option on a process that's hung, you need to complete the following steps from a Linux or Unix terminal:

1. **Open a new Linux or Unix terminal and search for the process by typing** `ps -aef |grep <process name>` **at the command prompt.**

2. **Press Enter.**

3. **Locate the PID (process ID number) in the second column from the left.**

4, **Type** `kill -9 <PID>` **at the command prompt, as shown in Figure 20-2.**

5. **Press Enter.**

The process goes off to electronic Never-Never Land, and you return to the command prompt.

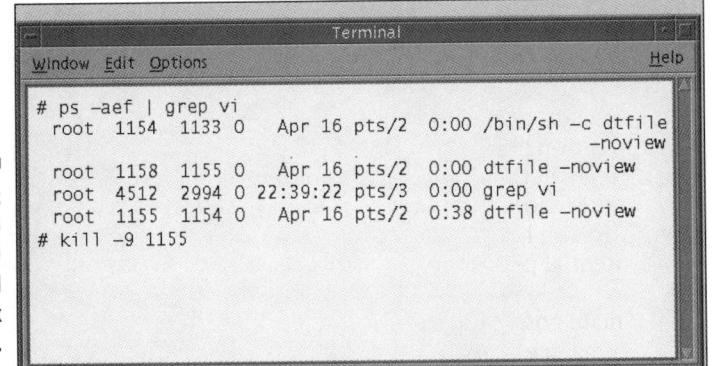

Figure 20-2:
Using the
`kill -9`
command
On a Unix
terminal.

```
                              Terminal
 Window  Edit  Options                                    Help

# ps -aef | grep vi
  root  1154  1133 0   Apr 16 pts/2  0:00 /bin/sh -c dtfile
                                                    -noview
  root  1158  1155 0   Apr 16 pts/2  0:00 dtfile -noview
  root  4512  2994 0 22:39:22 pts/3  0:00 grep vi
  root  1155  1154 0   Apr 16 pts/2  0:38 dtfile -noview
# kill -9 1155
```

Part VII
The Part of Tens

The 5th Wave — By Rich Tennant

"As a candidate for network administrator, how well versed are you in remote connectivity protocols?"

In this part . . .

1t's an old folk saying that good things come in packs of ten. This is in all likelihood because that's as high as you can count on all of your fingers. Whatever the real reason, it holds true here. Good things are coming your way!

Chapter 21

Ten Resources for Windows and NetWare Administration

*B*elieve it or not, the World Wide Web is actually good for more than the three things that 99 percent of the public thinks it's good for. That is, you can actually do more than the following:

✔ Buy stuff online.

✔ Hang out in AOL (America OnLine) chat rooms and talk about collecting Pokemon cards.

✔ Download pictures of the your favorite rock star(s).

Whether you use NetWare, Windows 2000, or other forms of Windows, you're sure to find the 10 sites that we discuss in this chapter particularly valuable if you want to do what the Web was *actually designed for:* search out and distribute information!

Oh, .com All Ye Faithful . . .

Whatever you're searching for, you're likely to find it on the World Wide Web. The problem isn't that you can't find information; it's that you find *too much* information on tangentially-related topics. So, now more than ever, searching on the Web's a matter of asking the right question instead of looking for the right answer.

Otherwise, you may end up spending days wading through the sea of information that comes pouring through your monitor screen. The techniques, sites, and groups that we recommend in the following sections can at least give you some ideas on where to go to ask the right question for your needs.

Remember that if the Internet's known for one thing, it's *change*. Take the addresses and links that we describe in this chapter with a large tablespoon of salt, because what's here today may very well be gone tomorrow . . . .

The Microsoft Web Server

As you may guess, the all-time best spot to answer your mainstream questions about Windows is (drum roll, please) the Microsoft Web site itself (at www.microsoft.com). In fact, as we warn you in the preceding section, your main task isn't to find information about your subject but to separate out the information that you need and can use from the stuff that you don't need.

This problem is especially difficult if you're searching for information about Windows 2000, given that this version of Windows is the "flagship" piece of software around which Microsoft is building the world for its next line of software models. Microsoft, therefore, maintains oodles and oodles (and, yes, we know that we're using highly technical terms here) of documents and resources through which to sift.

To help you make your way through this embarrassing rash of plenty, Microsoft equips its Web site comes with its own search engine. (We describe search engines in more detail in Appendix C.) In this case, your best bet is to type as exact a question as possible into the search text box on the Web site and then click the Search button.

As a rule, the Microsoft site is the best for answering mainstream questions — those concerning fairly general networking or system setup.

Notice that, most of the time, you don't get a quick answer in response to your question. Microsoft publishes many different documents that it divides into broad categories and usually organizes by function. If you're asking a question about networking, therefore, make sure that you specify whether you want information on workgroups, domains, or other specific topics.

The plus side is that, unless your question is extremely obscure, a Microsoft staff member has probably already written a product paper on it. Of course, if you need to find out how to network your Windows 2000 with your Nintendo Game Boy, you're best off visiting a newsgroup, Web search engine, or the local house of worship for an answer to your question.

Searching for Licensing Information

A subdirectory of the Windows site that you may easily miss is one that we want to point out to you, particularly if you're in charge of a medium to large network that's growing. If you're in growth mode, you're going to bump into the limitations of either the number of CAL licenses or of the license mode that you choose.

To further determine what you need for the full suite of Microsoft BackOffice products, you want to visit the following site:

```
www.microsoft.com/backoffice/
```

As on the main Microsoft site, you're best off using the built-in search engine on this site to locate the information that you want. Among the most valuable pieces of information you find here is the latest updates as to which Microsoft BackOffice products work in Per Server versus Per Seat mode, which drastically affects how you structure your license for your server system.

FTP Resources — Enormous, Anonymous, and FREE

Many Microsoft files are large enough to require a special FTP (File Transfer Protocol) server dedicated to their downloading onto user's computers.

These files normally fall into two groups: small applications (applets) that you can use to enhance your system or correct small software bugs or fully formatted documents, complete with graphics and hypertext links to direct you back to the main Microsoft sites. If your local computer is short on space, therefore, make sure that what you're trying to download isn't bigger than the space available on your hard drive.

To access this resource, open your Web browser and surf your way across the Net to the following site:

```
http://ftp.microsoft.com
```

Be forewarned: This site is *big*. And while you're going to find tons of interesting material, try to stick to what you're looking for. Although Microsoft usually logically and efficiently names these files, you can't guarantee that what you pick up is exactly the document you need.

To get an idea what exactly is inside the gift you're downloading, go to the /doftlib directory and double-click the README.TXT file. This file is a text file, usually in WordPad, that resides on the site before you begin your download and that gives you a quick synopsis of the underlying files and the subjects they cover in detail.

Don't go surfing around the FTP site without it!

Some excellent subdirectories to check out underneath the vast caverns of the Microsoft FTP server include the following:

- **/softlib/mslfiles:** An excellent directory, full of fun stuff to take home on your hard drive.
- **/peropsys/GEN_INFO/KB:** The complete set of articles from the Microsoft Knowledge Base.
- **/peropsys/Win_News:** Selected News articles, How-to information, and the archives of various Windows mailing lists. Particularly good if you're running a network with earlier versions of Windows on it.

The Mail's in the Check (box)

If you run Windows NT or even Windows 2000 Server (which is part of the Windows NT 4.0 legacy, after all) we suggest that you also consider subscribing to the NT mailing list run by Beverly Hills Software. Because an estimated more than two-thirds of Microsoft networks run versions of Windows NT through 2000 and on, you may find that this mailing list's a good resource to help you administer a mixed network of Microsoft machines.

To get on the mailing list, point your Web browser to the following site:

```
www.bhs.com/microsoft.winntnews
```

You must fill out a form there, and you may need to select some checkboxes to agree to conditions or determine whether you want to receive the newsletter under the default setup.

If you want to subscribe by e-mail instead, e-mail the following address:

```
winntnews-admin@microsoft.bhs.com
```

Make sure that you include the command **subscribe winntnews** in the first line of your message. This phrase acts like a CGI command to the server that receives your message. You get information on the Windows software's latest connectivity advances, techniques, and service packs, roughly once per week.

Usenet Newsgroups on Windows

Newsgroups are postings on a particular subject from people around the world who share an interest in that subject. At last count, more than 25,000 groups are out there on various topics, trading the latest information of interest. Of course, if you run any sort of Windows product on your network, your interests probably run toward Windows information!

For your purposes, you need to focus on newsgroups that talk more specifically about the Windows product line. Windows 2000 groups are still in their infancy as of this writing, but for now, the three best newsgroups to watch are the following:

- ✔ `comp.os.mis.windows.nt`: Miscellaneous topics on all versions of Windows NT.

- ✔ `microsoft.public.windowsnt`: A similar, Microsoft-specific newsgroup.

- ✔ `comp.os.windows.advocacy`: A newsgroup dedicated to advancing Windows in the networking world.

- ✔ `msnews.microsoft.com`: A general Microsoft question and answer forum.

You may need to sign up with the Microsoft Internet service to access this final group.

Just the FAQs, Ma'am . . .

A *FAQ* is a list of answers to what the acronym *FAQ* refers to — *F*requently *A*nswered *Q*uestions! You pronounce it *"fack."* The next time that your cat gets a hairball, that can remind you how to pronounce it. One of the best lists of frequently answered questions is on the following site:

```
/www.ntfaq.com/
```

From this site, you can search for answers from a list of topics that include the following (and many more):

- ✔ Active Directory
- ✔ Compatibility
- ✔ Environment — desktop
- ✔ File systems
- ✔ Group policy
- ✔ Installation
- ✔ Internet Explorer 4.0/5.0
- ✔ Network performance
- ✔ Problem solving
- ✔ User configuration

An NT Administration Tool Site

You can find another good site at the following URL.

```
www.ntadmintools.com/info.html
```

This Web site specializes in technical support and samples of Windows NT and Windows 2000 Administration Software. You find information on where to get and install software on backups, bug fixes, and network monitoring. Most of the information you find here is still oriented toward NT 4.0, but the Windows 2000 section is likely to grow through the year 2000 and on.

The Mother of All NetWare Sites

Of course, we can't start out any list of sites without directing you to the place where it all happened: the Novell corporation home page. Navigate to the following site to start:

```
www.novell.com
```

From the Novell home page, you can visit directories containing information on the latest NetWare product releases, find answers to many basic questions on the operating system, and get information about new products that work with NetWare. Of particular interest are the areas of the site that provide information on technical support and training. Like Microsoft, Novell is a major software vendor and hence offers all sorts of additional options you can choose from to acquire service contracts, gain certification on the product, or have a trainer visit your company to train you (or your network staff) in the ways of NetWare.

All of this assistance comes at a price that your pocketbook may feel quite heavily! If you're running a stand-alone system or a small network, you may be better off checking other resources for documentation and/or network newsgroups for answers to your questions. We cover this topic in more detail in Appendix C.

NUINet — As Cool to Use as It's Funny to Pronounce

You pronounce the abbreviation for *NetWare Users International* (*NUINet*) as "*Noon*-net" or "*New*-wee-net," depending on who you ask. The more important information, however, is constant — that NetWare Users International is an association of Novell networking professionals that supports NetWare user groups worldwide. NUINet offers information on technical forums, user groups, conferences and exhibits, and the NetWare online connection.

You can find several Web links to NUINet chapters around the world, but the best starting point is to go to a subdirectory on Novell's own Web site, which you find at the following address:

```
www.novell.com/corp/community/nui/index.html
```

USENET Newsgroups on NetWare

Because newsgroups are postings on a particular subject from people around the world who share an interest in that subject, you can bet that you find a bunch on NetWare. As with other popular operating systems, different groups dedicate themselves to various topics within the software realm of NetWare, trading the latest information on troubleshooting, news, and other topics. Some of the most useful groups you can find include the following:

- ✔ `comp.os.netware.advocacy`: Dedicated to advancing NetWare's share of NOSes in the networking world.

- ✔ `comp.os.netware.connectivity`: Information and troubleshooting questions on connectivity products.

- ✔ comp.os.netware.misc: General NetWare topics.

- ✔ comp.os.netware.security: NetWare Security issues.

- ✔ comp.os.netware.announce: Moderated NetWare announcements.

Incidentally, many newsgroups, particularly those with a corporate or formal association or affiliation, are *moderated*, which means that a particular person or group of people screens out messages that are either unrelated, offensive, or simply *spam* (that is, Internet ads posing as legitimate posts).

As a rule, you're likely to find more useful information on a moderated newsgroups, although you still have no guarantee of the accuracy or the legibility of the information that you may find!

Chapter 22

Ten Resources for Linux and Unix Administration

***

In This Chapter

▶ Linux vendor Web sites

▶ Links to Linux online

▶ Linux in the public eye

▶ Unix newsgroups

▶ A site dedicated to Unix gurus

▶ Unix tips and tricks

***

*W*e always like giving Web addresses for sites on Linux and Unix, because we enjoy demonstrating to you that you're going to discover just what a valuable resource the Internet is, both in terms of finding the information you need to help you run your network or solve vexing questions on administrative needs. You always want to know just what kind of information you can tap into on-line and why you need it. You also want to keep in mind that, although Unix and Linux are very similar operating systems, the discussion topics and suggested fixes for each system can prove very different. Be wary, therefore, of substituting a troubleshooting fix for Linux on your Unix system and vice-versa. Instead, go directly to a site or newsgroup that discusses the operating system that you're running.

Your Linux Vendor Web Site

Of course, we can't start out any list of Web sites without directing you to the home page of your chosen flavor of Linux. Because you can buy many forms of Linux via a vendor as well as download it for free from the Internet, you often can purchase (or may already have) a vendor service agreement that directs you to the vendor's Web site. If you purchase Red Hat Linux, for example, you want to check out the following site:

```
www.redhat.com
```

If you purchase the TurboLinux flavor of Linux, check out the following site:

```
www.turbolinux.com
```

Even if you're using the open-software version of Linux, Debian/GNU Linux, you still can check out a Web site — namely, the following site:

```
www.debian.org
```

Notice that, instead of a .com site, you're going to a site that's a .org, indicating that an organization runs it and not a formal company. Because of Debian's large number of users and all the developers in the organization, even if you purchase the VALinux version of Debian, you probably can get more information from the .org site than you can elsewhere.

Keep in mind that all forms of Linux are close enough to be cousins. So if you want a friendly family reunion (or you just want some information you can't find in one branch), check out another version's way of doing something, and you may find the vital piece of information that you need.

Regarding the preceding tip: It's valid, but don't try it for installation or configuration questions; if you do, you may experience some rude shocks!

Newbie Administrator Guide

If some administrative challenges face you (such as being the root), take a peek at the Linux Newbie Guide site. You find solutions to problems that relate more to adding users than to changing your screen saver, so if you're feeling more advanced, you're likely to enjoy this site's contents. You find it at the following URL:

```
http://sunsite.auc.dk/linux-newbie/
```

A *newbie* is just Linux speak for a new person who just got into most anything online, such as e-mail, administration, or networks. (Luckily for people such as me, no such term as *oldie* is in use.)

Slashdot Discussions

The *Slashdot* organization's discussion area is a good connection for true Linux wizards to make. This site is a discussion forum for Linux issues. If you have a question about Linux and you can't find the answer through books, intuitive deduction, or reading tea leaves, post it at the following address:

```
www.slashdot.org/
```

As you need to do with any discussion group, remain polite. Exhaust other avenues first; massive posting of questions (especially simple ones) only annoys other readers and may cause people to avoid your posts.

Linux Online

Occasionally, you come across a site on the Internet that isn't so much about its material contents as its links to so many other places to find information. This site is one such great link site. You find connections to Linux topics galore from here. Just point your browser to the following URL:

```
www.linux.org/apps/index.html
```

Cut! Print It!

One of the most useful sites on the Web for Linuxphiles and their ilk is this site on printing. Specifically, if you inherit an older printer that looks as if NASA used it on the early moon shots, you can find out whether trying to get it to work is worth the effort. This site contains a very good database of printers that do and don't work with Linux. Go to the following address for the Linux Printing site:

```
http://linuxprinting.org
```

Linux in the Public Eye

If you're curious about what kind of hoopla Linux is generating, make sure that you check out the following Linuxworld - Putting Linux to Work site:

```
www.linuxworld.com/
```

This site is also the best to keep you up to date on the latest Linux conferences, expositions, and Linux comedy clubs. (Okay, we're kidding about that last part.)

Unix Newsgroups

Unix boasts several major newsgroups because of its popularity and venerability (that is, it's been around a long, long time). You can find Unix groups that discuss all the different flavors of Unix. For the most popular form on the market, Sun's Solaris version, the following groups are your best bets to join and post your Unix questions:

- ✔ `alt.solaris` (for general Solaris information)
- ✔ `alt.solaris.x86` (for running Solaris on Intel PCs)
- ✔ `alt.sys.sun` (for questions on running Sun systems)
- ✔ `comp.sys.sun` (for more issues on Sun systems)
- ✔ `comp.sys.sun.admin` (for topics relating to administration)
- ✔ `comp.sys.sun.apps` (for applications running on Sun boxes)
- ✔ `comp.sys.sun.hardware` (for hardware compatibility issues)

Sun Solaris Product Line

Sun Microsystems is about the closest thing that you find to a dominant vendor in the Unix market. Although you get the most out of the following site if you run Solaris, SunOS, or other versions of Sun's products, you can still get good pointers here if you run other versions:

```
www.sun.com/solaris
```

Much as you can on the Microsoft Web site, you can search through the massive quantities of data available on this site. Most of the time, however, you don't get a quick answer in response to your question. Most Sun documents divide up into broad functional categories, such as networking or network file system rather than into specific how-to documents.

Many areas of Sun's documentation may seem a bit incoherent to those who aren't Unix experts in a given area. If you're asking a question about networking, therefore, you want to make sure that you phrase your question as specifically as possible if you're requesting information on NFS, networking, or other specific topics.

If you purchase a technical support agreement from Sun, consult your documentation that comes with the agreement for special locations or e-mail addresses that you can visit to gain special information. Most likely, you have a customer code or ID number that you can use to gain access to more esoteric support answers buried in this labyrinthine Web site.

The Unix Guru Universe

Billed as the "Official Home Page for the Unix Guru Universe," the following site is a very good place to pose your most troubling questions:

```
www.ugu.com/
```

This site acts both as a gateway for you to pose your questions to experienced system administrators and as a repository of administration information ranging from the basic to the jaw-droppingly profound.

Interestingly enough, this site presents you with two additional options via the contacts you make on it:

- ✔ If you're in charge of a Unix network and need additional help, you can locate many independent contractors from this site.

- ✔ If you're in the Unix area and are considering a move to a different company, you can find out who's been there already and can give you inside information on the place.

Unix Tools and Tips

The address of a final site that's worth visiting can give you calluses just from typing it, but it's definitely worth the effort. Get your fingers pounding away on the following URL for the NACSE, or Northwest Alliance for Computational Science and Engineering:

```
www.nacse.org/demos/coping-with-unix/coping-with-unix/
                  node144.html
```

This site's an excellent resource for finding out about and downloading Unix administration tools and also for locating tips to enhance your Unix experience.

As far as that line of reasoning goes, the best that you can make of your Unix experience is to gather information from this site that enables you to solve problems and reduce your stress level, thereby improving the experience!

Chapter 23

Ten Truths (or Constants) about System Integration

In This Chapter

▶ The importance of planning

▶ What you can never have enough of

▶ Standards that you must obey

▶ Attitudes you want to cultivate

*A*s you're working with a bunch of machines that are as unruly as a bunch of third graders on a major field trip, you may start wondering what possessed you to take up system integration. You can at least take heart in the fact that a few constants do exist in that area. These constants derive from years (if not decades) of experience culled from system integrator to system integrator by the oldest, most traditional method of information exchange of all: oral transmission. These constants aren't *laws* that you need to obey to cure all your network's ills. They're more like preventive guidelines for ensuring that your network runs correctly and for heading off most problems before they occur. But your life is likely to prove less stressful and more productive if you keep the following ten truths in mind.

The Three Most Important Words in System Integration: Planning, Planning, and Planning

Don't fall into the trap of thinking that planning is useful only in the stage where you're in between doodling out a new network on a piece of scrap paper and submitting the budget request to your manager. In fact, planning is an integral part of your game from the get-go, and you also want to make it part of your daily routine.

Planning is especially important if you want to truly fix a problem instead of just putting a temporary bandage on it. You can pinpoint exactly what's causing the problem and then plan a solution that can forever banish the problem from your network. If you have a frozen machine, for example, an easy but temporary cure is to reboot it and empty out a portion of the full disk. But a much better, long-term solution is to track down the reason the disk is filling up and then remedy the situation that's causing the entire problem in the first place. In other words, try to follow a format that assists the Vulcanlike, logical portion of your mind to come up with your answers.

Follow these basic steps for a logical method of tracking down the source of a problem and creating a solution for it:

1. **Organize your reports or observations.**

   Most likely, you can organize the events leading up to a problem in chronological order. Finding that a serious problem on an integrated network mysteriously raises its head less than once a day is relatively rare; often, the problem recurs several times a day.

2. **Go back and confirm your observations.**

   Be wary of painting your conclusions with strokes that are too broad. In other words, just because event X precedes disaster Y, that doesn't necessarily mean that X *causes* Y to happen.

3. **Distinguish symptoms from the problem.**

   If you were a doctor, would you diagnose a patient's problem as "having stomach pains" or "aching in the head"? Of course not. These conditions are symptoms — medical road signs that clue you in to the patient's potential problem, whether it's heartburn, an ulcer, a migraine, or a concussion.

   Amazingly, however, many administrative types are willing to invest hours at a time trying to solve the so-called *problem* of "the server is acting funny." That's *not* a problem; it's a symptom of the real problem — something that's causing the server to act oddly. Always take the time to distinguish between the symptom and the problem, or you can expect to spend a lot of time chasing down electronic phantoms.

4. **Determine what's new or different on the system.**

   If you run a lab with several different administrators, yours may be the case of too many cooks spoiling the soup. Anyone who spends time in administration starts developing his own quirks and ways of doing things. Until you prove them innocent, make sure that you scrutinize what all these administrators installed, edited, or configured prior to the initial occurrence of the problem.

5. Look for patterns.

If you deal with multiple systems, you're especially wise to look for patterns in the problem. Look for patterns in two areas: time and operating systems. In a time pattern, you can see when a problem occurs, whether it occurs as a given script runs at 2 p.m. or as people start logging in at 8 a.m.

An operating system pattern enables you to reduce the size and scope of the problem effectively. You may, for example, conduct a quick survey of users who report a recurring problem and find out that all of them are Windows 2000 users. Then you know that you don't need to waste time working first on the Linux server that hooks up to these machines. Instead, you can start looking into the specific operating system's software; you may even find a new bug.

6. List what you try.

As you start trying to fix the problem, keep tabs on what you do. Doing so not only prevents you from duplicating an effort later on, but it also enables you to take advantage of the quirks of fate — where you fix one part of the problem but not another. By backtracking to see what you did right, you may stumble on the complete solution.

7. Document the solution.

This step is the most important one. Why? Because hardly anyone ever seems to do it. Nothing is more frustrating than needing to backtrack through the same problem if it pops up again when you could have the answer in the palm of your hand if you just keep records of all your successful fixes.

You Can Never Have Too Much Documentation

You never — repeat — *never* face a time when you have too much documentation. If you have multiple operating systems, you need multiple manuals, multiple Help files, and multiple books about each subject. Granted, this truth may make for your task of sifting through all the information — page by page by page — much harder. Here's a hint, however: After you work through the problem (separating it from the symptom, identifying a pattern, and so on), turn to the book's index or table of contents to zone in on the specific topic. Doing so is a lot easier than thumbing through various chapters with the hope that you may eventually find something useful for your situation.

You Can Never Have Too Much Information

You can never really have too much information. Keeping your finger on the pulse of the technology world serves you in good stead. Ideally, try to keep up with at least two Web sites: one that focuses on the business use of the machines in your mixed network and another that acts as a clearinghouse of data for experienced troubleshooters and gurus. One can keep you ahead of the game, and the other keeps you *in* the game if something breaks.

Following are some Web sites that may serve your needs:

- ✔ **CNET:** The CNET site (at `www.cnet.com/`) is a good, all-purpose site of the first kind. Although it's not hard-core technical (in that you don't, for example, find bug fixes anywhere on this site without digging for them), it's an excellent place to read about what's going on in the world outside your lab. It especially comes in handy if you're planning to spend $100,000 on a new operating system from a software company and you find that a major whoopie-cushion manufacturer just bought the company.

- ✔ **Slashdot:** Gandalf hung out with the wood elves, and Merlin hung out in the castle (polishing the Round Table), but other types of wizards? *They* hang out here at the Slashdot site (at `www.slashdot.org/`). If you have a vexing technology question, you can pose it to technowizards at this site. Slashdot acts as a sort of discussion forum for all sorts of software issues — even if the software is outdated, outmoded, or plain out of sight.

- ✔ **Linuxberg:** *Linuxberg* is a sort of take-off of the term *iceberg* because this site (at `www.linuxberg.com/`) is certainly large and imposing and could take down the Titanic if it hit it. But for the budding integrator, this site is a boon because it contains links to new Linux utilities as well as just general news.

- ✔ **Microsoft:** Microsoft's Web site (at `www.microsoft.com/`) is so amazingly immense that it would take you years to search for an answer. But you're almost certain of finding it. Speed up this process by making use of the excellent search engine on this site.

- ✔ **NetWare:** If you're running NetWare, consider getting your information right from the source (at `www.netware.com/`). You can also see when (and if) NetWare continues to evolve on the software scene.

- ✔ **Sunsolve:** Make this site (at `www.sunsolve.com/`) part of your daily reading if you plan to use Sun's version of Unix, known as *SunOS* or *Solaris*. Although you don't find much about breaking news stories on the Unix scene, you can find bug fixes galore here.

You Can Never Have Too Many Spare Machines

Trust me on this one. Although placing that old box in the atrium as an orchid planter or donating it to the charity of your choice may seem tempting, consider keeping it around as a reserve. If you need to replace a fried print server or a personal computer for the CEO's visiting cousin, that old machine is just what you need. And remember that, if you're talking slow, old machines, *slow going* is a lot better than *no going*.

File System Compatibility Is Paramount to Run Things Smoothly

No matter how much computer designers like to show off the fact that their operating systems work with anything, anywhere, under any conditions, the fact is that file systems still don't work well together. The method that each operating system uses to handle and organize its data is distinctly different. Unix and Linux use different systems, usually named the *Unix, swap,* and *Linux* file systems. Windows 2000 and NT use *NTFS*. And the stand-alone Windows systems still on the market use the *FAT* file system.

Because none of these systems really enjoys one system writing a file to another, you're best off if you avoid creating a feuding roommate situation. If you do install multiple operating systems on a machine, give them separate partitions.

You Must Obey All Other Standards

Although file systems have their own standards about how to work with files, keep in mind that, throughout this book, other standards are covered. The chapter on protocols and the chapter on wiring, for example, go into detail about how you must meet standards or your system becomes a complete oddball — stranded by itself if it tries to work or communicate.

Here's a specific example: Don't deviate from the standards for setting up the Ethernet cabling. If you have 100Mbit network interface cards but use Category 3 wiring, you're deviating from the standards. Not only do you experience poor performance, but unless you correctly install Category 5 wiring, you're also likely to find that consultants and part-time staff refuse to work on your non-standard system. Why? Because they don't want to be liable for working on a system that may crash because they can't figure out what file or wire goes where.

You Must Know What's Where and Why It's There

If you're looking for a hoary old chestnut on network administration advice, "Know what's where and why it's there" ranks right up there with some of Confucius's best.

Always make sure that you know where every switch and plug resides on your system. To use an extreme example, if a blackout hits, are you familiar enough with your network environs that you can find your way to the switches in the dark?

You Can't Always Be the Alpha Geek

Alpha Geek is a relatively new term for a technical person who considers his own knowledge at a level that surpasses that of others. Although perhaps an admirable goal to strive for, it leads to a certain kind of administrative blindness.

Don't become too proud, stubborn, or afraid to call for outside help if you can't solve a problem. You may be the world's next Linus Torvalds in working with Linux, but you may need a tried and true MCSE to come along and get you out of a really tight Windows 2000 jam. Swallow the pride and accept the help.

Dual-Boot Systems Are Bad for Your Health

A dual-boot machine is one single computer that runs more than one operating system. You can configure almost any PC as a dual-boot machine — for example, to run Windows 2000 and Windows 95. But as a rule, try to avoid doing so. No matter how seamlessly manufacturers claim that two operating systems can work in tandem on a machine, don't believe them. Perhaps it's merely coincidence, but survey after survey shows that dual-boot machines have a higher percentage of conflicts and failures than single-boot ones. Anything in the integrated network that can cause you more maintenance hassles you want to avoid or limit.

If you plan to run Windows 95 and Windows 2000 on one machine, making it a dual-boot machine, never install Windows 2000 first. The reason is that the Windows 95 installation process writes over the Windows 2000 startup files. You get a single-boot machine where you want a dual-boot one.

The Most Awful Truth of All . . .

The simplest integrated network to administer is one that's *not* integrated at all.

Does that statement sound like something that's at odds with the ideas in this book? Well, in reality, it's not at all. Your goal is always to reduce the number of variations in operating systems on your network. If possible, you even want to try to reduce the number of operating systems on your network. The reason is that, no matter how easy working with both Unix and Windows, for example, becomes, a mixed network of these machines is always a little less efficient than a *pure* network, where you can standardize everything to your heart's content. So play the budget and department manager games correctly to achieve this goal. Otherwise, you may end up servicing a dozen TRS-80s, a half-dozen Amigas, and the old Atari 2600 that your boss uses to play *Missile Command* on her lunch break.

Part VIII

Appendixes

The 5th Wave   By Rich Tennant

"We take network security very seriously here."

In this part . . .

This part of the book is full of resources to make your life easier. We explain the CD, define common networking terms, show you how to make system recovery disks, and introduce you to a world of references on network operation.

Appendix A

Glossary

● ●

*T*his appendix is helpful if you come across some terminology in one of the chapters that you just can't quite understand or remember.

Access Control List

These lists of the permissions assigned to a Windows 2000 resource also identify which users are allowed access. Access attempts are logged here.

Active Directory

A utility used in Windows 2000 to locate, track, and change any object on a Windows network.

ADSI

Commonly used acronym for the Active Directory Service Interface.

Active Directory Service Interface

Utility window allows applications to communicate with the Active Directory.

Active Server Pages

A script executed on the Windows 2000 server before it's passed on to the user as an HTML (Hypertext Markup Language) page.

Backward compatibility

The successful functioning of a new product with older versions of the product.

BOOTP

Commonly used acronym for the Bootstrap Protocol.

Bootstrap protocol

Allocates IP information to clients upon completion of the machine startup.

Bridge

A piece of hardware that links networks and performs some of the intelligent functions of routing communications to the right locations.

Central Processing Unit

The part of the computer that performs the calculations and computations.

Cluster

A group of systems brought together for the express purposes of clustering them.

Clustering

Combining multiple systems to act as a single unit, usually for redundancy.

Command prompt

The small amount of text lined up on the left side of a UNIX or Linux terminal. Typed commands appear to its left.

Command line

The line in the UNIX or Linux terminal where you type the command.

CPU

Commonly used acronym for the Central Processing Unit.

CPU throttling

Kernel-level capability that limits the number of CPU cycles taken by a process. This prevents a process from monopolizing the system.

DFS (Distributed File System)

A file system mode that allows Windows 2000 Server file shares to be maintained simultaneously on multiple machines for backup and security.

DHCP (Dynamic Host Configuration Protocol)

A component protocol of the TCP/IP family, used by Windows 2000 to configure clients with an IP address and other IP information for communication between clients and the Internet.

Directory

An object in UNIX or Linux where you can store files for organizational purposes. It's also called a *folder* when it's displayed in graphic terms on the desktop.

Disk quota

A set amount of disk space set aside for a specific user account's storage. Under this system, a user cannot store more data than is allocated under the quota.

DNS (Domain Name System)

A directory or database object that translates domain names into IP addresses that your networked computers can understand.

EFS (Encrypting File System)

A security feature that allows data encryption on the NTFS disk. This makes impossible for someone to bypass the operating system to retrieve the given information.

Ethernet

Both a type of network and a form of cabling that allows networked communication between computers.

FAT

A file system that provides backward compatibility with Windows 95, Windows NT, and MS-DOS.

FAT32

A file system that supports the later Windows products, such as Windows 98 and Windows 2000. It is distinguished from regular FAT by its ability to handle larger spaces.

File

Any object in a NOS, including text documents, directories, and pictures.

Folder

An object in Windows where you can store files for organizational purposes. It's also called a *directory* when it's displayed as text in a command-line display.

Forest

A group of Active Directory trees that trust each other.

FTP (File Transfer Protocol)

Name for protocol and process of transferring large amounts of data between machines or networks.

Gigabtye

A term of measurement for approximately one billion bytes of information.

HTTP (Hypertext Transfer Protocol)

The basic protocol used for the majority of Web communications.

Home directory

Your starting point whenever you log into a UNIX or Linux environment. It's also where your account stores files you create.

Hub

A piece of hardware that links network subnets. Hubs are not normally considered to be as intelligent as bridges or routers.

IIS (Internet Information Services)

This is Microsoft's newest Web Server Product, designed to complete with Apache and other products.

IPX/SPX (InterNetwork Packet Exchange/Sequences Packet Exchange)

Protocols that work like TCP/IP. This is a protocol that is native to NetWare and is semi-compatible with Windows 2000 so you can run these machines together.

Internet Protocol Address

The quartet of numbers that designate a machine's organization and location. An example of such an address is 166.100.20.4.

ISP (Internet Service Provider)

A company that provides dial-in connectivity to the Internet via your modem, ISDN line, cable modem, or T1 telephone line.

KB (Kilobyte)

A measurement of approximately one thousand bytes of information.

Kerberos

A popular security system that focuses on user authentication and is whose protocol is natively supported by Windows 2000.

LAN (Local Area Network)

The standard network setup for small companies.

MB (Megabyte)

A unit measuring roughly one million bytes of information.

MMC (Microsoft Management Console)

A utility allowing you to compose or configure the full suite of administrative tools in Windows 2000.

NetBIOS

The standard Windows network communications protocol.

NetSync

A NetWare administrative tool to administer a NetWare 3 and NetWare 4 mixed environment from the NetWare 4 utilities.

NetWare

Network operating system by Novell that allows multitasking. NetWare can be used on desktop operating systems, such as Windows, DOS, OS/2, and UNIX.

Network File System (NFS)

Any software and network protocols that support the sharing of files by users over a network. On UNIX systems, this is usually implemented using the NFS protocol, which relies on UDP/IP. On Windows systems, this is usually implemented with the SMB protocol, which in turn can be implemented over IPX, NetBEUI or TCP/IP. On NetWare systems, this is usually implemented with the NCPFS protocol, which in turn relies on IPX.

Network interface card (NIC)

Printed circuit board containing the necessary hardware that connects a computer to a network.

Network model

System structure in a group of interconnected computers that allows each data file to be accessed from more than one location.

Network operating system (NOS)

Operating system software that allows computers to work together and communicate. Examples of network operating systems include UNIX, Linux, NetWare, and Windows NT.

NTFS (NT File System)

The preferred system to use with Windows NT or 2000.

Password

Security measure that tells the computer to allow you to use its system resources.

Plug & Play

A standard that allows hardware to be automatically detected and configured when plugged into a system.

Pop-up menu

A menu of options that 'pops up', normally when an object is right-clicked upon.

Pull-down menu

A list of options that appears to drop from a point on the screen. Normally these can be found by clicking on options that are on the main toolbar of a given screen.

RAID (Redundant Array of Inexpensive Disks)

A system that allows multiple hard drives to act as a backup system.

Remote Storage

Windows 2000 process that performs hierarchical storage tasks.

Removable storage

Windows 2000 process that tracks data on storage devices that can be removed and moved to a different location. This includes CD-ROMs, floppy disks, and external floppy, tape, and CD-ROM drives.

Repeaters

A signal booster that repeats a network packet communication down the line so it isn't lost. Comparatively rare today, but useful when you're running a large Ethernet network.

Root

The administrative account in UNIX or Linux. There's only one root account, and you should keep its password private.

Root directory

The starting point of a UNIX or Linux file tree structure. It's denoted as a slash mark, /.

Router

A piece of hardware that acts as a more intelligent bridge for communication transmissions from one network to another. On rare occasions, there are software tools that can perform these functions, albeit in a more limited fashion.

Subdirectory

A directory located a level below a main directory.

Subfolder

A folder located a level below a main directory.

Submenu

A menu located a level below a main directory.

Subtree

A part of the Active Directory domain located below a level of the main directory tree.

Tape drive

Less commonly seen on stand-alone systems than CD-ROM or floppy drives, a tape drive is a machine (usually external) that saves data on magnetic tapes.

TCP/IP (Transmission Control Protocol/Internet Protocol)

The standard Internet communications protocol suite.

Terminal

A window you create on your desktop where you can run Linux commands on a command line.

Token Ring

An older, mostly outdated network system that prevents network collisions by providing an electronic token for machines to pass around for communication.

Trees

A directory style or structure.

User account

A set of data that includes a home directory, user name, and password for a user to connect to a network system.

WAN (Wide Area Network)

A larger network area than is normally covered by a LAN, or Local Area Network.

Windows Terminal Services

Service that allows multiple graphical sessions to be created and used on a single Windows 2000 server.

WINS (Windows Internet Name Service)

A component of Windows 2000 Server that provides NetBIOS name resolution and allows client systems to locate network servers for communication.

Wizard

A utility that guides you through a series of tasks by automating the tasks and asking you to select settings that will be applied.

Zero Administration

A paradigm where administration of the network takes minimal time and effort. A stated goal for the Windows 2000 suite.

Appendix B

About the CD

On the CD-ROM

▶ SpyGuru, a suite of System monitoring tools

▶ NwQuota, which monitors the amount of free space in your home directory

▶ Virtual Network computing, a remote display system utility

▶ Sockclnt, a useful tool for diagnosing TCP links on NetWare servers

▶ Diskcheck, a useful utility to protect and warn you about disk errors

▶ Logwatch, which automatically monitors your various system logs for errors or security breaches

This book includes a CD with plenty of resources for you to use while administering your system. This appendix explains how to use the CD and what you'll find on it.

System Requirements

Make sure your computer meets the minimum system requirements listed below. If your computer doesn't match up to most of these requirements, you may have problems using the contents of the CD.

✔ A PC with a Pentium or faster processor, or a Sun Sparc 5 or faster processor.

✔ Microsoft Windows NT 4.0 or later, Solaris 2.5 or later, or Red Hat Linux 6.1 or later.

✔ At least 64MB of total RAM installed on your computer.

✔ At least 500 MB of hard drive space available to install all the software from this CD. (You'll need less space if you don't install every program.)

✔ A CD-ROM drive — double-speed (2x) or faster.

✔ A sound card for PCs or UNIX boxes.

✔ A monitor capable of displaying 256 colors or grayscale.

✔ A modem with a speed of at least 14,400 bps.

If you need more information on the basics, check out *PCs For Dummies,* 6th Edition, by Dan Gookin, and *Networking With NetWare For Dummies,* by Ed Tittle.

For more Windows information, see *Windows 2000 Administration For Dummies* by Michael Bellomo, *Windows 98 For Dummies,* or *Windows 95 For Dummies* all by Andy Rathbone and all published by IDG Books Worldwide, Inc.

For more basic Linux information, you can also check out *Linux For Dummies,* 2nd Edition, by Jon 'Maddog' Hall, or *Linux Administration For Dummies,* by Michael Bellomo (both published by IDG Books Worldwide, Inc.).

How to use the CD with Microsoft Windows

If you are running Windows 95, 98, NT 4.0, or Windows 2000, follow these steps to get to the items on the CD:

1. **Insert the CD into your computer's CD-ROM drive.**

   Give your computer a moment to take a look at the CD.

2. **When the light on your CD-ROM drive goes out, double-click the My Computer icon. (It's probably in the top left corner of your desktop.)**

   This action opens the My Computer window, which shows you all the drives attached to your computer, the Control Panel, and a couple other handy things.

3. **Double-click the icon for your CD-ROM drive.**

   Another window opens, showing you all the folders and files on the CD.

How to use the CD with UNIX (Solaris 2.5, CDE Desktop)

If you are running UNIX, follow these steps to get to the items on the CD.

1. **Insert the CD into your computer's CD-ROM drive.**

   Give your computer a moment to take a look at the CD.

2. **When the light on your CD-ROM drive goes out, double-click the CD-ROM icon in the top left corner of your desktop.**

   A window displaying the contents of the CD-ROM is opened on the desktop.

Using the CD with the Linux GNOME Desktop on Red Hat Linux

If you are running UNIX, follow these steps to get to the items on the CD.

1. **Insert the CD into your computer's CD-ROM drive.**

   Give your computer a moment to take a look at the CD.

2. **When the light on your CD-ROM drive goes out, double click the CD-ROM icon in the top left corner of your desktop.**

   The Disk Manager window opens.

3. **Click the Mount button next to** /dev/cdrom.

4. **Open a window displaying the contents of the CD-ROM by double-clicking the File Manager icon and navigating to** /dev/cdrom.

What You'll Find

Here's a summary of the software on this CD arranged by category.

Linux Utilities

The CD contains these Linux utilities.

Logwatch

For Linux Systems and Windows Machines Running Linux. Logwatch, which automatically monitors your various systems logs for errors or security breaches. An excellent add-on to your Linux system due to its good security coverage and lightweight processes.

Diskcheck

For Linux Systems and Windows Machines Running Linux. Diskcheck runs hourly (unless you configure it otherwise) in the background and warns you if you're running low on disk space or are prone to other developing problems.

NetWare Utilities

The CD contains these NetWare utilities.

NwQuota

This utility monitors your home directory and warns you with its taskbar icon when the directory is close to filling up. This product works on NetWare 3.x, 4.x, 5.x, and Windows 95/98/NT.

Sockclnt 2.00

This is a useful tool for diagnosing TCP-related problems on NetWare servers. It will work with NetWare 3.x, 4.x, 5.x

Windows Utilities

The CD contains these Windows network utilities.

Virtual Network Computing

A remote display system much like a Linux/UNIX terminal. This utility allows you to view a desktop environment from anywhere on a network or the Internet. This program supports such varied architectures as Win32, WinCE, Mac, Java, and X Windows.

SpyGuru

This utility includes several system monitoring tools. Users can monitor network traffic, CPU usage, and available free space. They can also select their own counters and readouts to display the data.

If You've Got Problems (Of the CD Kind)

We tried to compile programs that work on most computers with the minimum system requirements. Alas, your computer may differ, and some programs may not work properly for some reason.

The two likeliest problems are that you don't have enough memory (RAM) for the programs you want to use, or you have other programs running that are affecting installation or running of a program. If you get error messages like Not enough memory or Setup cannot continue, try one or more of these methods and then try using the software again:

- ✔ Turn off any anti-virus software that you have on your computer. Installers sometimes mimic virus activity and may make your computer incorrectly believe that it is being infected by a virus.

- ✔ Close all running programs. The more programs you're running, the less memory is available to other programs. Installers also typically update files and programs. So if you keep other programs running, installation may not work properly.

- ✔ Have your local computer store add more RAM to your computer. This is, admittedly, a drastic and somewhat expensive step. However, if you have a Windows PC computer adding more memory can really help the speed of your computer and allow more programs to run at the same time. This may include closing the CD interface and running a product's installation program from Windows Explorer.

If you still have trouble with installing the items from the CD, please call the IDG Books Worldwide Customer Service phone number: 800-762-2974 (outside the U.S.: 317-596-5430).

Appendix C

H-E-L-P and Where to Find It

- -

In This Chapter

▶ Package documentation

▶ Online and self-documentation

▶ Newsgroups

▶ Search engines

▶ Getting Linux software

▶ If you like to read books . . .

- -

*B*elieve it or not, a time may come when you're in need of resources beyond what this book can provide you. So first of all, remember the Golden Rule about needing help to solve a vexing and time-critical problem:

Don't panic.

The science fiction series *The Hitchhiker's Guide To The Galaxy* first stated this rule, but the principle is amazingly relevant. Remember that system integration isn't a walk in the park for the vast majority of people. It's a skill that's taught nowhere on Earth (although it should be), because courses and certifications, by design, teach you only one segment of a network, such as cabling, routers, Windows, or the Unix operating system.

So you're not the first one to run into the problem; you just need to start gathering information to solve it. Don't panic, and you can find the solution. Or, as an old, wise system administrator once told me, "Panicking is uncool. Uncool dudes get stomped on."

Package Documentation

Always make your first step consulting your package documentation, which consists, logically enough, of all the books, flip cards, white papers, or comic books that come with your software or hardware after you order it. Although this step sounds too straightforward to cover in detail, surprisingly few people really take the time to go through the documents that come with the packaging.

Why? A couple reasons for this oversight come to mind: First, unless the documentation carries a stamp such as "ADMINISTRATION MANUAL" in bright-red, 36-point uppercase block letters, a lot of people assume that it's a warranty card or sales propaganda for the corporation that's sending the equipment. Second, the documentation may not carry an obvious label, or the company may even bury it as part of a given manual.

You may think that a manual carrying the label "New User Guide," for example, can't help you troubleshoot a vexing network problem. But you really can't tell just from the title whether the manual contains a hidden appendix, as carefully concealed as the Ark of the Covenant, that covers all the administrative information you need. So act like the network administration equivalent of Indiana Jones and don't give up searching for what you want until you first check all available sources at hand.

If nothing else, 99 percent of the time your package documentation includes a 1-800 user support number that you can call for help. Of course, normally you face a cut-off period of a few months after you purchase the product before the number's no longer valid, but then you can either fib a little as to the date you made your purchase or you can negotiate some kind of support deal with the company on the phone. Trying never hurts!

Another sad fact concerns the new form of documentation that you receive today. Instead of a book, you get a CD-ROM usually with an even more misleading label than you find on manuals. This problem probably results from a CD-ROM's lack of a huge cover or table of contents — it offers no room to sufficiently label what it contains. You really never know, therefore, what's on a CD-ROM unless you pop it in the drive and view it. So if you're looking for answers and you have a CD-ROM from the company from which you buy your system, check out its contents — even if its label merely reads "Install Disk."

Online Documentation

Never, ever pass up the possibility that the company that makes the software or hardware you need info on maintains a Web site of its own. Again, the vast majority of the time, the package documentation points you to the site — for example:

"For more information on how to activate the ACME Gee-Whizzo-Matic Photon Torpedo Router, visit us on the Web at www.gee-whiz.com."

If the documentation is sloppy, however, or you buy off-brand parts for your network (shame on you!), use a search engine as described in the section "In Search of the Best Engine," later in this appendix, to locate a company's Web address.

Sleuthing about for a company's Web site may give you information that's not necessarily pleasant from a support point of view. A fellow administrator of mine, for example, once tried to find information on an off-brand zip drive he picked up for a significant discount at a Silicon Valley superstore. In searching for the Web site, he discovered that the company had gone out of business several weeks earlier, leaving him with zero support other than a few white papers that came with the box!

Self-Documentation

The most useful (or most frustrating) form of documentation is what's known as *self-documentation* or *site documentation*. This documentation is any that you compose yourself to note how you solve particular problems that crop up on your site. More frequently, you must sort through this type of material if (as is true of the vast majority of people who run mixed networks) you inherit a network system run for years by an administrator who's moved on to make zillions on stock options with the new startup, BurnpilesOfmoney.com.

Self-documentation is useful in that it often addresses problems that crop up on a regular basis. It's frustrating, however, if no one compiled any documentation or it's written in a particular form of code or shorthand that the prior administrator used. Unless you can swipe a leftover ENIGMA machine or lease the Rosetta Stone for a week, good luck in figuring this one out!

To avoid complicating the life of any administrator who may follow in your footsteps, a good idea is to write down what works whenever you solve a particularly hairy problem. Such documentation is also a good insurance policy if you fall into the same problem again — so that you don't need to waste time hunting around over the same ground for the solution that, ideally, lies right at your fingertips.

If you're farsighted enough to take my advice on this matter, keep your written records in an *Administration Binder*, label it accordingly, place it on your shelf, and make sure that you keep it in a locked room or drawer. You'd be amazed at how desperate some people may become to solve a problem — so much so that they may end up "borrowing" your hard-earned knowledge and conveniently forgetting to put it back . . . .

Usenet Newsgroups

Newsgroups are postings on a particular subject from people around the world who share an interest in that subject. At last count, more than 25,000 groups on various topics were trading the latest information on their professions, studies, and hobbies. If you visit Chapter 21 or 21 in the "Part of Tens" section of this book, you can view a few newsgroup suggestions as to where to begin searching for information. This section goes into a little more detail about how newsgroups work and how you can find more groups that cater to your particular software interest, whether NetWare, Windows, or Linux.

Believe it or not, the whole process starts whenever user writes a message on his topic of interest and posts it to the Net. This message is usually known as a *post* or an *article*. You can post articles to one or more newsgroups. Existing newsgroups are organized in a kind of hierarchy, with each group's name indicating its place. At the top level, you determine a newsgroup's hierarchy by looking at the first part of its name, as shown in the following list:

 - ✔ `alt`: A sort of catch-all hierarchy name for topics other than those of the following two groups.
 - ✔ `comp`: Indicates newsgroups devoted to computers of some type.
 - ✔ `rec`: Indicates newsgroups discussing recreational activities.

Articles that the local news system generates or receives it then forwards to the other news servers that carry that site. To distinguish articles and recognize duplicates, articles carry a message identification section that combines the posting site's name and a serial number in a special field. The news system logs this identification field into a history file. It then checks any incoming articles against this field and throws any away if it's a duplicate of an existing article.

Newsgroup names are specific as to the content of what people are talking about in that group. You can, for example, find newsgroups for discussions on any of the following topics:

 - ✔ **Advancing Windows issues in the tech world:** `comp.os.windows.advocacy`.
 - ✔ **Advancing NetWare issues in the tech world:** `comp.os.netware.advocacy`.
 - ✔ **Restaurants located in the San Francisco Bay Area:** `sf.ba.food`.
 - ✔ **Discussions about an annoying character by the name of Wesley, from the TV show *Star Trek: The Next Generation*:** `alt.wesley.die.die.die`.

If you want to search for other newsgroups on the topic that interest you, you have two choices: You can use a search engine, as detailed in the following section, or you can visit the following Web site:

```
www.egroups.com
```

The Egroups Web site is an area dedicated to searching for and updating the vast (and ever growing) list of available newsgroups. If you visit this site, you can search for groups by entering topic keywords (for example, **Windows**, **2000**, and **networking**) in the site's search text box.

Note: A minor point to notice is that Egroups function as a catalog of newsgroups and not as a provider or enforcer. You have no guarantee that, even if Egroups lists a newsgroup, that newsgroup's still in existence (or at least active enough that you see a few dozen postings there a week).

In Search of the Best Engine

Search engines are Web sites that connect you up to an online database of stored information markers. You simply type the terms you want to search for in the search text box, click the site's Search button (both appearing prominently on the site), and you get back a truckload of Web site addresses (URLs), documents, or links that can at least provide you with a decent lead.

URL stands for *Uniform Resource Locator,* which is the bit of information that your system uses to locate and display a given Web site. Although saying "URL" (pronounced *Earl*) is fun, the more functional designation remains *Web address.*

Depending on which search engine you use, you get different results. Search engines differ dramatically in the coverage and returns that they give you. This discrepancy is primarily because of their different search techniques — some search for words embedded in the text of the Web page; others search by topic and matching auxiliary words; and others search by looking at Web registries.

Some of the more popular search engines include the following:

✔ **AltaVista:** The AltaVista search engine (at `www.altavista.com`) specializes in looking through Web-page contents for the words you're searching for. This feature makes AltaVista especially good if you're looking for someone's home page with a specially developed utility.

✔ **Hotbot:** Hotbot's search engine (at `www.hotbot.com`) gives you both Web-page and established-site addresses. Hotbot is especially useful for finding information that Yahoo! or AltaVista misses.

- **LookSmart:** LookSmart (at www.looksmart.com) bases its search on the frequencies of past searches people make on its engine and its own text-based system. This type of search is a useful alternative to that of the more mainstream engines such as Yahoo! or Hotbot.

- **Yahoo!:** Yahoo! (at www.yahoo.com) is easily the most popular search engine, as it incorporates a standard text search engine and the Web's best directory structure, which can help you find large, well-established companies that supply software and/or hardware for your system.

Most of the early search engines couldn't handle regular English expressions. You may, for example, have received entirely different results from the phrases *windows nt printer* and *how do I install a windows NT printer*. Today, search engines are equipped to handle such phrases (or so the search engine companies claim), but typing just the key words or phrases of a question usually works best.

Say, for example, that you have a question on setting up Windows 2000 printer drivers. You may search for just that: *Windows 2000 printer driver installation*. Simply searching for *printer drivers* or, heaven help you, *Windows 2000*, may take you until the next century to sift through all the returns.

On the other hand, the almost inconceivable may happen: You get no *hits* (as search-engine responses are known) from your query. If so, start peeling back the layers of specificity until you start getting some leads. Using an example like the preceding one, suppose that you search for *Windows 2000 printer driver installation Hewlett-Packard Ramjet Inkmeister Model 666*. If you get no responses, remove the most specific piece of information — in this case, the model number. Continue, if necessary, by removing the Inkmeister model name and then the Ramjet make from your search. By the time you get down to the hardware's brand name, you're almost 100 percent guaranteed to find something.

Other *For Dummies* authors, such as Ed Tittel, Mary Madden, and Earl Follis recommend a second interesting site. For what they term the "Ultimate Web Search Tool," check out the following site:

```
www.metacrawler.com
```

Searching the News

One of my favorite search engines, Excite.com (at www.excite.com), is very useful in finding terms leading to Web documents for your use. Quite a few people, however, don't know that Excite.com also features a special tool that helps you where other engines fail by enabling you to search newsgroup postings.

The News search button's migrated a couple times in each revision of the Excite.com web site. Currently, you can find it toward the bottom of the site, bearing the label *Message Boards*, because that's essentially what Internet newsgroups are. Click it to go to the news search engine.

From there, use this engine just as you use the regular one. If you're running into a problem restoring your NetWare or Windows system, for example, you can type **Operating System Restoration** and click the Search button. This phrase tells the engine to search for any news postings within the last week from people who've asked or answered questions about restoring operating systems.

You can also set the *time back* function on a newsgroup search. That is, you can look for all messages posted to newsgroups on the topic you want within the last week, month, or year.

If you want more information about navigating and searching the Internet for Windows, NetWare, or other topics, check out *The Internet For Dummies*, by John R. Levine (published by IDG Books Worldwide, Inc.).

And, of course, if you want to find out how to become a search term wizard, consider also picking up a copy of *Yahoo! For Dummies*, by Brad Hill (also published by IDG Books Worldwide, Inc.), if you get the chance.

How Do I . . . ?

One of the best How To guides out there is the Tucows.com site. Although you can certainly get plenty of software there, you can also browse through a substantial database of tips and tricks on various software products. You can visit the Tucows site at the following location:

```
http://howto.tucows.com/
```

Windows and NetWare: To CompuServe and Protect

Full service *ISPs*, or *Internet Service Providers* such as CompuServe and America Online can prove helpful to an administrator. Being full-service and full-fare organizations, in addition to Web browser interfaces, they also come with memberships and easy access to chat groups and other news resources.

CompuServe seems to be making the most headway in this area as it turns the corner into the next century. Not only are its forums known for slightly better technical content (as opposed to the chat rooms that focus on the latest doings of Garth Brooks or the Spice Girls), but it's also making a push for inclusion as a service on all new computer sales to consumers.

Whether this trend continues, it currently makes CompuServe an attractive alternative as a place to hunt for usable Windows or NetWare information. The signup and setup process for a CompuServe or AOL connection is beyond the scope of this book.

For more information on CompuServe or AOL, Make sure that you check out the books *Internet For Dummies*, by John R. Levine, and *AOL For Dummies*, by John Kaufield (both published by IDG Books Worldwide, Inc.).

Be aware, however, that each forum you enter on a full-service provider generally includes three files or "Web objects" that enable you to get the most out of your connection, as the following list describes:

- ✔ **Conference Room:** This type of Web object is a virtual room, where you interact with users in real time. It's also known as a *chat room*. Make sure that your typing skills are up to snuff here or you risk the collective boredom of those who may want to respond to you!

- ✔ **Message Board:** This type of Web object consists of electronic conversations, organized by topic, that you post to a given area. A message board is really the same thing as a Usenet newsgroup but with slightly better graphics (usually). (You can read more about Usenet newsgroups in the following section.)

- ✔ **File Library:** This type of Web object is a collection of the files that sites archive from a message board or conference room that those running the site consider particularly useful. Always make time to search for your answers here in this instant answer repository; otherwise, you're missing out on a very valuable resource.

You don't, of course, need to join a full-service provider to work with any of the other Internet hot spots mentioned in this chapter. Any low-budget ISP (also known as *thread* or *coach* service providers) can hook you up to the Web, sometimes at substantial savings.

Where to Get Linux and Unix Software

Although you can purchase the Linux operating system from many places (your local Barnes and Noble, for example, even carries it today!), you can locate Web sites where you can download Linux for free onto your computer by visiting the following page on the Linux organization's Web site:

```
www.linux.org/aps/index.html
```

This site also contains an excellent list of Linux applications that you can locate and download for use on your system.

A good spot to search out vendor-related Linux products is the following site, which is laid out like a virtual mall (so bring your mall walkers):

```
www.linuxmall.com/
```

Keep in mind that, because most Linux products are freeware and/or come from organizations that may not support the code, the term *YMMV* definitely applies!

For the abbreviation-challenged, *YMMV* stands for *Your Mileage May Vary*. It's a new, nifty term for suggesting caution in installing Linux (or any software) product.

Another site that you want to visit, particularly if you run Solaris or SunOS from Sun Microsystems, is the *Sunsite* at the following URL:

```
ftp://sunsite.unc.edu/pub/Linux
```

The Sunsite contains oodles of Linux software from Sun Microsystems. Although download times can prove slow during business hours, your benefit is that most of the items from this site at least go through a basic QA process.

Okay, one more abbreviation: *QA* stands for *Quality Assurance* and at the very least means that your computer's not going to burst into flames as you're installing a given product.

If you're running Linux and you visit Tucows (or any other site dedicated to Linux), you may wonder what's with the Penguin? Simply put, he's the official mascot of the Linux operating system!

He's sort a visual metaphor for Linux in that he's cute and harmless looking but can survive the harshest environments without blinking an eye. Or maybe Linus Torvalds likes penguins. (The authors don't remember seeing any penguins waddling around Finland. Maybe they were at the University of Helsinki doing graduate work in computer science.)

For Those Who Prefer Wood Pulp and Ink to Silicon and Light Beams . . .

Of course, you may be one of those impossibly retro people who want to actually hold your information in the palm of your hand. (Bless you if you are. We writers like to go on making a living, too.)

If this description sounds like you, several sites cater to your love of buying books with the information you need. Two catch-all sites that you can visit are Amazon.com and Barnes and Noble's online bookstore at the following URLs

  ✔ www.amazon.com

  ✔ www.barnesandnoble.com

The pricing, service, and selection are fairly similar, although we find that Amazon.com has a slightly better search engine and normally offer more information to the person looking for facts about a given book.

Search Amazon.com, for example, by using the name *Michael Bellomo.* You see a raft of information, ranging from user reviews to interviews with the author. These connections enable you to research the available material for your topic more quickly and efficiently. Just watch that postage meter as you're calculating your savings.

More specifically tailored sites can prove helpful in purchasing technology information. The sites managed by IDG Books, for example, contain their own search engines, enabling you to find the exact title match for the book that you want. Some of the sites in this vein that we recommend are as follows:

  ✔ **IDG Books Worldwide, Inc.:** IDG Books (at www.idgbooks.com) publishes the *For Dummies* series, of course, but do you know that the company also publishes even more advanced technical reference books? The IDG site is well worth a visit to view and order books from the Blueprints, Master Visually, and Bible series on any of the NOSes that we mention in this book.

  ✔ If you still consider yourself a beginner, however, or you just like the friendly, informative style of the For Dummies series, you need to visit IDG's Dummies books site (at www.dummies.com), which groups its titles by broad subject matter (Technology, Consumer, and so on). You quickly find more Dummies books on more topics than you may think possible.

  ✔ **O'Reilly Publishing:** O'Reilly Publishing (at www.oreilly.com) has long been a standard in the world of technical books. Although not for anyone below intermediate level, O'Reilly's publications are particularly good for Unix and Linux users, as the company's been publishing in this areas for quite some time.

  ✔ **Fatbrain.com:** Fatbrain.com's online book store (at www.fatbrain.com) is another excellent technical-book Web site where you not only can buy books, but also view comments and reviews by technically astute users. If you're considering buying an extremely advanced book that may cost $100 or more, this site's well worth the visit.

Again, watch the postage on some of these selections — and keep your eyes open for ordering specials.

Appendix D

Creating and Using Boot/Rescue Disks

• •

*P*eople in the network field have nightmares about failing to bring the system back up if it crashes. To facilitate your evening rest, understanding what happens if a key machine goes on unpaid administrative leave (that is, *crashes*) and refuses to boot from the CD-ROM is worth your time (and far better than counting sheep).

The answer to your prayers is a *boot disk*. A boot disk that you inherit or create enables you to boot off a disk instead of your hard drive. If the damaged installation doesn't recognize your CD-ROM or CD-ROM drive, you can boot your machine from a set of boot disks to accomplish either of the following goals:

- ✔ Get the system back into shape.
- ✔ Salvage as much data as possible before the machine sinks into cybernetic oblivion.

A related form of disk that many operating systems use today is a *rescue disk*, which fixes problems that may arise during the lifetime of your computer. You use rescue disks if the machine can boot but can't fix the underlying problem. Rescue disks can help you fix the following problems:

- ✔ Corrupted sectors on a hard disk.
- ✔ Files in a corrupted program.

No matter which operating system you're using, *label* the disk as a rescue disk or a boot disk. You don't want to find that you inadvertently copied over the files that you need with Mom's recipe for Chocolate Anchovy Truffle Pie!

Creating a Linux Boot Disk

Although Linux is one of the most reliable operating systems on the market, something can happen to make the system go haywire and refuse to boot up. A sudden surge of power from a lightning strike, for example, can cause a lockup so severe that booting becomes slow or simply impossible.

You may also run into this kind of problem if one of your hard drives is failing. In that case, booting up the system one final time is crucial for you to salvage as many of the files on the old drives as possible. You can perform this feat only if you have a boot disk available.

To create a boot disk under Red Hat Linux, complete the following steps:

1. **Insert a blank disk into the floppy drive.**

2. **If you're using the GNOME desktop, the disk automatically mounts for you.**

3. **Open a Linux terminal by clicking the Terminal button on the GNOME desktop toolbar.**

   The button displays a picture of a computer screen.

4. **Change the directory by typing** `cd/lib/modules` **at the command prompt and pressing Enter.**

5. **At the prompt that appears, type** `ls` **and press Enter.**

   The kernel version number for the version of Linux you're running appears. You need that number for the command that creates the boot disk.

6. **At the prompt, type** `mkbootdisk -- device/dev/fd0 2.2.5-15` **and press Enter.**

   Linux asks you to confirm that you want to create a boot disk.

7. **Press Enter to begin the creation of your boot disk.**

   The creation process takes approximately two minutes, depending on the speed of your machine. After completion, Linux returns you to the command prompt.

8. **Remove the newly created boot disk from the drive, label it** *Emergency Boot Disk* **or something similar, and store it in a** *safe* **place.**

When do you want to make a boot disk for Linux? As soon as possible! In fact, as you install Linux, it asks whether you want to create a boot disk during the installation process. If you get the chance, always choose Yes at this prompt.

Creating a Linux Recovery Disk

As long as your crashed or malfunctioning system is still bootable, you can use a *recovery disk* to boot up. A recovery disk is different from a *rescue disk* in that it doesn't help your machine boot up, but it can assist you with repairing problems that your machine may experience after it completes the boot-up process. Sometimes you can't get to the root of the problem from the GUI or even the terminal side of things. In such a case, you need to boot the machine by using a recovery disk, which can scan and repair file systems and even entire hard drives on a machine with comparative ease.

A recovery disk stores procedures and system diagnostic tools that you copy over from the CD-ROM. If you actually activate and use the tools on the disk, it automatically completes these tools' repair functions or, at most, with a little prompting from you in a user menu. You always want to make at least one recovery disk, as you do a boot disk, and keep it somewhere in your lab or equipment room.

To create a recovery disk, follow these steps:

1. **Insert a disk into the floppy drive.**

2. **Insert the CD into the CD-ROM drive.**

3. **On the GNOME toolbar, click the Main Application Button to mount the CD-ROM.**

4. **On the pop-up menu that appears, choose System⇨Disk Manager.**

5. **Click the Mount button next to the line for the** /mnt/cdrom **file system to mount the CD-ROM.**

6. **On the toolbar, click the Terminal button to open a Linux terminal.**

   This button displays a picture of a computer monitor. After you click it, the terminal window appears.

7. **At the prompt, type** cd/mnt/cdrom/images **and press Enter to switch directories.**

8. **At the prompt, type** dd if=rescue.img of=/dev/fd0 **and press Enter.**

   This action copies the rescue file from the CD-ROM to the floppy disk.

Making boot disks in Debian Linux

If you're working with the Debian flavor of Linux, the procedure to create a boot disk is markedly different. To create a boot disk for Debian, follow these steps:

1. **Boot your computer normally.**

2. **Insert the Debian Installation CD-ROM into your CD-ROM drive.**

3. **If you're using Windows and not MS-DOS, go to the MS-DOS prompt by choosing Start➪Programs➪MS-DOS Prompt.**

   The MS-DOS Prompt window appears on your desktop.

4. **At the command prompt, change to the drive letter that corresponds to your CD-ROM drive by typing** *<CD-ROM drive letter>:* **and pressing Enter.**

   Note: In this book, if you see text between angle brackets in italic-style font, as in the preceding step, we don't mean that you type this material as it appears in the step. What we mean is that you replace both the brackets and the text between with whatever element the text calls for. If we tell you to type **<CD-ROM drive letter>:**, for example, we mean that you need to substitute whatever letter your drive is, such as **D:**, for **<CD-ROM drive letter>**. On most systems this drive is D: or E:.

The MS-DOS prompt changes to the letter of the drive that you specify.

5. **At the MS-DOS prompt, type** \tools\rawrite2\rawrite2 **and press Enter.**

   Linux prompts you to enter the *disk image source*, meaning that the computer is asking where you want to copy files from.

6. **Type** boot\resc1440.bin **and press Enter.**

   Your computer prompts you for the drive letter of your floppy drive.

7. **Type** *<floppy drive letter>:* **at the DOS prompt and press Enter.**

   Your computer prompts you to place a floppy disk in the floppy drive and press Enter. The floppy drive on most Windows/MS-DOS machines is normally A:.

8. **Insert a blank floppy disk in the floppy drive and press Enter.**

   The computer spends a minute or so creating this installation boot disk and then returns you to the MS-DOS command prompt.

9. **Eject the installation boot disk from the drive, label it, and store it in a safe place.**

Creating Boot Disks in Unix (Solaris)

To create a boot disk for the Solaris 7.0 flavor of Unix, complete the following steps:

1. **Insert a blank disk into the floppy drive.**

2. **To open a terminal window, right-click anywhere on the desktop and choose Tools➪Terminal from the pop-up menu.**

3. **In the terminal window, determine whether you're using Volume Manager (vold) by typing** `volcheck ls -l /vol/dev/aliases/floppy0` **at the command prompt and pressing Enter:**

   If a message appears on-screen that's similar to the following line, go to Step 4:

   ```
   lrwxrwxrwx 1 root 34 Jan 21 17:28
           /vol/dev/aliases/floppy0
   -> /vol/dev/rdiskette0/unnamed_floppy
   ```

   If you see the following message, skip to Step 5:

   ```
   /vol/dev/aliases/floppy0 not found
   ```

4. **Type** dd if=filename of=/vol/dev/aliases/floppy0 bs=1440k eject floppy0 **and press Enter.**

5. **Type** dd if=filename of=/dev/rdiskette bs=1440k **and press Enter.**

Unix creates a boot disk from the floppy that you insert in the drive. After the process is complete, you return to the command prompt. Remove the disk from the drive, label it as your Unix boot disk, and store it someplace safe.

Creating Boot Disks in NetWare

The latest version of NetWare contains an executable program that's a self-extracting boot-disk image — that is, you can create a boot disk on demand by placing a floppy disk into the disk drive and activating the self-extracting boot disk image program.

Earlier versions of NetWare, similar to products in the Microsoft line, automatically came with company-made boot disks. Be aware, however, that trying to boot one version of NetWare from a boot disk for a different version of NetWare produces unpredictable results.

Creating a Windows NT 4.0 Boot Disk

First, to create a boot disk in Windows NT 4.0, you must have access to the i386 directory on your Windows NT CD (or possibly your hard disk drive). (*Note:* On some networks, you can't access the i386 directory without logging in as the administrative account.) If you have such access, follow these steps:

1. **Log in to a computer running Windows NT 4.0.**

2. **Insert a floppy disk that you want to turn into a Windows NT boot disk in the floppy drive.**

3. **Next, click the Start button and choose Programs⇨Windows Explorer⇨i386 from the Start menu.**

4. **Copy the** `boot.ini, ntdetect.com` **and** `ntldr` **files to the floppy disk by clicking and dragging these files from the Explorer window to the floppy disk icon on your desktop.**

   If your computer doesn't display the floppy disk icon on the desktop, double-click the My Computer icon. A window opens that displays the floppy disk icon.

5. **After you finish copying these files, eject the floppy disk, label it as an NT boot disk, and store it in a safe location.**

If you're using any SCSI devices that you need to access, you also need to copy these drivers onto the disk.

Creating Windows 2000 Boot Disks

The typical Windows 2000 installation kit that Microsoft sends you normally comes with a couple copies of boot disks, but you can't count on these disks. They can become lost; or if you're inheriting a Windows 2000 system from another administrator, the system executor may not will them to you.

Although the good folks at Microsoft swear they haven't added special sensors that detect a human being's stress level, empirical evidence seems to indicate the contrary. Don't believe me? Try going without boot disks, and you see that more than 90 percent of your crash times occurs whenever someone of higher authority comes to visit or a big project's near completion. So unless you can defuse the stress sensors hidden somewhere in Windows 2000, go and make those system boot disks at the next commercial break!

Remember that the emergency repair process can potentially wreak havoc on your system, so make sure that it's a power that only you, the administrator, can call on.

To create boot disks in Windows 2000, complete the following steps:

1. **Beg, borrow, or steal four 3.5-inch, 1.44-megabyte floppy disks.**

2. **Format the disks (if necessary) on a Windows 2000 machine by inserting the disks into the machine and right-clicking the A Drive icon and choosing Format from the pop-up menu that appears.**

   The Format window appears, displaying your format options as check boxes on the left.

3. **Select the Quick Format check box if the disk is already formatted but contains inconsequential data, such as Mom's Key Lime Pie Recipe or a GIF of the latest Guess Jeans models.**

   Of course, if it contains something important, such as Company Payroll Files, eject the disk and insert a different one!

4. **Click the Format button to begin the format process.**

   A Format Complete screen appears after formatting is complete.

5. **Click OK to continue.**

6. **After you finish formatting the disk, insert it into the floppy drive on a computer running any version of Windows or MS-DOS.**

   Repeat the formatting process for the remaining three disks if necessary.

7. **Insert the Windows 2000 compact disc (CD) into the CD-ROM drive.**

8. **From the Start menu, click Start⇨Run to open the Run dialog box.**

9. **In the Open text box, type** *<CD-ROM drive>*:\bootdisk\makeboot a: **and click OK.**

   On most systems, the CD-ROM drive is drive letter D. The A that we mention here is, of course, your floppy drive, to which you copy the boot-up information.

10. **Follow the on-screen prompt that follows.**

Remember that, if you create a boot disk from the Windows 2000 Professional CD-ROM, you can't boot up Windows 2000 Server. And no amount of hacking, pleading, or prayer enables you to boot up a Windows 2000 Professional machine with a boot disk made off a 2000 Server CD-ROM.

Don't just label your boot disk something comfortingly generic such as *Boot Disk*. Make sure that you identify whether it's a boot disk for 2000 Professional or Server!

Creating and Using a Windows 2000 Emergency Repair Disk

Ever want to play George Clooney's role on *ER* so you can shout "Gimme 60CCs of Supra-Hemoglobin, stat!"? Get to drive that cool looking white van with the sirens?

Well, we can't guarantee that level of excitement, but believe me, your heart's going to be racing if you suffer a system outage without an Emergency Repair Disk. (Also known as an *ERD* — but only if you want to look really cool to the network neophytes.)

You can use your Windows 2000 Emergency Repair Disk (ERD) to fix problems preventing you from starting your computer. Of course, you don't get very far unless you can boot your machine, so you may need to use the system boot disk to get to the stage where you can even pop the repair disk into the drive and read it.

The Emergency Repair Disk doesn't back up data or programs and isn't a replacement for regularly backing up your system. Keep in mind, too, that the repair process on the ERD doesn't help you with registry issues.

To create recovery disks in Windows 2000, complete the following steps:

1. **Beg, borrow, or steal a 3.5-inch, 1.44-megabyte floppy disk.**

2. **Format the disk on a Windows 2000 machine by inserting the disk into the machine, right-clicking the A Drive icon, and choosing Format from the pop-up menu that appears.**

3. **Select the Quick Format check box in the Format window that appears if the disk is already formatted but contains inconsequential data, such as the latest Beanie Babies catalog or your brother's recipe for chili with crushed Oreos and click the Format button.**

4. **After you finish formatting the disk, insert one of the disks into the floppy drive on a computer running Windows 2000.**

5. **From the Start menu click Start and choose Programs⇨Accessories⇨System Tools⇨Backup.**

   The Backup screen appears sporting several tabs at the top.

6. **Click Emergency Repair Disk tab.**

   The Emergency Repair Disk screen appears.

7. **Follow the instructions on-screen.**

Using Your ERD in System Repairs

One afternoon *it* happens: A machine goes down — hard. The junior administrators call you on your cell phone, and in a flash, you're off to repair the damage. You bring the tape backups out from the basement. You check The ERD and CD-ROM drives. The theme from *ER* is playing loudly in the background . . . .

What do you do next? Just follow these steps:

1. **Insert the Windows 2000 Setup CD-ROM and power up the system.**

2. **If the CD-ROM drive is dead or the CD-ROM is missing, insert the first of the four floppy disks you created as system boot disks in the appropriate drive and reboot the computer to boot from the floppies.**

 If the CD-ROM drive is working and you have the CD-ROM, you can use either the CD-ROM or the floppy disks. The CD-ROM just tends to be a little faster; of course, if your system is an older one with a dual- or quad-speed CD-ROM drive, that may not be the case. In any event, follow these steps next:

1. **Restart the computer.**

   If you're using the four floppies formatted as system boot disks, respond to the prompts that request each floppy disk in turn.

2. **As the Setup process starts, select the Repair/Recover option by pressing the letter *R* on your keyboard.**

3. **As the system prompts you, insert your Windows 2000 Setup CD-ROM in your machine's CD-ROM drive.**

   Even if you experienced a problem with the CD-ROM drive, as long as it's not a hardware issue, it should come on-line now.

4. **As the system prompts you, select the emergency repair process by pressing the *R* key.**

5. **As the system prompts you, you must choose between the following two types of repair:**

   - (M) Manual Repair: If you choose this option, you can also choose to repair your system files or startup environment problems.

      Unless you're *very* experienced with the Windows 2000 system, avoid this option, as you may miss an area that needs repairing. Essentially, unless you're feeling really lucky, only advanced administrators want to consider this option.

   - (F) Fast-Repair: The Fast-Repair option automatically attempts to repair system files, the partition boot sector, and your startup environment. Unless you have any concerns about saving some system setting, you always want to select this option.

6. **Follow the on-screen instructions that appear after you select an option.**

   The instructions are slightly different for each option.

7. **As the system prompts you, insert your Emergency Repair Disk in the appropriate disk drive.**

   During the repair process, the repair disk replaces missing or corrupt files with files from the Windows 2000 CD-ROM. If these files aren't available, it may grab the files from the `systemroot\Repair` folder on your system partition. You receive an on-screen notification if the repair is successful.

   At the point at which the repair is successful, the system prompts you to click Finish to complete the job and restart the computer.

8. **Click Finish.**

After you first complete the setup process, your computer saves the information about your original system settings in the `systemroot\Repair` folder on your drive's system partition.

Whenever you use your Emergency Repair Disk to bring your system back to life, it can access the information in `systemroot\Repair` folder. Never change or delete this folder or you reduce your chances for restoring your system.

Index

• *M* •